THE
POWER
OF
PERSUASION

Also by G. Ray Funkhouser

The Ropes to Skip and the Ropes to Know (with R. Richard Ritti)

THE POWER OF PERSUASION

A GUIDE
TO MOVING AHEAD
IN BUSINESS AND LIFE

G. Ray Funkhouser, PH.D.

BOOKS

Library of Congress Cataloging-in-Publication Data

Funkhouser, G. Ray.
The power of persuasion.

Bibliography: p.
Includes index.
1. Power (Social sciences) 2. Persuasion (Psychology)
3. Human behavior. I. Title.
HM201.F94   1986   303.3   86-5730
ISBN 0-8129-1318-3

Grateful acknowledgment is made to the following for permission to reprint previously
published material:

Dow Jones & Company, Inc.: Excerpt from "Battle Tactics: Carl Icahn's Strategies in His Quest
for TWA Are a Model for Raiders" by William M. Carley from the *Wall Street Journal*, June
20, 1985. Reprinted by permission of the Wall Street Journal, copyright © Dow Jones &
Company, Inc., 1985. All rights reserved.

Harcourt Brace Jovanovich, Inc.: Excerpt from "Lear, Tolstoy and the Fool" by George Orwell
from *The Orwell Reader*. Canadian rights administered by A. M. Heath & Company Ltd.,
London. Reprinted with permission of Harcourt Brace Jovanovich, Inc., and A. M. Heath
& Company Ltd. as agent for the Estate of Sonia Brownell Orwell and Secker and Warburg
Ltd.

News America Syndicate: Excerpt from Ann Landers column from the *Philadelphia Inquirer*,
June 19, 1985. Reprinted by permission.

Designed by Robert Bull

Manufactured in the United States of America

9 8 7 6 5 4 3 2

First Edition

To Judy

CONTENTS

PART III: **HOW TO USE PERSUASION, POWER AND CONTROL**

CONTENTS

INTRODUCTION

The Power of Persuasion covers a topic that has puzzled, vexed and fascinated the human race since the first day it appeared on this planet. The book is based on a new theory of persuasion and power, the result of research I have been conducting in several areas over the past twenty years. Although I did not realize it at the time, I began laying the book's foundation in graduate school, where my doctoral dissertation in communication reported some research I had done in psycholinguistics—how language influences our thought processes. Subsequently as a professor of communication I published a number of articles on the topics of attitude change, information diffusion and the dynamics of public opinion. I then spent seven years in commercial marketing research and management consulting, directing studies on advertising, marketing and organizational behavior.

For the past several years I have been a professor of marketing, from which platform I have concentrated on developing this theory. It began as an attempt to analyze the tactics used by successful sales people, but soon expanded into a model of how people in general influence what other people do. As I explored the implications of the model and extended my inquiry beyond marketing, selling and advertising, I found my theory to have an eery compatability not only with writings on the topics of human behavior and power through the ages, but more importantly with how people *actually have behaved* since the beginnings of recorded history.

I mention my background and the origins of the theory only so that a reader will begin with a proper perspective. Contrary to the impression that may be conveyed by the informal style in which this book is written, considerable research stands behind the theory on which it is based (reported in several articles I have published in the professional literature). However, I chose not to write a strictly scholarly book. The subject matter is not only interesting but important to just about everyone, but to write a book that would satisfy an academic review committee would limit the audience to but a handful of experts. Another topic on which I have done considerable research is improving the techniques of communicating specialized science to educated non-specialists. This seemed like an appropriate time to apply my own findings.

The purpose of *The Power of Persuasion* is twofold: to outline a theory of power based on a synthesis of several streams of modern social science research; and to reconcile the insights this theory provides with thoughts and ideas about power that have come down to us over the centuries. Throughout the text I mention sources of information and ideas, but any sort of thorough, in-depth critique on the history of thought about power would only distract most readers from what I have to say. The bibliography at the end of the book gives an idea of the range of sources from which my theory emerged. I urge you to read anything or everything on that list (not that it comes close to exhausting the possibilities). It is not my intention to expropriate other people's ideas, but filling the book with footnotes would have made it impossible for the non-professional reader to plow through.

To give some credit where it is due: My colleagues at the Rutgers University Graduate School of Management, particularly Robert R. Rothberg, have been a source of stimulation and support. At the inception of my academic career, Wilbur Schramm, Nathan Maccoby and Edwin Parker, of the Institute for Communication Research at Stanford University, introduced me to social science research methodology and to theories of communication and attitude change. More recently, professors Thomas S. Robertson, of the Wharton School, and Eugene F. Shaw, of Temple University, were helpful and supportive when it made a difference, as was David Pope, an old editor friend. Dick Ritti, a colleague when I was on the faculty of Penn State University, guided me to priceless wisdom and knowledge on how organizations *really* function. Raphael Sagalyn, my agent, and Jonathan Segal, my editor, each had the vision to see beyond the early drafts, to the book that could be.

Thanks also to my many students, who never realized how much *they* were teaching *me*, and to numerous friends, relatives, acquaintances and chance encounters who put up with what must have seemed to them irascible argumentation and impertinent probing, but which actually were only attempts to test and refine my ideas.

Operational Philosophy, by Anatol Rapoport, was an early inspiration that among other things helped move me from a career in chemical engineering toward one in communciation research. The body of research by psychologists such as Carl Hovland, Irving Janis, William McGuire, Martin Fishbein, Alex Bavelas, Stanley Milgram, Donald Campbell, Amos Tversky and many others has been an invaluable source. Transactional analysis psychologists such as Eric Berne, Thomas A. Harris and Claude Steiner provided practical insights into human behavior and power relationships that can be found nowhere else.

Much useful information on power and persuasion may be found in the *Journal of Marketing*, the *Journal of Consumer Research* and the *Wall Street Journal*—the first two for theory and research, and the last for examples from the real world. Numerous syndicated columns by Darrell Sifford and Ann Landers have kept me in touch with the many ways in which power pervades the lives of ordinary people. Some of the richest and most fascinating sources on the topic of power are time-honored works such as the Old and New Testaments, the Koran, *Canterbury Tales*, Shakespeare's plays, Homer's *Iliad* and *Odyssey*, Plutarch's *Lives*, Plato's *Republic* and Tolstoy's *War and Peace*. For anyone wishing to probe the intricacies of political power, George Orwell is required reading.

The most valuable sources of my understanding of persuasion, power and control, however, are the salespeople, hustlers and power-players I have personally encountered and had to learn to deal with. Three individuals were especially important to my writing this book. The ways in which their lives intersected with mine motivated me to figure out how they managed to get away with the things they did, the initial spark that touched off my research into persuasion and power.

May we all profit from their examples.

PART I

PERSUASION, POWER AND CONTROL

1

WHY POWER CONCERNS US ALL

The Pervasiveness of Power in Our Lives

" 'Tis love that makes the world go round!" One of America's most cherished sentiments! What do you suppose would be the reaction if someone publicly proclaimed: " 'Tis *power* that makes the world go round!" Yes, unless the speaker had chosen his audience carefully, chances are that he would be hooted and hissed right off the stage. Were a typical reporter to take an interest in the story, he would likely portray the speaker in the news media as a suspicious, if not downright sinister, character.

Let me hasten to emphasize that I am not, in this book, coming out against love in favor of power. In fact I strongly advocate both. I use that particular beginning only to illustrate an important point: Power makes most Americans very uneasy. And why shouldn't it? Isn't power what wars and violence are all about? People with power push other people around, don't they? Wouldn't the world be a much nicer place if it weren't for all the politics and power games? And yet . . . who among us (be honest now) wouldn't consider selling just a smidgen of his or her soul for a little bit more power for ourselves?

Americans, the truth be known, are obsessed with power, but we don't know how to deal with it. We crave it, but we shrink from it. We fear and distrust it, but nevertheless we are fascinated by it. We constantly use it, but at the same time we thwart and undermine it at every opportunity. We are entertained by it, yet we abhor it. It is difficult for many of us to conceive that there could possibly be the least thing good about it.

Why the ambivalance and confusion? Mostly semantics, cultural bias and personal insecurities. As a result, power pervades every level and every context of our lives, but few clearly understand what it truly is or how it really works, in spite of the bookstores sporting literally shelves of books on the topic. The bestseller list has been topped both by books about how to get more of it (for example, *How to Win Friends and Influence People* by Dale Carnegie and *Power!* by Michael Korda) and books about warding it off (for example, *The Hidden Persuaders* by Vance Packard and *Your Erroneous Zones* by Wayne Dyer). But even to most people who have read these books, the essence of power remains a mystery.

All right. So Americans are confused about power, don't understand it and yet are obsessed with getting it. What does that have to do with the price of eggs? It has plenty to do not only (literally) with the price of eggs, but with the tone of American society in general and the quality of our personal lives in particular. Our confusions, obsessions and hangups concerning power affect our society and our day-to-day lives in many ways, including:

- Our hostility toward "bigness" in government, business and people.
- The childish delight we take in getting away with petty little scams and mischiefs.
- Our distrust of salespeople and advertising.
- Our rampant divorce rate.
- The popularity of smart-ass anti-authority movies such as *Animal House*, *Porky's*, *Butch Cassidy and the Sundance Kid*, *One Flew Over the Cuckoo's Nest* and (the original) *M*A*S*H*.
- The rising tide of crime and drug use.
- Our fondness for underdogs.

4

- Our worldwide reputation for spoiling our children.
- The prevalence of stress at home and on the job.
- The popularity of jazz music, spoofs and "jazzed-up" versions of serious works.
- Increasing homosexuality and other forms of deviant sexual behavior.
- Americans' worship of money and our susceptibility to "get rich quick" schemes.
- Our hunger for a world with a black-and-white, comic book format, in which the good guys never fail to clean up on the bad guys.

Power does not *cause* any of these, for power is not a thing. "Power" is a word referring to certain psychological and social processes. If you want to understand how it works, make your mind up about one thing right now: Always look reality straight in the eye. Shy away from reality, and in matters of power you will be shafted every time. And realistically, power, not love, does make the world go around. Love is a fine thing—it makes life much more enjoyable, and we all need as much of it as we can get. But, sad to say, what it can accomplish by itself is limited. No one has ever succeeded in even defining what "love" means, though countless thinkers, poets and writers have tried. We can't always rely on its being there when we need it, and distressingly, it often tends to wane over time. It operates best between individuals, not in large groups. And when it does work to accomplish something, it succeeds only because it ties into power.

Power has never deserved the bum rap we have given it. By definition, it makes the world go round, because power is the process by which people *do things* and *get other people to do things*. Love and power are quite compatible, although people who don't understand power tend instinctively to feel that they can't be. *Control*, which just about everyone mistakes for power, is the real culprit. Power is a positive force, while abused control is evil in its purest form. In a few pages we will clear that distinction up, as well as straighten out many other common misconceptions about power.

The purpose of this book is to explain how persuasion, power and control work, not to disparage anyone's beliefs about love. It contains plenty of practical advice and guidance, but it is not, strictly speaking, a how-to book. That is, there are no "Ten Easy Steps" to being more powerful. As you will soon see, the topic of persuasion, power and control is far too vast, subtle and complex to permit a "one-minute Machiavelli" approach. Even so, I am prepared to make some guarantees. Depending on what *you* contribute to the venture, here is my offer:

- *If you read the whole book*—A better understanding of how power and control affect your life than you ever had before.
- *If you put in the necessary effort*—The ability to more effectively reach your important life objectives.
- *If you put in the effort and have a little luck*—An increase in success, contentment and control over your own life.

Plus, although I can't guarantee it, I think you will enjoy reading this book. It is about psychology, religion and philosophy, but without being a "heavy read." And it covers the most fascinating topic there ever was—POWER! How can you lose? I can't think of any way that can happen. Just for the sake of self-defense alone, you'll not likely regret the time you spent on it.

There are so many books about power, ranging from *The Prince*, by Machiavelli, to *Winning Through Intimidation*, by Robert Ringer. Why should there be yet another? There are three reasons why I think this book is necessary:

1. If you are reading this book, you probably have read others on the topic of power, not to mention articles in magazines and newspapers. You probably have wondered about it, and you may even have given the matter some serious thought. I would be surprised if you *understood how it works*, however, because none of the books or articles you have read tell you that. This book does.
2. Most other books about power look at it from a single viewpoint—interpersonal relationships, getting ahead on the job, politics, marketing and salesmanship, self-fulfillment and so forth. Books on persuasion invariably concentrate on what amounts to tech-

niques of selling or negotiating. This book *approaches power and persuasion from a number of different angles*, and therefore it is the only book that can convey to you how power permeates and affects virtually every aspect of your everyday life.

3. Almost everything currently available and popular on the topic of power or persuasion is based on current research, contemporary problems and fashionable issues. Such books can be useful, but only in a limited way. The modern social sciences such as psychology and sociology tend to discount ideas that cannot be "proved" and knowledge that cannot be measured, according to their own standards. This means that virtually all thought on the topic of power prior to the twentieth century, plus a lot of more recent thinking, is given short shrift by many of today's writers. Most books written today are shaped around today's trends. But today's trends are tomorrow's old news; the essence of human behavior has not changed for thousands of years. This book is unusual in that it is rooted in *both ancient and modern sources of knowledge*. Modern social science has provided some powerful analytic tools and some valuable insights into behavior. But the mission of science is strictly to discover knowledge, not to resolve spiritual issues; and so it shouldn't surprise us that social science has proved to be more clever than wise (Donald T. Campbell made this point both cleverly *and* wisely in his elegant, iconoclastic presidential address to the American Psychological Association in 1975). Ancient thinkers, on the other hand, have provided considerable wisdom on the topic of power, but not at the operational depths that can be reached using modern analytic techniques. Integrating both approaches, this book provides a more thorough understanding of power than could be achieved by relying on either body of literature by itself.

Why should the average lay reader need such a great depth of understanding about power in the first place? As a practical matter, persuasion, power and control are vital concerns for every one of us. Power is how we make our way through the world, and persuasion is how we influence what people around us do (and they, us).

- On the job, advancement depends on your performance and on your ability both to use your subordinates productively and to deliver results to your superiors. The difference between success and failure hinges on your skills in using power and persuasion.
- At home, your household is a network of power relationships among you, your spouse, your parents, your children and/or your neighbors. A happy home is one that uses these relationships in a positive way.
- In the marketplace you are pressured on all sides and at all times by well-financed and expertly designed attempts to influence your behavior. If you want to maintain control of your own destiny, you had better be alert to what is going on out there.
- Out on the street, in public, power-playing goes on even between strangers, in chance encounters. The better you understand persuasion, power and control, the more smoothly your days will go.

Power, as we all commonly experience it, is an endlessly varied and fascinating process, but the essential mechanisms of power and persuasion are relatively simple. If you have read very much at all about those topics, you may be having some trouble believing that. After all, every book is different from every other, and each has its own list of principles, strategies and tactics. The problem is that after reading any (or all) of those books, we remain as mystified as ever. At best we get a glimpse at how "they" do it. "They" sit at rosewood desks in the corner offices, while we are stuck behind the copying machine. "They" keep the rest of the family under their thumbs with psychological guerrilla warfare, using tricks and tactics that we of course would be loathe to employ. "They" pull the wool over our eyes with hypnotic sales pitches and sophisticated, mind-controlling advertising campaigns, poor innocent dupes that we are.

But how does it work? The fact is that even the expert persuaders can't tell you. They can tell you what they do, and they can tell you why they do it. They can describe their results. They can expound their own personal beliefs, opinions and philosophies, and the more articulate of them can give you a list of one-liner rules of thumb. But like anyone who is an expert at doing something, expert persuaders can tell you only so much. They do not entirely understand what they are so good at doing.

When people think about expert persuaders, they tend to visualize lawyers, politicians, salespeople and advertising copywriters. Many of these are in truth highly effective persuaders (although many others are not). But most of us rarely cross swords with these kinds of experts, while we are surrounded in our lives by persuaders who can run rings around the average lawyer or salesperson. Children can be masterful manipulators. Spouses constantly play power games, with wives traditionally believed to have the upper hand (if you follow any of the family-oriented comic strips you know what I mean). Lovers do their share of persuading, as do friends, neighbors and relatives. Persuasion and power operate even in chance encounters on the street (the automobile is one of our favorite instruments of power and control). You have probably noticed that some people seem to get their way as a matter of course, while others seem always to lose in a one-on-one situation.

We are talking here about power and persuasion in the sense of one person getting another to *do* what he or she wants him or her to do. From the point of view of practical persuaders, action always is the ultimate goal. A manager wants his people to work more productively. A child wants mom to buy her a candy bar in the grocery store. An attorney wants the jury to find for her client. A girl wants to be asked out on a date (by a boy who wants a little loving). An advertiser wants shoppers to buy his brand. A wife wants a new kitchen. A husband wants some peace and quiet. Two women both want the last good dress on the bargain counter. Two men both want the same taxicab on a rainy night in Manhattan. A salesman wants us to sign on the dotted line, and we want a better deal.

Rhetoricians tell us about persuasion in terms of changing another person's beliefs or point of view. Social psychologists tell us about persuasion as a means of changing someone's attitudes. These approaches take us only so far, because ultimately what is the point of changing someone's beliefs or attitudes unless it results in his *doing* something differently, something *we want him to do*?

All practical persuaders—friends or strangers, children or adults, professionals or amateurs—operate according to the same principles and employ the same basic tactics, according to the same basic strategy. Power and persuasion finally come down to information management.

- People do things because they *decide* to do them.
- In making these decisions, they go through a decision process.
- By understanding that decision process, we can influence it.

Persuasion, as I will use the term here, is the basic process for influencing what other people do. It means *engineering people's action decisions through the effective use of information.* Persuaders do not *make* people do anything. Rather, they *get them to decide* to do things. What about when people have no choice but to do something? We'll take that up later, but for now go on this assumption: Any time there is a possibility, there is a choice.

Power, a more general term, is the ability to act effectively and to accomplish objectives. *Control*, which most people confuse with power, is the ability to influence, direct or dominate what other people do. This distinction (straight out of the dictionary) is one of the keys to understanding how power works in our lives. Both power and control work through the persuasion process, whether we are looking at a salesman convincing someone to buy a car, or a military officer ordering his unit to attack an enemy strongpoint. This book will describe the persuasion process and will clarify the differences among persuasion, power and control. That done, you will realize that we all do these things, all of the time, according to the same principles. The only difference is that some of us are better at it than others. You may be surprised to realize, after reading this book, that you are a lot better at persuasion, power and control than you had ever imagined.

Common Myths About Power

With all the concern and confusion about power, it isn't surprising that many people hold inaccurate beliefs about power. Let's examine some of the more common of these.

Power Myth 1: *Power is bad.*

Power is about the most taboo topic in America today, even more so than sex and money (both of which are closely tied to power). Friends and acquaintances rarely discuss their power relationships frankly. Teachers in public schools get in big trouble if they seriously bring up power in their classrooms. Powerful people and powerful institutions have few friends among the American public. We are usually pleased to see them toppled or at least successfully attacked by "the little fellow."

However, the notion that all power is bad is nonsense. Through power we have the ability to accomplish things, and without it life literally could not proceed. In mythology, in religion, in literature and in popular entertainment we find both *good* and *bad* power. The conflict between God and Satan is central to Christianity and Islam. Great literature has protagonists (good guys) battling antagonists (bad guys). *The Wizard of Oz* featured *two* sets of witches: Good Witches of the North and South, and Bad Witches of the East and West. The forces of good prevail over the forces of evil in the great myths and stories, and audiences cheer at the movies when the cowboys with the white hats out-shoot the cowboys wearing the black hats. We enjoy seeing "good power" triumph in real life as well.

Because of our lack of understanding, "power" has gotten a bum rap. It is the *abuse* of power—control—we don't like. Realistically, the person who complains about power is often the one who turned out to have the lesser amount and therefore didn't prevail.

Power Myth 2: *Our obsession with power is an outcome of the stressful, modern world in which we live.*

Not at all. Read the Book of Genesis and you will find that power struggles began with Adam and Eve, and that the serpent was the world's first persuader. The Koran contains the same myth (Surah XX, 120), apparently adapted to the Arabian culture, in which women had much less power than they did in the Hebrew culture. Muhammad has the devil working on Adam, not Eve: "O Adam! Shall I show thee the tree of immortality and power that wasteth away not?" Hundreds of years later John Milton expanded this drama in *Paradise Lost* into

11

a primeval power struggle between the Ultimate Power Guy (God) and the Ultimate Jerk (Satan).

The Old Testament, dating back three thousand years or so, is replete with stories about people using power and good advice about dealing with it. Many of the Psalms, for example, are pleas to Yahweh by the Hebrews for more power over their enemies. Jacob prospered through manipulation, Joshua through military force. The Book of Proverbs contains numerous bits of good advice about power, and Ecclesiastes comments on what it is really worth. At about the same time Greek dramatists were writing plays hinging on power problems. Greek and Latin philosophers left behind them a legacy of sage discussions on the topic of power, and *Plutarch's Lives* amounted to a casebook on men of power in the ancient pagan world.

Machiavelli wrote *The Prince*, essentially a manual of practical advice for rulers who had to deal with newly emerging political systems, around 1514. About one hundred years earlier, Chaucer had shown a keen practical understanding of a wide spectrum of types of power in his *Canterbury Tales*. To this day there exists no better rendering of the quintessential man-eater than his "Wyfe of Bath." One hundred years after Machiavelli, Shakespeare made power struggles the vehicle for several of his plays. *War and Peace*, written by Tolstoy around the turn of the twentieth century, contains a number of textbook discussions of power as it applies to individuals, armies and governments.

People have *always* been interested in power. It stands to reason: when have people not wanted things to go their own way?

Power Myth 3: *We have no business influencing what other people do.*

Doctors influence their patients. Teachers influence their students. Parents influence their children. Pastors influence their congregations. People influence their friends. Where is the harm? Often we influence people to do things that are beneficial for them, as indeed we should. But when someone controls another person for his own benefit, at the other's expense, that is another matter. Then we are talking about manipulation and control, and *that* is what offends us.

Power Myth 4: *Powerful people are outgoing, self-confident and aggressive.*

The "supersalesman" is an American mythological hero—the Harold Hill "Music Man" who moves right in and fast-talks his way to fame and fortune. He might be a salesman, a Hollywood agent, a high-powered politico, or a silk-smooth con artist; whatever the role, he is blessed with the gift of gab. In reality a few people like that are powerful, but most are merely obnoxious. On the other hand, some very powerful people are soft-spoken, or even shy and diffident. Some people have proved to be powerful even though they were literally helpless. There are many ways of influencing what people do, and slapping them on the back, shoving a cigar in their mouth and proposing a deal is not necessarily even one of the best.

Power Myth 5: *With a little "sales resistance" it is easy to keep from being influenced by other people.*

As fearful as many of us are about being controlled by others, we like to believe we can hold our own. To some extent that is true enough: If someone is obviously trying to persuade you to do something you don't want to do, he probably won't succeed if you are determined not to do it. But when a *really* artful persuader works on you, you may never be aware of it, not even after you have done whatever it is he persuaded you to do. Make no mistake—this happens to you all the time.

Power Myth 6: *It is easier to influence weak people than it is to influence strong people.*

If we define "weak" and "strong" in terms of how easily people are influenced, this is true by definition. But really, nobody, "weak" or "strong," is immune to persuasion or control. Samson was undone by Delilah. Othello was brought down by Iago. P. T. Barnum, America's legendary supersalesman, time and again fell victim to someone else's slick sales pitch. A surprising number of ancient heroes were felled not on the field of battle by their opponents, but at home by their own women. Remember the principle of judo: An opponent's strength can be used against him. Many of the character traits we consider strengths can leave us vulnerable to manipulation by unscrupulous people. Character traits such as trust, honesty, openness, and tolerance are considered to be hallmarks of strong people. If they seem to be waning these days, it may be because our society has reached the point where it is too easy for sharp operators to get away with taking advantage of them.

Power Myth 7: *The key to being powerful is to get into a powerful position.*

This can, of course, help, but it is far from the whole story. People in powerful positions—presidents of companies, commanders of armies and navies, and even rulers of empires—still have the problem of being in command and having subordinates carry out orders. Weak people in powerful positions are nevertheless weak people, and people skilled in power (or control) who have no official position can be very influential. More than one nation, corporation and family has been run by someone other than the one whose name was on the door.

Power Myth 8: *Power is a mysterious quality that some people have and others don't.*

In their book (*The Only Living Witness*) about Ted Bundy, a convicted serial murderer suspected of killing twenty-five, and possibly more than thirty, young women, Stephen Michaud and Hugh Aynesworth said Bundy had "a preternatural power to manipulate, a capacity whose effect was akin to magic. It was this power that made him such an effective killer and so impossible to track down. It was a key to his two successful escapes from Colorado jails." Michaud and Aynesworth are thorough and insightful reporters, but here they make an all too common error, attributing to magic and supernatural forces that which they do not understand. This myth is wrong on two counts. First of all, everybody is capable of accomplishing things and influencing the actions of others. So having power is a matter of degree, not an either/or. Second, and more important, there is nothing mysterious about power (even that of people such as Ted Bundy). By the time you finish reading this book you will understand exactly how it works.

.

Power Myth 9: *Revealing the truth about power
and discussing it openly will make it easier for people
to control and take advantage of others.*

This is the biggest myth of all, in spite of how many believe it. Power is a positive force, not something evil. The whole point of education is to increase people's power. The same is true of religion. If we understand how persuasion, power and control work, it becomes that much more difficult for other people to jerk us around. Controlling people is more a matter of motives than of technique. The real controllers and manipulators know how to do that much better than any book could ever tell them, and they always have. In fact, the major source of my own understanding was watching them in action and analyzing what they did. Most people are not interested in controlling others, but simply want to live their own lives more effectively. For them, learning how persuasion, power and control work can only be liberating and empowering. If anyone objects to *that*, I would question his true motives.

Why Does Power Make Us So Uncomfortable?

Not everyone craves power, at least not in the grand sense; the notion of power makes many uncomfortable, to say the least. Among Americans the reasons for this seem to be three: religious, political and personal.

America, although it enjoys perhaps the widest range of religious worship of any nation, is essentially founded on Christian principles and assumptions. Scorning earthly power and wealth, Christ taught that love and salvation were the supreme values. These continue to be honored as important social values in America, but they also are directly contrary to selfish, personal drives and, increasingly, the tone of our society. Few of us will instinctively deny material rewards, humble ourselves and turn the other cheek. Later we will see how the opposite of Christian love is not hate but control. Wagner, in his *Ring* cycle, made much the same point: The power of the Ring to control the universe could be realized only by someone who had renounced love. So, as much as we might desire wealth and power (and the marketing emphasis in our modern society strongly pushes us in those directions), the American culture contains many religion-based messages contradictory to those desires. The more a person was influenced by Christian assumptions, the more uncomfortable that person might feel about one form or another of secular power.

Politically, Americans historically have been against "power." As far back as the 1830s, Tocqueville observed this tendency and theorized that it might owe to the strong pressures of democracy toward equality and concommitant feelings of helplessness. Thus our officials (at least in theory) are elected to exercise limited amounts of power for limited periods of time. Offices or positions may wield substantial power, but the individuals who occupy them use that power at the pleasure of the voters. To further constrain the exercise of arbitrary power, government in the United States historically has acted to keep business politically weak. So there are strong "anti-power" assumptions underlying the American political system, which to a great extent reflect the sentiments of Americans.

On the personal level, we can again go back to our historical roots. The colonies were founded and populated by people in search of freedom of one form or another. At least until the late 1800s "independence" was a part of life for most Americans, and it still remains a strong cultural value and myth. Any exercise of power could be interpreted as encroaching on a person's freedom and independence, and this too contributes to our discomfort about power.

What This Book Will Do

Here is what this book will *not* do. It will *not* necessarily make anyone who reads it rich, famous, successful, healthy, happy or twenty pounds lighter. The purpose of the book is to explain the mechanisms of persuasion, power and control, and to show how they affect us all in our everyday lives. The rest is up to you, the reader. If you want to be more powerful, I offer you some useful knowledge that may help. If you want to learn how to resist other people's attempts to manipulate and control you, you will find plenty of handy hints in the pages that follow. If you opened the book hoping to get a line on how to jerk other people around, be my guest. You will find plenty of passages to make your ears burn, and you may even find reason to change your purposes. You are not likely to gain any real advantage over others, especially if they also have read this material.

We start by examining the natures of persuasion, power and control. We will explore the four types of power and will see how individual decisions, the building blocks of power, are analogous to atoms. The ability to make effective action decisions is *performance power*. Tolstoy claimed in *War and Peace* that history is the totality of moment-to-moment decisions made by ordinary individuals. But people do not always act alone. *Persuasive power*, the ability of one person to influence what another person does, we might say is analogous to a reaction between two atoms. Carrying the atomic analogy even further, "molecules of power"—influence between people that operates over time—are created by *agreement power*. People make agreements about what they mutually will do, or will not do. A business contract is an example of agreement power, as is a vow of marriage. The most prevalent, and most sought after, form of agreement power in America at the present time is . . . money. Yes, we will look at the fascinating implications of viewing money as a form of agreement power.

The fourth form of power, *structure power*, like the other forms of power, is ultimately based on individuals' moment-to-moment decisions. Just as living organisms are structures comprised of single atoms, so social organisms such as families, churches, clubs, cities, corporations, armies and nations are structures of agreements among people that direct the kinds of action decisions they make. The tragedy of Shakespeare's King Lear was that he confused these four types of power. Many of us make the same kinds of mistakes in our everyday lives, although rarely on such a dramatic scale.

Next we will clarify the crucial difference between power and control, the major mix-up that prevents most people from dealing with power effectively. Americans typically believe that "power" means being in a position to make other people do their bidding. Accordingly, "freedom" means being in a position so that others can't do that to them. Anyone who operates strictly according to these views of power and freedom is virtually guaranteed of being neither powerful nor free. Why is that so? I don't want to spoil the surprise by giving away too much in the first chapter, but it comes down to a difference in motives as decisive as the difference between good and evil. The processes of power and control are the same, and the key to the direction in which these processes are employed lies in the heart of the person using them. People tend to be either Power People or Control People, although there are few pure examples of either extreme. Those who take neither path commonly are called "victims." Which do I advocate in this book? No question—power all the way.

To understand how persuasion, power and control work, we must understand why people do what they do. Over the centuries history's great thinkers have left a rich treasury of ideas on what motivates human behavior, but for the purpose of understanding precisely how power works what others have said tends to be either incomplete or imprecise, or both. Combining the wisdom of the philosophers with the analytic tools of modern social science, we can reach a clearer understanding of how these processes work. We begin with the premise that people do things because they *decide* to do them. We will dissect the decision process preceding every action into simple, specific steps so you can easily grasp all the ways in which this process can be influenced and how people can improve their ability to make more effective action decisions. Let me stress up front that understanding this process will require a little effort. Even though the basic mechanisms are simple, the human heart and mind are subtle and complex, and so can be the decisions that lead to action. This book explains those mechanisms more simply and straightforwardly than you can find elsewhere, but even so, be warned that this will *not* be a compilation of some snappy one-liners, entertaining anecdotes and a list of ten how-to's. There are plenty of other books that can give you that, but they also will not further your understanding of how persuasion, power and control work.

Knowing why people do what they do, and how they make their decisions to act, we can analyze the persuasion process. Most people, and most how-to-persuade books, see persuasion as convincing someone of all the good things that will result if he does what you want him to do. Master that approach to persuasion, and you have a fair chance of becoming a successful advertising copywriter or commission

.

salesperson. However, leave it at that and you risk being taken to the cleaners in just about every other sphere of your life.

From the action decision process, ten basic persuasion tactics emerge. Five of these work to change people's perceptions of the choices they are considering. The other five are tools for manipulating the persuasion process itself. You will see how all the various types of power and control you encounter in your everyday life can be boiled down to this one basic process, and you will learn the eight-step strategy for successful persuasion.

We also will correct another error many people make, that persuaders get other people to do things. We will see how sophisticated persuaders succeed by using persuasion to get people *not to* do things. Why is that approach so effective? Because it takes advantage of people's natural inclinations, to the extent that they usually aren't even aware that it is happening. We will examine in detail that and all the other persuasion approaches used by the hustlers, the hucksters, the fast-talkers, the manipulators . . . and yourself! It may strike some as a little farfetched that all persuasion can be represented in only ten tactics; but recall that every book in the English language can be down into the twenty-six letters of the alphabet. The trick in both instances is to understand how the elements fit together.

The analysis of persuasion, power and control, in all their forms, prepares us for an in-depth exploration of how they work in everyday situations. We will see how the theories presented here apply to the marketplace, the workplace, and to our lives in general.

We operate in the *marketplace* as independent agents exercising free choice. The marketers, advertisers and salespeople have nothing going for them but their ability to persuade. How much power they have over us depends entirely upon how much power we are willing to let them have. We will review the leverage points that give the advantage to the marketplace persuaders. We will examine the various powertools they use, and exactly how they use them.

In the *workplace*, structure power prevails. We are boxes in the organization chart, little cogs in the big machine. Or are we? Look around at work. In spite of the job descriptions, the policy manuals and the reporting relationships, people get away with murder and even prosper by doing so. How can that be? What does it take to succeed? We will take a realistic look at how power works at every level of an organization, from the people on the assembly lines to the ones in the executive suites, bringing into the analysis the crucial distinction between power and control. The reasons why some organizations succeed and others fail will then become clearer. Essentially, organizations are successful to the extent that they enable their members to be powerful. Organizations based on controlling what their members do are in the long run headed for disaster. We will see why organizations almost inevitably degenerate from power structures to control structures and thus have limited lifespans.

The final chapter will outline how to have power. There are two sides to this: following the eleven paths to power, and subverting the levers of control. Neither by itself will get you there. Coming as it does after our analysis of the processes of persuasion and power, this chapter will help you to appreciate the wisdom of the ancient thinkers. Truly, as Ecclesiastes tells us, there is nothing new under the sun. However, the tools of modern social science, if properly applied, can give contemporary meaning to ancient wisdom. That, I hope, will be the ultimate contribution of this book.

What follows is a somewhat different way of looking at the moment-to-moment activities of everyday life. It requires analyzing your behavior (and that of other people) as a continuous stream of discrete, precise steps. Most people tend not to look very deeply into themselves, but rather prefer just to go about their business. Not everyone agrees with Socrates that "the unexamined life is not worth living," but you probably are reading this book at least in part to learn more about yourself. A book this size can't answer *every* question you have about power—that would require a whole library. What it *can* do is give you a framework for analyzing how power works in your own life. Once you are aware of the basic process, you will realize that it is not mysterious at all.

This book is based on a theory, but it takes a practical approach. I am not reporting on a new trend, nor disclosing previously hidden secrets. No, all I did was discover a new way of looking at life as it goes on around us every day. In doing so I have, I believe, achieved a better understanding of matters that have perplexed the human race for countless centuries. I hope to share it with you in the pages that follow.

2

THE FOUR TYPES OF POWER

King Lear's Big Mistake

As you may recall, Lear, King of Britain, had reached four score and upward. He determined to divide his kingdom among his three daughters, thus to retire from the throne. As part of the ceremony, he asked each daughter in turn to declare her love for her dear father (that is, himself). Goneril and Regan, the two eldest (and least constrained by integrity), had no problem with that, but Cordelia, his youngest and favorite, had love richer than her tongue, and declined to speechify. Outraged, Lear disinherited her and split the kingdom between Goneril and Regan, with the understanding that they would support him and one hundred knights, him to spend alternate months with each daughter. "I do invest you jointly with my power, pre-eminence and all the large effects that troop with majesty," he declared.

It wasn't long before Goneril and Regan saw their enthusiasm for this arrangement wane. First they cut his entourage to fifty knights, and then to none. Soon Lear was stumbling through the countryside, lurking in hovels and babbling his regrets to all who would listen. Finally the connivance and ambitions of Goneril, Regan and Gloucester's bastard son, Edmund, demised him completely. Lear was reduced to a "poor, infirm, weak and despis'd old man," in the final scene holding the dead body of Cordelia in his arms, having too late realized her true qualities. Small consolation that Goneril, Regan and Edmund had in the meantime perished by their own treachery.

Possibly Lear could have used the services of a good management consultant. Some therapeutic counselling might have helped too. One thing is for certain—had he understood the differences among the four types of power, he could have avoided a lot of grief.

While Lear was on the throne, he had *structure power*. He was king, and therefore everybody did what he said. When he passed the crown on to his daughters, he fancied that he had *agreement power*—after all, they did say they would support him and his knights. However, when Goneril and Regan welched ("How sharper than a serpent's tooth it is to have a thankless child!"), Lear was suddenly on his own. He soon discovered he didn't have sufficient *persuasive power* to get anyone but a couple of loyal retainers to do anything. As for *performance power*, his youthful vigor was years behind him; more to the point, he was a dotty old fool. Not that he'd ever played with a full deck (Goneril: "The best and soundest of his time hath been but rash." Regan: "'Tis the infirmity of his age; yet he has ever but slenderly known himself"). Evidence of his inability to judge character was compelling. Lord knows he had been warned early on by the Earl of Kent ("When power to flattery bows . . . and majesty falls to folly"). Even his Fool knew the score: "Thou madest thy daughters thy mothers . . . thou gavest them the rod and puttest down thine own breeches. . . . I am better than thou art now; I am a fool, thou art nothing."

By Act IV, Lear was finally catching on: "Thou hast seen a farmer's dog bark at a beggar? And the creature run from the cur? There thou mightst behold the great image of authority; a dog's obey'd in office." Alas, it was one more case of old too soon, wise too late.

Having been a mad king, Lear never analyzed his situation, but assumed that the fact that people invariably did whatever he told them to do (and always so agreeably!) had something to do with *him*. Not that he is the only one ever to have made this mistake. Retired executives or police officers, puzzled why no one any longer pays attention to them, err in the same way. So do retired department store buyers who wonder why colleagues from their supplier firms who formerly wined and dined them suddenly seem to have perpetually full calendars. Sooner or later it dawns on them that the wining, dining and joviality wasn't for *them*, but for "the pencil" they used to command—their authority to write orders.

There is only one process of power, but it operates in four ways. To ensure that you don't make the same mistakes King Lear did, let's see what they are.

Performance Power: Making Effective Action Decisions

We do things because we decide to do them, and performance power is our ability to make effective action decisions. People with high performance power accomplish their objectives by deciding to do the right things, at the right times.

What kinds of things? Anything that will advance a person toward his or her objectives. Floor traders who time their buys and sells right have performance power. Managers who allocate their resources so as to achieve their M.B.O.'s have performance power. So do military commanders who marshal their forces to capture a key position, reporters who get the important facts and write them up in a way that their audience can't resist reading, and secretaries who manage their workloads so that they keep the boss happy and also go home at quitting time leaving a cleared desk behind them.

Baseball Hall of Famer Lou Brock, former star of the St. Louis Cardinals, had so much performance power that he holds the all-time record for number of bases stolen. How he did it holds some lessons for us all.*

Lou Brock was a fast runner, although at any time there were others in baseball who could beat him in a footrace. He has the record, and they don't. The difference lies purely in decision-making. What's to decide? First, *whether or not* to go for that next base. Second, *when* to go.

---

* Adapted from an article by Bruce Keidan, "How Lou Brock Has Come to Steal Immortality," *Philadelphia Inquirer*, August 8, 1977, p. 1-E.

Whether or not to go is a matter of knowing whether he can beat the ball to the base. To perfect his steals, Brock timed himself, and he studied his footprints to ensure that he was running in the straightest possible path from one base to the next. He also timed the pitchers. He found that from the time the pitcher commits to releasing the ball to the time the catcher's throw reaches second base, somewhere between 3.0 and 3.5 seconds will pass. His own time from first to second base ranged between 3.2 and 3.4 seconds. So most of the time, he and a *perfect* throw were going to arrive at the base pretty much simultaneously. With Brock on base, the catcher knew that he had to make a perfect throw, which forced him and the pitcher to pay a lot of attention to nailing Brock, *if* he ran. We can't, of course, forget the batter at the plate who is trying to get a hit or at least draw a walk. So Brock had distraction working in his favor—the opposing battery must split its attention between two objectives.

Through extensive study, Brock determined the best posture to be in for maximum acceleration when he took off for a base, and he started with an invisible shift of weight to get him going. He also worked out a way of standing at an angle which, through optical illusion, created the impression that he was standing closer to first base than he actually was.

He exploited the rules. The rules say that the pitcher must come to a set position before he pitches. Brock, however, can be in motion. To find the cue to tip him off when the pitcher was committed to throwing the pitch to the plate, Brock studied films of pitchers' feet. He discovered the pitcher's heels to be the giveaway, signalling the decisive shift of weight that meant either a pitch to the plate or a pick-off throw to first base. After that point the pitcher could not change his mind, and thus Brock knew precisely *when* to take off.

To gain a little more edge, Brock enlisted the aid of the player who followed him in the batting order, Ted Sizemore. Sizemore learned, instead of stepping into the ball, to step *back* toward the catcher. This slowed the catcher up just enough to mean the difference many times. Sizemore would often bluff bunts, to get the bat out into the catcher's field of vision for the sake of yet more distraction.

Teams tried various tactics to stop Brock, ranging from intimidation to fancy maneuvers. Ordinary pickoff plays failed at the outset.

They only showed Brock the pitcher's move, so he could study it. One team tried having the first baseman sneak out behind him, then having the pitcher throw directly at Brock. At first this confused him, but then he figured out how to put it to use. He waited until the last instant before dodging the ball. Usually the first baseman, having been screened by Lou from seeing the ball coming, couldn't react fast enough to catch it. As the ball bounced off him and rolled into right field, Brock went all the way to third. Pitchers soon abandoned that tactic. They tried speeding up their deliveries. They spent long hours perfecting their pickoff moves. None found "The Answer."

Lou Brock's example is the essence of performance power. He had a clear objective—steal that base—so he knew exactly what he wanted. By careful study and practice, and through well-digested experience, he made maximum use of his natural abilities. He knew exactly what those abilities were, and he knew exactly when and where to employ them. Finally it all came down to a matter of decision-making—the right action at the right time. That, in a nutshell, is performance power, and Brock had enough of it that he was only the fifteenth player elected into the Hall of Fame his first year of eligibility for that honor.

Ancient heroes like Achilles, Hercules, Odysseus and Sir Lancelot had performance power. American heroes like Charles Lindbergh, explorers Lewis and Clark, Thomas Edison and General George Patton had performance power. Superstar athletes have performance power. Certain fictional heroes—the various Humphrey Bogart characters, James Bond and Travis McGee—appeal to us because of their performance power. Great scientists (e.g., Albert Einstein) and great artists (e.g., Vincent van Gogh, Wolfgang Amadeus Mozart) have it. So do successful serial murderers and terrorists.

Structure Power: Social Roles, Rules and Hierarchies

As King Lear discovered to his great distress, structure power goes with the crown, only then to the guy who wears it. To understand structure power, think of the tollbooth on a bridge. Whoever sits in that tollbooth—you, me, Victoria Principal, Attila the Hun or the

VISTA

Speaker of the House—has the power to demand the amount of toll from anyone in an automobile who wishes to cross the bridge. Whoever is in the automobile—you, me, the Boston Celtics, the Emperor of the East and West or Frank Sinatra—is obligated to pay that amount (well, maybe not Sinatra). Once the motorist pays, he is privileged to pass through the gate. The fee paid, the tollkeeper can't stop him. And once the tollkeeper steps out of the booth, he has no special right to demand anything from anybody.

The principle of structure power is that positions or social roles are defined as having certain rights and responsibilities vis-a-vis other positions or social roles. Within the boundaries of those roles or positions, the people occupying them theoretically have no latitude as to the actions they can take. They do it as the organization chart, the policy manual, the sacred scrolls or tribal custom dictates.

This clearly applies to people's jobs. It also is the basis for families, cultures, associations, professions, tribes, religions and every other form of social organization. If a culture doesn't have an organization chart, at least it has a variety of social roles that its members play. In middle-class American society most of us sooner or later play the roles of adult, employee, parent, child, spouse, consumer, student, voter, driver, guest, pedestrian, innocent bystander and churchgoer, among many others. Performing one of those roles, we know that certain things are expected of us, and that there are other things we are not to do. The rules may not be written down, yet we and others around us have a pretty good idea of what they are.

Bureaucrats, constitutional lawyers and corporate attorneys are the present-day masters of structure power. The laws of the land represent legal structure—actions we must, and must not, take. Corporations and governments are constituted as networks of do's and don'ts. Performance in a structured situation depends upon how well you follow the rules. Deviate at your own risk. If in doubt, check it out. Call in the legal department, or get out the policy manual. If doubt still persists, kick it upstairs, consult the priest or the rabbi, or take it to the Supreme Court. Ultimately, it must be resolved within the context of the power structure. No exceptions. How many times have you come up against the Ultimate Solution: "Yes, I can see your point, but if we let you do that, then we would have to let *everybody* do it. I'm sure you understand."

Structure power establishes systems of "have to's" that occupants in positions or roles must respect. As annoying as the rules can be from time to time, without them there would be no such thing as society, civilization, government or any other organizations. Custom, tradition, mores, laws, principles, guidelines, policies, procedures— all these and more represent the structure power that holds organizations together.

Perhaps because of our hunger for freedom from control, Americans have elevated very few masters of structure power to the status of cultural hero. About the only ones we celebrate are the Founding Fathers, who in 1776 ended our relationship with Britain as one of its colonies and following the Revolutionary War drafted the Constitution of the United States, the basis for our nation's legal and political structures. Moses and Saint Paul are revered in their respective religions, but few of their adherents explicitly realize that their great contributions were matters of structure power. Moses codified the laws of the Hebrew religion and culture. Saint Paul took the initial, important steps toward founding an organized religion on Christ's teachings.

Business historians, on the other hand, recognize a number of "structure power" heroes. Economist Adam Smith described the principle of "division of labor" upon which modern industry depends. Daniel C. McCallum, of the Erie Railroad, in 1855 developed what came to be the model of the structure of the modern managed industrial corporation and laid out one of the very first organization charts ever printed by an American company.* Theodore Vail at the turn of the century designed the remarkably successful management system of the Bell Telephone Company. Alfred P. Sloan, Jr., restructured General Motors Corporation in the 1920s and left Henry Ford choking on its dust. Frederick W. Taylor, the father of "scientific management," developed the principles of time and motion study. These people, and

---

* Alfred D. Chandler, Jr., *Strategy and Structure* (Cambridge, MA: M.I.T. Press, 1962), p. 21.

many others like them, helped bring about the modern industrial age with their innovations in organizational structures, but their names are not exactly household words.

Agreement Power: Mutual Influence Relationships

Structure power operates between abstractions—positions or social roles. Agreement power operates between individuals (including legal "individuals" such as corporations). Two individuals agree on the terms of mutual rights and obligations. It may be a two-hundred-page contract spelling out the details of a Hollywood deal (these get down to specifying the size of the type in which the stars' names will appear in the ads). It may be an exchange of marriage vows. It may be a couple making a date. It may lie in the act of accepting a job offer. It may be two nine-year-old boys swapping three Spiderman comics for two G.I. Joes and a Superheroes.

In theory the terms of agreement power are binding, so the essence of using it lies in negotiating favorable terms. In practice, it is also a good idea to provide some means for enforcing the agreement should there be any "misunderstandings." Agents, labor negotiators, industrial buyers and sellers, and marketplace hagglers all live by agreement power, and by their negotiating skills they keep their families fed. Formalizing their agreements through legal contracts, they rely on the legal system for enforcement. The informal agreements made between friends, lovers, neighbors, buddies and parents and children tend to depend more upon good faith. Broken agreements are often the cause of shattered relationships. If a person will break one agreement, why risk trusting him with any more?

Structure power, in spite of its apparent absolute do's and don'ts, is only as binding as the parties involved agree it is. The codes of a religion, the rules of a club, the laws of a land, or the policies of a firm have the power to obligate only individuals who agree to be bound by them. Thus the nature of authority: The office, or the person, or the laws have the power to direct the behavior only of those who agree to be directed. Chester Barnard, in his management classic *The Functions of the Executive*, noted that the army is actually among the most democratic of institutions. Its formidable authority structure notwithstanding, orders are issued only if it is certain that they will be obeyed, and that is a matter of securing the consent of the troops through training and morale. In agreement power lies the strength of freely elected authority, for all concerned agree that the winner of the election should exercise the powers of the office—the majority chose him, and the others agree to abide by the majority vote.

Nietzsche's proclamation that "God is dead" was, as Richard L. Rubenstein pointed out in his book *Power Struggle*, a theological code word for the *collapse of authority*—political authority, moral authority, social authority and religious authority. Nietzsche had sensed that as modern times marched relentlessly on, the old rules were going by the boards. More and more people were declining to follow them. That same erosion of authority has continued to this day, with progressively less consensus as to what rules, if any, an individual should use for guidance, and what social entities or institutions, if any, we should recognize as authoritative. Recent examples of this social tide include the student demonstrations of the late 1960s, which represented a rejection of school and political authority, and the women's liberation movement of the 1970s, largely aimed at rejecting traditional notions of relationships between the sexes. To some extent this is the result of a mistaken belief among some segments of society that discrediting authority necessarily enhances the freedom of individuals. Thus we have the news media, activists, intellectuals, gadflies and professional dissenters deliberately tweaking authority tradition, government, business and the military—at every opportunity and then triumphantly parading all the gaffs, blunders and ill-considered statements that they are able to provoke. It is all great fun, but more often than not it only serves to unravel a thread or two more of our social fabric.

In America at present (and perhaps throughout most of our history), the most revered form of agreement power is *money*—the almighty dollar. The idea that money is power is nothing new, of course. However, we don't always recognize the particular type of power money represents. Without money people make mutual agreements for goods and services—"Chop that wood, and I'll give you a nice home-cooked meal." "Bring home the bacon, and I'll be a hot number."

"Help raise my barn this week, and I'll help raise yours the next." In ancient Sparta, Lycurgus created a semicommunistic society by decreeing that money be in the form of large, virtually worthless lumps of iron. This proved so ungainly a medium of exchange that little money changed hands, and citizens acted out of duty to the state rather than in pursuit of wealth.

Such transactions are the result of face-to-face negotiations, or of mutual obligations represented by roles. Money is agreement power honored by strangers, and with fixed pricing no one needs to negotiate. We work eight hours for X dollars' worth of agreement power. Taking it to the store, people whom we have never seen before are obligated to give us X dollars' worth of groceries in exchange. Money thus is an excellent medium for discharging agreements in an anonymous, mass society. Many of the exchanges formerly made by virtue of obligations among family, village or tribe members now can be made with others whose relationship to us begins and ends with that transaction. Money unquestionably is necessary in a modern, technology-based society; but in another sense, a high per-capita gross national product is an indicator of a nation's degree of social alienation. It provides the bearer with agreement power, but not the kind of agreements that bring people together. It also is an inherently *weak* form of agreement power: When the chips are down, loyal supporters are almost always worth more than hired guns. Few people are willing to die for money, but millions are willing to die for their beliefs and their sense of duty.

That money represents agreement perhaps accounts for the outrage many Americans feel in response to inflationary price increases. One thing Americans do believe for certain is that money is worth something. So, if we work our forty hours and the X dollars we receive for it buys less than it did a year ago, has not an agreement been broken? And is such a betrayal not cause for anger? In the face of quantum jumps in gasoline prices during the oil crises of the 1970s, many otherwise upright citizens were provoked to surliness, vandalism, violence and gratuitous theft. The fact is that money, as with anything else, is worth only what others agree it is worth. It may be the preferred lubricant for a lonely, anonymous and mobile society, but as a god, it is no more immortal than any other. Americans tend to value everything in terms of money, and as both Erich Fromm in *The Sane Society* and Ernest Schumacher in *Small Is Beautiful* have observed, nothing with a price tag on it is sacred. From time to time events demonstrate the wisdom of this, but many of us continue to miss the message.

Charismatic leaders operate through agreement power. Popular figures such as Franklin Delano Roosevelt, John F. Kennedy and Martin Luther King, Jr., as well as disastrous figures such as Lenin, Hitler and the Reverend Jim Jones (of the Jonestown massacre), are able to persuade significant numbers of people to agree to transfer the disagreeable burden of decision-making to them. Whether "charismatic leadership" is for better or for worse ultimately depends upon the outcomes of the leadership.

We tend to be guarded in extending our admiration to people skilled at agreement power—public "agreement power heroes" are not numerous. But people with a flair for it have certainly made their marks in the world, as well as in fiction. One of the early masters of agreement power was the biblical Jacob, who got his brother Esau to trade his birthright for a mess of pottage. Wagner's monumental four-opera *Ring* cycle revolves about the god Wotan's doomed attempt to weasel out of the agreement he made with the giants who built Valhalla for him. Portia, the heroine of Shakespeare's *Merchant of Venice*, successfully got her lover out of an agreement to give Shylock a pound of flesh. Henry Kissinger received a Nobel Peace Prize acknowledging him as an agreement power maven. Perhaps the most notable modern failure in agreement power was Britain's Neville Chamberlain, who in 1938 signed Czechoslovakia over to Adolf Hitler in exchange for "peace in our times."

Persuasive Power: Influencing Actions

When no structure power applies to a situation, and when no agreement power exists, and yet one person wants another to do something, persuasive power comes into play. How does a salesperson get a client to sign on the dotted line? How does a young man get a young woman to go up to his apartment? How does a child get mom to buy a candy bar in the supermarket? How does a trial lawyer get a jury to find for her client? How does a con artist get a mark to part with his money? By persuasion, nothing else.

The persuasion process is the essential mechanism by which all forms of power operate, and we will examine it in more detail in the next section of the book. For the time being leave it at this: *Persuasion is a matter of engineering other people's action decisions so that they do what we want them to do.* The ancient Greeks and Romans, according to Plutarch, held persuasion to be the most noble way to influence people's actions, and the ability to persuade to be one of the highest virtues. The philosopher Aristotle was highly commended for his ability to persuade people whichever way he pleased. However, Plutarch had in mind a particular type of persuasion—*rhetoric*, or logically demonstrating that the advocated action is the Right Thing to Do. Other forms of persuasion throughout history have not been especially popular, as we tend not to appreciate other people's attempts at engineering our action decisions. (E.g., Plutarch Vol. I, page 135: " . . . with good reason thinking that being seduced into wrong was as being forced, and that between deceit and necessity, flattery and compulsion, there was little difference, since both may equally suspend the exercise of reason.")

In situations of structure or agreement power, there are mutual responsibilities. When the boss tells a subordinate to do something, the boss is responsible. But persuasion gets the *other* to decide, and our value system puts the burden of responsibility on the decision-maker. Thus a persuader can enjoy the best of both worlds—he gets what he wants, and the other person is responsible. Certain extreme forms of persuasion—extortion and blackmail—fall outside the law, but little everyday coercions, intimidations, scams and manipulations are legally permissible, even if socially disapproved.

Only in the twentieth century, and especially in America, has persuasion (not rhetoric in the classic sense, but advertising, salesmanship and political propaganda) become a predominant method of social control. When the gods expire, their former places may be filled by devils. A number of writers have commented on this transition, among them Daniel Boorstin, Daniel Bell and Christopher Lasch. Lasch in *The Minimal Self* puts it this way:

.

The decline of authority is a good example of the kind of change that promotes the appearance of democracy without its substance. It is a part of a shift to a manipulative, therapeutic, "pluralistic" and "non-judgmental" style of social discipline that originated, like so many other developments, with the rise of a professional and managerial class in the early 20th century and then spread from the industrial corporation, where it was first perfected, into the political realm as a whole.

It is not clear whether persuasive power became pervasive by design, as Lasch seems to imply, or simply by default, necessitated by the crumbling of previous belief and authority structures. Nor is it the first time that power style has shifted in this way. Plutarch describes Theseus's return to Athens when he attempted to resume the first place in the commonwealth and found that "the minds of the people were so generally corrupted that, instead of obeying commands with silence, they expected to be flattered into their duty."

Consider Shakespeare's character Edmund, illegitimate son of the Earl of Gloucester, in *King Lear*. The "policy manual" of his times left him on the outside looking hungrily in—children fostered out of wedlock had no structure-power claim on their father's heritage. Driven by ambition, and resentful of Edgar, the rightful heir to the title, he saw no option but to scheme, manipulate and connive. In the course of his adventuring he perpetrated Edgar's banishment, his father's mutilation and the falling out of Goneril and Regan (not an entirely bad guy, at that). Though he tried to repent on his death bed, it came too little, too late. From such as Edmund flow the connotations of the term "bastard." Quite likely men of uncertified birth gravitated toward manipulation, given the power structure in which they were forced to operate. Today we more often apply it to men who operate that way than to love children.

Persuasion is not necessarily bad, of course. As a power type it fills a social need, and most of the time it is harmless enough. It goes on between people as an everyday matter of course, whenever a circumstance arises not adequately covered by structure or agreement power. In fact, we often employ it to get people to enter into agree-

.

ments, or to join power structures, in the first place. Job recruiting (or any kind of recruiting) depends upon persuasion, as does selling, advertising, charitable solicitations, panhandling, confidence games, politics or any other power transaction in which there is no legitimate basis for saying that the one person has to do what the other one wants.

Americans recognize such people as Socrates, Aristotle, the Latin orators, Abraham Lincoln, Daniel Webster and attorney Clarence Darrow as heroes of persuasive power. These all are rhetoricians whom we perceive as having argued in favor of truth and justice. Our mythology, if not our pantheon, abounds with exemplars of other forms of persuasive power: Harold Hill, the "Music Man"; P. T. Barnum; the "city slicker"; the "Philadelphia lawyer"; the "Yankee peddler"; among many others. And who among us has not longed, at one time or another, to be blessed with just a bit more of it ourselves?

The Power of the Weak

How is it possible that the timid, the incompetent and even the helpless can make other people do things? The various forms of power provide even the "weak" with many avenues to influence.

Perhaps you know a family in which the "strong" members carry a hopelessly "weak" member—a drunken, chronically unemployed husband or a "delicate" and constantly ailing wife. Far from being weak, these in fact may be the true heads of their households— everything revolves around them, and nothing happens without their say-so. They do it through structure power, by exploiting the value structures of the rest of the family. It isn't by accident that we often find alcoholics married to virtuous, responsible women, or domineering hags espoused to virtuous, responsible men. Hey, they know a good deal when they see one. At the outset they realized that, once the agreement power of the wedding vows was consummated, the other was the type of person who would carry out the duties and responsibilities of the spousal role, come what may ("You agreed for better or for worse, didn't you? Were you lying, or what?")

So that is one way the "weak" can have power—they wheedle

themselves into a position or role that requires somebody else to be responsible for their welfare. All it takes is finding a sucker who will live up to those responsibilities, and then manipulating him or her into agreeing to it. A "Peter Pan" will seek out and charm his "Wendy." From the distaff side, the old "premature bun in the oven" ploy has long served well as the engine for just this kind of marriage, the groom-to-be having been preselected for his susceptibility to "doing the right thing." This has been known to succeed even when it is someone else's bun, or when there is no bun at all. This particular maneuver is greatly aided by another element of structure power, the tendency of our legal system to hold the father responsible for child support, regardless of the woman's role in getting him into that position.

Jobs with iron-clad security—for example civil service, tenured positions or slots in the family firm—also can mean safe havens for "weak performers" through the same mechanisms. Once they fake it through the probationary period they can safely revert to type, as the rules make it virtually impossible for anyone to get rid of them.

"Sympathy plays" also rely on structure power—the value that we who are better off are supposed to place on treating the unfortunate or afflicted with sympathy and charity. Beggars fake injuries or disfigurements; family members feign illnesses; criminal defendants show up in court in wheelchairs, with doctors in attendance.

People with no property, wealth, reputation or prospects may seem to be weak, but in some situations can have a lot of power. Challenged by such a one, a person with a lot to lose may find it prudent to back down. Thus a fanatic who is willing to die certainly has an advantage over an adversary who isn't. Respectable citizens are likely to come out poorly in confrontations with the disreputable. Small businesspeople fall prey to protection rackets, corrupt bureaucrats, and other extortionists and hustlers. Large corporations shrink from battles that might generate bad publicity. Downtrodden groups fighting for their rights can capitalize on publicizing the brutal tactics of their more powerful oppressors, as leaders such as Gandhi and Martin Luther King, Jr., have demonstrated (at least, this works in places where a free press and a spirit of fair play are operative). On the inter-

national scale, the United States is an easy mark for political terrorists and adventurers. Some of our greatest strengths as a nation
lie in the high values we place on human life, property rights, an
open society and due process of law. However, trying to live up to
these values leaves us, the wealthiest nation on earth, at a disadvantage before any handful of people willing to disregard those same
values.

Vulnerability also increases when a "stronger" target lacks the
resolve to act, one consequence of a corroded value structure. Michaud
and Aynesworth in *The Only Living Witness* reported some thoughts of
serial murderer Ted Bundy, a classic example of a certain type of
"weak" individual: ". . . the key is individual stress in a world running
toward anomie. It is not the meek but the weak who, Ted believes,
inherit such a world, the chronic losers who take power when 'The
System' begins to break down." (He felt that in other places and other
times, he might have lived a normal life.)

Even literally helpless people can have great power to affect what
others do, as witness Karen Ann Quinlan's impact. Falling into a
coma on April 14, 1975, as a result of mixing alcohol, tranquilizers
and aspirins at a party, she existed in a state of limbo between life
and death until June 11, 1985. During the intervening decade the
lives of the others in her family were drastically disrupted. Vast resources, both emotional and financial, were devoted to maintaining
her. Scholars, lawyers and medical experts debated the ethical issues
arising from her situation. Legally resolving it consumed endless courtroom hours. Ms. Quinlan's power had relatively little to do with her
as an individual, but rather stemmed from the ambiguity of her social
role. Our society extends certain rights to living people, but definitions
of the mid-1970s left unclear just what rights she was entitled to,
and what obligations others had to her. Thanks to Ms. Quinlan, some
of these elements of "structure power" have been updated to reflect
the realities of the late twentieth century.

Actively, passively or even when incapacitated, the weak can have
a significant impact on what other people do, which in the final analysis
is what power is all about. Without consciously intending to do so,
weak people can dominate a situation just by being there. Often
they are sensitive about minor things other people would ignore, or

have petty little requirements that would never occur to ordinary people. Others, trying to extend common courtesy, may discover they cannot be themselves in the presence of the weak person. They warp their behavior to be accomodating and find themselves walking on eggs, feeling uneasy and getting irritable, without understanding why.

But don't get the idea that the power of the weak is always a negative force. Let's close this section with a lovely and uplifting example of how the weak (in fact, the completely helpless) can be powerful in a positive way.

It's a story I found in the *Wall Street Journal*, by Christopher de Vinck, about his brother Oliver, blind at birth and incapacitated. Oliver spent all his thirty-two years in his bed, unable to do anything except eat, breathe and sleep. Nevertheless, de Vinck considers him one of the most powerful human beings he ever met.

Unwilling to institutionalize him, the family cared for Oliver at home. They found his presence to be not a burden but a blessing. He provided a gentle lesson in compassion for his brothers and sisters, who fed him, tickled him, and helped make him comfortable. When de Vinck reached courtship age he brought girlfriends home to meet his family. One, invited to see his invalid brother, declined. Another not only wanted to see him but was eager to help with feeding him.

What psychologist could devise a more compelling indicator of motherhood potential? The second girl and de Vinck were married and now have several children. In a very real sense they owe it to Oliver. To be responsible for the creation of a happy family—that is *true* power, the kind the world could use more of. How many can claim any accomplishments as important as that?

The Weak and the Meek

Power takes several forms, and each operates with infinite variations. Obviously there is a lot more to it than simply overwhelming the opposition. Do the strong and forceful really have the advantage? History, legend and everyday life prove to us time and again that the apparently weak can come out on top. "The race is not won by the swift, nor the battle by the valiant," sayeth the preacher Qoheleth. The ancient Greek king Agamemnon conquered the mighty city of Troy and was poisoned by his wife, Clytemnestra, upon his return home.* The immortal hero Hercules' jealous wife, Deianeira, gave him a poisoned shirt (she had been tricked into believing that it was a potent love charm) whose torments drove him to self-destruction. Samson defeated the Philistines on the field of battle only to be delivered over to them through the wiles of Delilah. Mohandas Gandhi dealt the final blow to the British Colonial Army in India with his non-violent campaign of passive resistance. Uncle Tom's humility and unwavering religious faith triumphed over the brutality of cruel Simon Legree.

Can we possibly be talking about the same thing in all these examples? We can hardly equate Ted Bundy with Gandhi. Surely there are some important differences between Oliver de Vinck and King Agamemnon's treacherous wife. Longshoreman/philosopher Eric Hoffer observed men in California's migrant labor camps during the Dust Bowl days of the 1930s and concluded that the weak have an inherent self-hatred that may give them formidable energies, and an intensity that can generate a special fitness beyond what other people realize in their ordinary struggles for existence. Yet blessed are the meek for, as both the Old and New Testaments tell us, they (not the weak) shall inherit the earth.

We have come up against one of the great mysteries of power, the major source of confusion preventing most people from understanding it. The meek shall inherit the earth. The weak hate themselves. An incapacitated brother brings blessings of love. People in "down" positions topple the mighty. The fact is that anyone, strong, weak or meek, can influence other people. But influence isn't always a matter of power. It depends on the person's basic approach to life. The meek may indeed be powerful—it takes a certain kind of strength to be genuinely meek. The weak cannot be powerful, because they lack that strength. Their energies may have tremendous impact on the world, not through power but through its opposite: control. Until you appreciate that distinction, a complete understanding of power will always elude you.

---

* Having previously sacrificed their daughter, staying out with the boys for the next ten years, he may have had it coming.

3

POWER AND CONTROL

The Difference Between Good and Evil

Power fascinates American audiences, and for that reason *Gone With the Wind* is (in "real dollars") the all-time movie box-office draw; and *Dallas* and *Dynasty* for several years running topped the TV ratings, right?

Wrong. The facts about GWTW and the two prime-time soap operas are true enough, but it isn't power that captures our interest. Look again at the central characters of these dramas. The schemes, manipulations and shenanigans of Scarlett O'Hara, J. R. Ewing and Alexis Carrington mostly only cause trouble for the other characters. By any standards of genuine accomplishment, J.R. and Alexis are losers. The most memorable line from *Gone With the Wind* was Rhett Butler's "Frankly, my dear, I don't give a damn," as he strode out of Scarlett's life. We are not talking "power" here at all—these folks deal exclusively in "control."

As for people of genuine power—strangely enough, American audiences find them rather boring when they are served up straight, with no evildoers to vanquish. *The Right Stuff*, based on solid, straightforward achievement, died at the box office and on television. Inspiring stories about people who scaled great heights are virtually guaranteed to put the average American audience to sleep, and to provoke school-children into passing sarcastic notes when forced to endure them through the medium of classroom films. Jesus Christ was a supremely powerful figure, and most Americans would be surprised to learn that worldwide, the most watched TV miniseries to date has been not *Roots* or *Shōgun*, but *Jesus of Nazareth*. Certainly we'd never guess it from its rank in the U.S. ratings.

Even scholars of English literature are seduced by control. Their consensus is that the more interesting character in Milton's *Paradise Lost* is Satan, not God. The contrast between power and control could not be drawn any more sharply than that, and the scholars go for control.

What is the difference? As I mentioned earlier, it comes straight out of the dictionary:* *"Power*: ability to do or act; capability of doing or accomplishing something."

A person of power gets things done, accomplishes his or her objectives. What kinds of objectives? Johann Sebastian Bach and Wolfgang Amadeus Mozart composed great music. Leo Tolstoy and William Shakespeare wrote great literature. Moses, Buddha, Jesus Christ and Muhammad founded great religions. The Duke of Wellington and Dwight Eisenhower won important wars. Isaac Newton, Marie Curie and Albert Einstein made great scientific discoveries. Florence Nightingale revolutionized medical care. Andrew Carnegie and Henry Ford founded industrial empires. George Washington and Thomas Jefferson helped create the American nation, and Abraham Lincoln and Franklin Delano Roosevelt helped preserve it. Mother Theresa touched the world's heart with her valiant war against poverty and suffering. Jim Thorpe, Mark Spitz and the 1928 New York Yankees overwhelmed their athletic opponents.

These are people of power, no doubt about it. We continue to admire and to benefit from their achievements, in some cases even thousands of years after the fact. But most people of power remain

---

* These are from the *Random House Dictionary of the English Language, College Edition*, 1968. Other dictionaries have similar definitions.

.

40

anonymous, known only to the handful of others whose lives they touch: the small businessperson who over long years serves customers cheerfully and with integrity; the corporation or government employee who, like the good soldier, hangs in there always giving the job his best possible shot; the amateur hobbiest who makes a boat, or a quilt, or a beautiful garden; the amateur athlete who moves up the tennis ladder, progresses toward an ever lower golf handicap, or leads the bowling team to victory; the citizen who gets involved in local politics and helps bring about needed services for her community; the parents who raise a family of solid, productive children.

The world over, people of outstanding power are celebrated with holidays, memorials and shrines, or at the very least a statue in the park. But we all have the potential to be powerful, to the limits of our abilities. That is, anyone can have important objectives, and power is the ability to accomplish them. How much power we have comes down to how effectively we can make action decisions. Power enables us to realize our dreams.

How is control different from power? "*Control*: to exercise restraint or direction over; dominate; command."

Doesn't say anything about accomplishment, does it? *A person with control influences what other people do.* People of power may use control to help achieve their objectives, of course. Any effective corporate manager or military commander is going to have to employ it to ensure that subordinates are doing their jobs properly. But pure control means simply having an impact on someone else, nothing more. A prankster who phones in a false fire alarm, or a computer hacker who diddles someone else's data base, is exercising control. So is a boss who delights in "keeping his people on their toes" with arbitrary, dictatorial commands. So is the wife who puts something extravagant on the family credit card to get even with her husband, or the husband who stays out drinking all night to get even with his wife, or the child who set the backyard on fire to get some attention. Think again about J. R. Ewing, Alexis Carrington and Scarlett O'Hara—what do they accomplish? Little if anything. Their outstanding characteristic is their facility for jerking other people around. (Interestingly, "control people" often have formidable talents or abilities, if and when they apply them to achieving objectives. Recall that Scarlett did rescue some measure of comfort for her family out of the aftermath of the Civil War, no easy feat. And J.R. is no slouch in the oil business, when he puts his mind to it. So it goes in real life. Though over-shadowed by the evils they wrought, Hitler, Mussolini and other tyrants did manage some positive accomplishments.)

People of positive accomplishment endure one way or another—if not as statues in the park, at least in the fond memories of their loved ones. Not so with people who take a control approach to life. On the commonplace level, unless they provide for memorials in their wills, they tend to die unmourned, leaving those whose lives they soured with a feeling of relief and perhaps a few stories to tell. The more prominent are remembered, but as history's great villains: King Herod, Caligula, King Richard III, Adolf Hitler, and on a more local level, Charles Manson and Reverend Jones of the Jonestown massacre.

Power and control literally represent the difference between good and evil. Anyone who does not appreciate that distinction will have a hard time putting power to positive use. Everyone has elements of both in his or her character. Although popular drama, fables and fairy tales often portray pure types, few if any individuals in real life can be classified as exclusively one or the other. Most people have a ten-dency in one of those two directions. To make the discussion easier, let's call people who characteristically operate in the direction of posi-tive accomplishment "Power People." Those who go out of their way to influence other people we will call "Control People." Those who aren't especially effective in either direction commonly are called "Vic-tims."

In our culture the Ultimate Power Person is the conception of God underlying Judaism, Christiantiy and Islam—the universal, om-nipotent, all-that-there-is, monotheistic supreme being. At the other extreme, the Ultimate Control Person is the devil, Satan, The Prince of Lies. Perhaps Miltonian scholars find God to be the less interesting because there isn't much drama, suspense or complexity in a character who can invariably do what He wants, whenever He wants to. Satan provides more entertainment because he reminds us more of ourselves, people we know and problems that trouble us.

A closer look at Satan and how he operates helps clarify the nature of the Control Person. Popular Hollywood movie portrayals of the devil as a supernatural force aside, Satan doesn't *make* people do anything. What he does is prey on our weaknesses and trick us into deciding to do other than God intends. His essential power over us lies in deception. According to the ancient Hebrews, the serpent was the world's first persuader, who smooth-talked Eve into tasting the forbidden fruit. Called to account for this (and for in turn persuading poor old Adam to join her sinful ways), Eve uttered those immortal words: "The devil made me do it." This is a Control Person reaction, Eve's attempt to con God into excusing her and letting her off the hook. Sorry, Eve, but nobody cons the Ultimate Power Person. Even the devil can't con the Ultimate Power Person. He can set snares for the unwary, but cannot prevail over those who follow the ways of God.

Why did Satan go to all the bother of getting Adam and Eve in dutch with God? As Milton tells it, Satan declined to put God first, his pride (in the sense of self-centeredness—"Nobody is going to tell *me* what to do") having led him to believe that he should be God's equal. As the Ultimate Authority in the universe, God deemed that unacceptable and cast Satan and legions of his followers out of heaven and down to the other place.

Meeting to map out strategy, the devils split over what to do next. One suggestion was to go back and try once again to take over Heaven, the idea being to settle it once and for all by either winning or being totally wiped out. Another possibility was to go on their good behavior and see if God sooner or later might take them back. A third faction felt, what the heck, let's make the best of it down here, as things could be worse. These in their own ways are "power" solutions—picking an objective and working toward it. However, Satan decided instead to go to a place he'd heard of, Earth, where God had put some new creatures destined to take the fallen angels place in Paradise. If we can't be there, Satan reasoned, why should those other creatures be allowed? He therefore made the long trek to Earth, hoping to find some way of messing things up for them. He soon learned that God had forbidden them the fruit on the Tree of Knowledge, and with a little probing found Eve to have certain vulnerabilities (as did Adam). We all know the outcome.

The point is that Satan's only intention was to cause trouble. He had no positive goal in mind, and that is the hallmark of Control People. Like any other jerk, bully or con artist, Satan's main payoff was negative—to destroy, or diminish, or cause pain, but especially to get away with something, to "defy the gods." He'd already lost everything, so why not make somebody else lose and even up the score? Whether or not we believe literally in the Old Testament account, mankind's Fall in the Garden of Eden does illustrate perfectly the essential natures of power and control. Perhaps significantly, it is the very first story in the Book. The minute you put two people on the face of the earth, you've got trouble.

The dark side of control is influencing other people *simply for its own sake*, and down through the ages Western Civilization has labeled that as "evil." Saint Augustine, in his *Confessions*, identified this negative streak we all to some extent share. He recounted an episode from his own childhood when he and some friends stole pears from a neighbor's garden not because they were hungry, but purely for the sake of doing evil. Although the enormity of the crime seems slight enough, the principle was decisive to Saint Augustine; and it is just as decisive in distinguishing power from control. Power People do not universally do "good," because after all not everyone is going to agree with their objectives. But their actions are aimed at accomplishing something positive, and if we don't agree with their point of view, at least we can respect that. Control People act from the negative motive of diminishing other people's power. They take advantage, they undermine, they perpetrate little obstructions and humiliations. Even at its most banal level—squalid little practical jokes and gratuitous put-downs—we recognize control for what it is, by the distaste we feel for it, by the sordidness and pettiness that characterize it.

Samuel Taylor Coleridge caught the spirit of it well. Commenting on Iago, the villain who destroyed Shakespeare's Othello, he said: "Iago's soliloquy, the motive-hunting of a motiveless malignity—how awful it is!" Iago betrayed the successful and admired general, Othello, out of spite, his "reasons" for doing it conjured up after the fact to rationally justify it. Iago's example points up another facet of Control People: They envy, resent and hate Power People, and will do what they can to thwart and frustrate them. That too began with Satan in the Garden of Eden. The backbiters, the gossipers, the carpers, the gripers, the people who make a career out of being stubborn, all are playing the same control game. They have no real objective—they just are doing their bit to ensure that others won't accomplish *their* objectives. Is Iago's treachery really any different from, or any more awful than, the situation described in this letter to Ann Landers?

Dear Ann Landers: My parents were divorced when I was an infant. Mom raised me but my dad was a part of my life until I was 11, when he moved to another state. I hated him for running out on me.

It wasn't until recently that I found out why Dad left. He remarried when I was 3 and had two children with his second wife. Mom resented this and made his life hell. The whole story came out when my grandmother died. I saw Dad at the funeral for the first time in 15 years. We sat together during the services and became reacquainted. I liked him instantly and felt very close to him.

It was awkward, but I got up the nerve to ask why he abandoned me. He said Mom took everything when she left him. He paid alimony and child support, but the alimony stopped when she remarried, so she kept increasing the child support to get even. She then hauled him into court whenever he was a little late with the payments just to embarrass him.

Dad never had much money. He worked on construction most of his life and had a hard time making ends meet. He ended up bankrupt trying to meet my mother's demands. He said there was no alternative but to go someplace where she couldn't hound him anymore.

Dad and I are good friends now. When I asked Mom why she was so vindictive, she said she wanted to wring every last nickel out of "the rat" for my sake. She admitted she didn't need the money, but it was a matter of principle.

I love Mom, but now I know her greed deprived me of a father. All those years without him certainly did not make up for the extras she dragged out of him.   —THE TRUTH IS OUT

Although few people are 100 percent Power People or Control People, many gravitate toward one or the other, recognizable in these profiles:

Power People

Power People know who they are and what they want out of life, and they have a realistic sense of how to get it. No matter what they are doing, they seem to have a game plan. They aren't loners, but they chart their own course and do their own thinking. When they lead, others follow. They are effective. They usually manage to get good results, seemingly without a lot of strife or stress, whether they are doing a job, raising a family, playing a game or whatever.

Power People are builders and creators, making positive contributions to the world. In the process they may sometimes cause harm or distress, but not for its own sake. Because, realistically, no matter what their objective is, any accomplishment can be judged from different points of view, and almost inevitably some will disagree with them. When two Power People go after the same objective, if they can't come to a mutually agreeable resolution, something may have to give. Power People are straightforward, and they try to follow the rules they live by. We know where they stand, whether or not we agree with their positions.

Power People place a high value on achievement, and they get satisfaction from their accomplishments. They often have open, generous spirits, and find joy in their lives and good in the world. You can beat them or destroy them, but you can't defeat them.

History's prominent Power People are celebrated as our great saints, heroes and leaders. You can find plenty of examples in places such as various "halls of fame," history books and lists of Nobel Prize winners. In the context of your own life, you will find them active in community affairs, selected as "citizens of the year," enjoying successful careers, doing well in school and/or raising happy families. Generally they are pleasant people to spend time with. You leave them feeling better for their company.

Control People

Control People are up only if someone else is down. They don't contribute much to building anything worthwhile, but rather work at destroying or tearing down other people and their accomplishments. Around them we never feel comfortable. We can't drop our guard, and we can't let them out of our sight. You can't do business with them and stay honest yourself.

They are the bastards and the bullies, the witches and the bitches, the ones who delight in throwing their weight around and who stab others in the back. They pick on anyone who is helpless or will let them get away with it. With those who can fight back they are more circumspect, working against them behind the scenes with treachery, lies, gossip and sabotage. Whether their style is raw physical violence or subtle psychological warfare, their only aim, ultimately, is to control others' actions and reactions.

The sorry truth is that Control People are nothing but insecure, miserable souls who can't be powerful; for control emerges when the impulse to power is thwarted, by lack of inner resources and/or by circumstances. Certain types of relationships tend to breed control behavior: Dependence brings out impudence. Abuse provokes revenge of one form or another. Tyranny is answered by rebellion. Over the long term, control begets its counterpart. Control People in authority foster it in those under them, and controlling parents pass a talent for it along to their children. Mass outbursts of control behavior such as riots, lynchings and even ritualized events such as socially sanctioned orgies and Detroit's notorious "Devil's Night" seem to arise in response to repressive social conditions, and are commonly explained as ways of "letting off steam."

The Control Person's hatred and obstruction of Power People spring from envy and resentment, as by comparison his own life seems unfairly blighted by frustration, disappointment and anger. The most extreme Control People are the crazies who go on lethal rampages, mowing down whoever is handy, or who quietly kidnap and murder dozens of children, prostitutes or teenaged runaways. Crimes, lies and perversions have their roots in impulses to control. History's great villains, criminals, tyrants and monsters are Control People. Dante assigned various categories of them to their appropriate circles of his Inferno, reserving the deepest part of the pit for traitors to their kindred, their country, their guests and their lords. These he left frozen in ice until the devil got around to devouring them.

Tolstoy nicely epitomized the Control Person in his character Dolohov in *War and Peace*:

> Anatole sincerely liked Dolohov for his cleverness and daring. Dolohov, for whom Anatole's name and rank and connections were of use in ensnaring wealthy young men into his society for gambling purposes, made use of Kuragin without letting him feel it, and was amused by him too. Apart from interested motives, for which he needed Anatole, the process itself of controlling another man's will was an enjoyment, a habit and a necessity for Dolohov.

Dolohov was an asset on the battlefield, and a boon drinking buddy. However, he also cheated Nikolay Rostov (one of the good guys) out of 43,000 rubles in a crooked card game out of revenge because Rostov's sister, Sonya, had spurned his marriage proposal, and he nearly succeeded in ruining another of Rostov's sisters, Natasha (Prince Andre's fiancée at the time), by seducing her into a fraudulent elopement that was foiled only at the last moment. He was a dutiful son to his impoverished and infirm mother, but the constraints and humiliation that imposed on him may have been part of his problem.

The transactional analysis psychologists provide some good insights into the workings of Control People. Claude Steiner's description of the "guerrilla witch" life script in *The Scripts People Live* is accurate to the nth decimal place (interestingly, Steiner provides no analogous male script). Bad guys in fiction invariably are painted as Control People, and we all have our favorite villains. The most chilling fictional Control Person I have yet found is Faye Doyle, in Nathanael West's dark novel, *Miss Lonelyhearts*. In real life, we also tend to cast our enemies and adversaries as Control People. In wartime, governments promulgate propaganda to create those perceptions and keep them vivid.

Here are the dirty little secrets about Control People. They get their biggest payoffs from getting away with things, and from being in control. Anyone can make them jump through hoops as long as he leads them to think they are getting away with something, or are in control. Recall Brer Rabbit's desperate plea for mercy—"Please, please, *please* don't throw me into dat briar patch!" Confidence men (one variety of Control Person) often play to the Control Person streak in others. Operating on the assumption that a little larceny lurks in everybody, they create a situation which leads the mark to believe he is getting away with a fast one. Witness the classic big con perpetrated by Paul Newman and Robert Redford in *The Sting*. What older brother or sister has not had a boring day or two brightened by assuring a younger sibling that "it's all right" to do some bit of mischief, then tipping off mom and standing back to watch the fun? One transactional analysis game, "Now I've Got You, You Sonofabitch," revolves around enticing, tricking or goading the other person into doing something wrong and then pounding on him for it.

If you want to ruin a Control Person's good time, deny him control. Let him know you are on to his game. Laughter hits where it hurts, as it demonstrates that his machinations are so transparent as to be amusing. To destroy him completely, get him into a position where he is forced to admit, publicly and to himself, that *he is in the wrong*.

This last point is literally true. For example, it is a very effective method for curing small children of lying, stealing or sneaking things. Make them own up to their "crimes" by having them apologize to their "victim." It may be spectacularly traumatic for them at the time, but unless they already are past the point of no return, it teaches the lesson indelibly. Adult Control People keep their games going by denying to themselves and others that they are blameworthy. Alcoholics Anonymous has found that nothing can be done for alcoholics (a notorious variety of Control Person) unless they are willing to admit being responsible for their own situations, and to stand up and ask the group for help. Often this doesn't happen until the person's drinking has so destroyed his or her life that AA is the only remaining hope. Criminals are not apt to reform so long as they can get away with denying their crimes or blaming them on someone else. Once they accept their own guilt, they can work on getting rid of their Control Person. Perhaps this principle has contributed to the longevity and the continuing vitality of the Catholic church, for the Catholic institution of confession enables the faithful to own up to their wrong-doings without risking the pains and embarrassments of doing it publicly.

One word of warning here—pulling this tactic on an adult Control Person who didn't volunteer for it is dangerous. They see it as public embarrassment or humiliation, which they enjoy about as much as a vampire enjoys a stake through his heart. The aftermath may be ugly, and it may never be forgotten nor forgiven. Control People have been known to kill themselves rather than own up to the fact that they are wrong. One thing Control People are not is good sports. (However, should someone object to something *they* do, they have no problem with telling him that *he* should be a good sport.)

Victims

Control People can operate only if Victims are available (Power People don't need them). A Victim can be a type of person, and also, as with Power and Control, being a Victim is a tendency present in just about everyone. Victims are the objects of someone else's control, and without them the Control People would be out of business. But that's not likely, as there has always been an ample supply, and as P. T. Barnum once remarked, "There's a sucker born every minute." Victims are confused and ignorant people who lack direction, motivation, strength, and competence. They are the fools, the pigeons, the marks, the chumps, the fall guys, the johns, the prey, the patsies, the rubes, the dupes and the rabble. Life just doesn't work out well for them, but darned if they can figure out why. If they could only get a handle on it. . . . If they could only get a break. . . .

Turn a Control Person around, and you will find him working on a Victim. Turn a Control Person *over*, and you will find a Victim on the other side. Similarly, Victims are prone to use control out of self-defense. Street derelicts are an extreme example of Victims, and what is their filth, their bizarre appearance and behavior and their refusal to participate in normal society but a wretched attempt to control other people (who in their experience have mostly tried to control *them*), to keep them at a distance? Consider the oft-made observation that instances of crime, delinquency and self-destruction may be "cries for help"—people lashing out in reaction to their own sense of being victimized. Perhaps in this nexus between control and victimization lies the basis for the Christian ethic of forgiveness: Hate the sin but love the sinner, for sin arises not from strength but from weakness.

Consider also the "games people play," so delightfully described by transactional analysis psychologist Eric Berne. The TA games are transactions between people that go round and round to no avail, mean little exercises in futility. The game-players operate from an "I'm not OK," or an "I'm OK but you're not" position, and fit well with the Control Person notion. The games (e.g., "Uproar," "Now I've Got You, You Sonofabitch," etc.) heap trouble, inconvenience and/or humiliation on the one who is "it," who in operating from the position of "I'm not OK" conforms to our idea of Victims. The game-player gets strokes from jerking someone around, and even the Victim reaps a few "cold pricklies," which the TA people tell us are better, in a situation of stroke-starvation, than no strokes at all. The TA people also have documented how participants in these games often switch off among the roles of "persecutor," "victim" and "rescuer."

Not everyone to whom something terrible happens is a "Victim" in this sense. A person struck by lightning, killed in an epidemic, mugged by a stranger, or blown to bits in an aerial bombing raid is a victim, but in the sense of being an innocent bystander. "Victims" in the context of persuasion, power and control are people who as a result of their approach to life, or their ill-conceived moment-to-moment actions, allow other people to influence them to their own disadvantage. We are talking about the woman trapped in a hopeless, sadistic marriage; the mark who is shorn of a ten-dollar bill in a street hustle; the sucker who buys an underwater piece of real estate, or who is cheated out of his farm, or who gets elbowed out of a job. All of us may be Victims from time to time; some make a career of it.

Victims don't make it into the history books, except as statistics. The most desperate live on the margins, having dropped out of normal society in an effort to keep their victimization down to a minimum.

Keeping Power and Control Straight

How do those profiles fit you and the people you know? Most of us are a mixture. We are Power People in some areas of our lives, able to effectively accomplish our goals. In other areas our vulnerabilities leave us open to other people's control, making us part-time Victims as well. And who is entirely innocent of Control? We all have our favorite little hustles, scams or fast ones we pull from time to time. We "sample" treats in the supermarket. We stiff the phone company. We merrily clip along at 75 miles per hour, but drop instantaneously to 55 when our Fuzzbusters alert us to a speed trap. We get a twinge of excitement from putting somebody in his place. We load slugs into subway turnstiles. We fudge on our tax returns. We sidle into the express checkout line knowing full well that we're five items over the limit. We turn in "creative" expense accounts and fill our pockets from the supply room at work. Significant numbers of teenagers and elderly people have found shoplifting to be an exciting form of recreation. Would drugs or underage drinking be nearly so popular if they didn't represent "getting away with something"?

It isn't that Power People never do anything wrong, but when they do, usually they do it with awareness. And they don't take pleasure from it: "I'm ashamed of myself, but I stole this loaf of bread so my family wouldn't go hungry." A Control Person, by contrast, might say: "You bet I ripped off a loaf of bread. Why be a sucker? That store rips off customers with its high prices. I'm just getting even."

The distinction between power and control helps us avoid some of the confusions that exist about power, because often "power" is applied when "control" is more accurate. For example, George Orwell in his essay on "Lear, Tolstoy and the Fool" says:

> There are families in which the father will say to his child, "You'll get a thick ear if you do that again," while the mother, her eyes brimming with tears, will take the child in her arms and murmur lovingly, "Now, darling, *is* it kind to Mummy to do that?" And who would maintain that the second method is less tyrannous than the first? The distinction that really matters is not between violence

and non-violence, but between having and not having the appetite for power.

Substitute "appetite for control" in place of "appetite for power," and we no longer risk mistaking what Orwell describes for the kinds of impulses that motivate people to build skyscrapers, write operas and launch new businesses.

Another confusion exists in the notion of power "over" another person. Yes, structure power and agreement power do put one person in a position to tell another what to do. But is it always "power"? As Solzhenitsyn describes the Russian Gulag in *One Day in the Life of Ivan Denisovich*, guards carry submachine guns and will mow down any prisoner who strays out of formation. What objective is a guard who does this accomplishing, beyond his own survival? If he fails to do his miserable duty, he will wind up on the other side of the bars himself. He has only *control*, in reality being as powerless as the people under his gunsights. Chairman Mao had it wrong: Control, not power, grows out of the barrel of a gun.

The how-to books about persuasion and negotiation almost always assume the reader will be dealing with a "rational" counterpart who, like himself, wants to solve a problem or achieve an objective; someone operating, as the transactional analysis people would put it, according to an adult script. The advice of these books usually is in the direction of striving for a "win-win" resolution—a fair exchange that leaves both parties better off than they would have been without the agreement. All well and good, when both parties are working from a power premise.

But how many times have you encountered someone coming from a *control* premise, who mostly wants to get his or her own way, irrespective of the outcome? What about the boss who loves to make his peons squirm? What about the buyer who delights in torturing his suppliers, in extorting wining, dining and women out of them? What about the road bullies who tailgate at sixty miles per hour? What about the husbands and wives who sabotage their spouses' careers to make sure they stay in a "down" position?

Dealing with Control People, the "win-win" model breaks down, because from their viewpoint, the main thing is to make sure that the other person *doesn't* win. They set up situations in which the other's position is hopeless at the outset. They manipulate people into no-win double-binds so that no matter what the other person does, he is *wrong*. They welch on deals, go back on their word or pull some kind of double cross. They may not win either, but that's not as important as making the other person lose. It's easy to dismiss this kind of behavior as "childish" or "irrational," except for two things:

1. Once you understand the Control Person's motive, this behavior is *perfectly* rational. He isn't interested in utility, satisfaction, positive outcomes or anything like that, but just wants to jerk somebody around. His actions are very neatly programmed to have exactly that impact.
2. No matter what name we tag it with, we can't dismiss it, because it is a common feature of life. Rational or not, we have to cope with it.

That is not easy. Control People refuse to admit guilt or to be saddled with responsibility, so it is difficult if not impossible to deal with them straightforwardly, as we would with a "rational" person. Extreme cases like criminals, drug addicts, spoiled children, manipulative spouses and con men, will lie, string people along, make empty agreements and blame somebody else for everything that goes wrong. It's all part of the game plan, as each of those is just one more way to jerk somebody around. Controlling spouses will convince the other to go into therapy, resolutely denying that they need help themselves (or else they will go along, seeing it as a chance to play games with both their spouse *and* the therapist). Convicts insinuate themselves into effective control of prisons, and patients in mental institutions have been known to take over by conning irresolute administrators in charge. Confidence men will offer to help law enforcement in return for leniency, perhaps by blowing the whistle on coconspirators, or by setting up cons to catch other criminals. Often the law is left holding an empty bag. One craftsmanlike example of this was a fellow under investigation for a laundry list of crimes. He offered to testify on some other matter if he were guaranteed immunity from prosecution for anything he might say. Immunity secured, he promptly confessed to everything for which he was being investigated and walked out a free man.

Power People and Control People use the four types of power differently, right down the line. Power People use their performance power to attain their goals. Control People, on the other hand, use their physical skills to bully or intimidate, their shrewdness to manipulate and take advantage, and their wit to embarass or humiliate. If they do accomplish laudable objectives (and there is no reason why Control People can't), they tend to use them as weapons. They wear their awards and diplomas on their sleeves, insist on being called "Doctor," and if a son or daughter is going to an Ivy League school or has a successful career, make certain that no one ever forgets it. Richard L. Rubenstein, a man about as far from being a Control Person as I can imagine, confessed in *Power Struggle* that originally one of his motives for getting a Ph.D. was to control how others saw him. "It was not enough to be Rabbi Richard L. Rubenstein; I wanted to be Dr. Richard L. Rubenstein, and the doctorate had to come from Harvard."

Power People use structure and agreement power to accomplish things with others that they could not manage alone. Control People see these types of power as great sticks to beat people with. "Drunk with power" describes a Control Person in office. They pull rank, take advantage of every privilege, and boss subordinates around for the pleasure of doing it. They insist that other people live up to the letter of agreements, at the same time taking great delight in violating agreements themselves. They usually don't flat refuse to meet their obligations, because that would put them clearly in the wrong. Rather, they show up late because "their watch was slow." They don't show up at all because "something urgent came up at the last minute." The check "must have gotten lost in the mail." Their part of the project fell short because "a subordinate [or a supplier] [or the equipment] screwed up." Accidents can, of course, happen to anyone; but with Control People they conveniently add up to a way of life.

People use sex and money as instruments of control. What are inch-long sculptured nails, iridescent makeup, slit skirts, string bikinis and braless breasts jiggling beneath gossamer blouses but calculated attempts to provoke reactions? Nikos Kazantzakis, in *Zorba the Greek*, refers to these as "women's weapons." The same goes for big spending, high rolling and heavy tipping. Power People tend to follow the philosophy of William Vincent Astor: "Each dollar is a soldier that does your bidding." Control People spend their dollars to make an impact on others, through flashy jewelry, exclusive club memberships, fur coats, one-hundred-thousand-dollar cars, bragworthy vacations and clothes and accessories whose designer labels are surrogates for astronomical price tags. They are suckers for get-rich-quick schemes, which hold out the lure of getting away with something. They want the money, it always seems, either so they can jerk other people around, or as a means of immunity from having to take orders. In the film *Treasure of the Sierra Madre*, Fred C. Dobbs, so brilliantly portrayed by Humphrey Bogart, is a perfect example.

Power People use persuasion to get help, enlist support or assist others to realize their own interests. But persuasive power is the Control Person's bread and butter. It forces the other person to make the decision, absolving the Control Person of responsibility. The Control Person manipulates his Victims into this position through the persuasion process. That is only one of the many roles the persuasion process plays. The next section of this book will tell you all about it. In the meantime, table 1 may help you get a feel for the difference between power and control.

Table 1
Power People and Control People

	Mostly Power	Fascinating Mixtures	Mostly Control
Political Figures	George Washington Mohandas Gandhi Abraham Lincoln	Lyndon Johnson Aaron Burr Huey Long	Josef Stalin Adolf Hitler Idi Amin
Military Figures	Dwight D. Eisenhower Robert E. Lee	George Patton Douglas MacArthur Napoleon	————
Business People	Robert Woodruff (Coca-Cola) Harold Geneen (ITT) William Hewlett and David Packard	John Jacob Astor William Randolph Hearst Cornelius Vanderbilt Charles Revson	Robert Vesco Charles Ponzi
Popular Fictional Characters	The Roadrunner Rhett Butler Luke Skywalker James Bond Any World War II hero played by John Wayne Dick Tracy Cordelia and Edgar The Dukes of Hazzard Butch Cassidy and the Sundance Kid	———— ———— ———— ———— ———— ———— ———— ———— ————	Wile E. Coyote Scarlett O'Hara Darth Vader Dr. No Nazis and Japs Pruneface Goneril, Regan and Edmund Boss Hogg Respectable Society

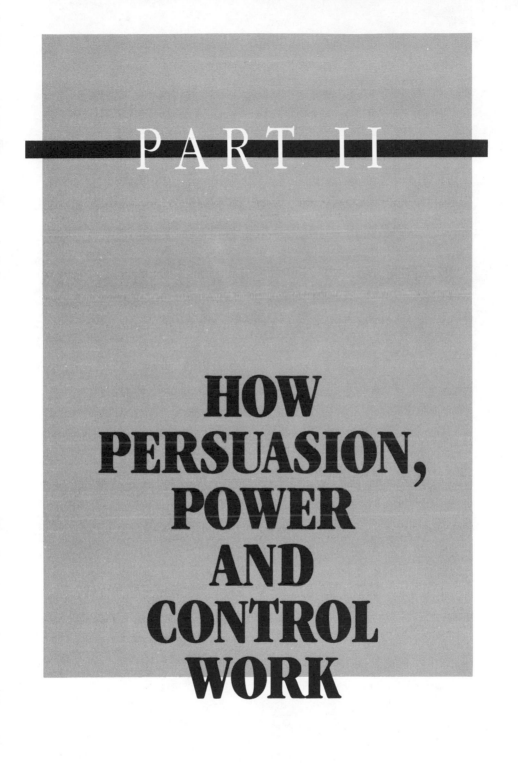

PART II

HOW PERSUASION, POWER AND CONTROL WORK

4

THE ACTION DECISION

Why People Do What They Do

Could there possibly be a more difficult and all-encompassing question than: Why do people do what they do?

Over the ages, thinkers, poets, writers, scientists and philosophers have proposed answers whose depth, complexity and profundity have aspired to the level of the question.

One theme has been that we do what we do because *we have no choice*. The ancient Stoics, Leo Tolstoy, Gestalt psychologist Kurt Lewin, the Calvinists and Russian mystic G. I. Gurdjieff each in his own way supported this idea. Fate, necessity, external forces, God or our machine-like natures dictate our behavior.

Another school of thought is that we are driven by *internal impulses to satisfy our needs*. The Epicureans, utilitarian philosophers Jeremy Bentham and James Mill, humanist psychologist Abraham Maslow, the classical economists, psychoanalysts Sigmund Freud and Wilhelm Reich, and poets Dante Alighieri and T. S. Eliot, all favored this notion, although each school of thought had a somewhat different type of impulse in mind.

During the nineteenth century the theory gained currency that we do what we do because *we are compelled to compete with and overcome other creatures, including each other*. Philosophers Schopenhauer and Nietzsche and psychoanalyst Alfred Adler saw it as a "will to power." Evolutionists Charles Darwin and Herbert Spencer saw it as "survival of the fittest." Economic philosopher Karl Marx saw it as the "class struggle." Modern-day sociobiologists such as Edward O. Wilson see it as genetic inheritance of behavior that increases the probability of passing on our own genes.

Finally, some thinkers contend that *we have dark and sinister motives for doing what we do*. Saint Augustine, taking his inspiration from the Epistles of Saint Paul, asserted that human beings are essentially sinful creatures, owing to Adam and Eve's original sin of turning away from God in the Garden Eden. Psychiatrist Ernest Becker contended that our inability to face the fact of our immortality, our "denial of death," has filled the world with evil. Psychiatrist Erich Fromm, Russian novelist Fyodor Dostoyevski and French existentialist Jean-Paul Sartre all made the point that free choice is too great a burden for most people, who therefore are happy to trade it away for security and relief from the anxiety it engenders.

History's great thinkers, of whom we touched above on only a handful, tried to answer this question at the lofty level of the soul, the heart, and the nature of humankind. While their thoughts shed light on the human condition in general, they do not, at the *operational* level, answer the question of why people do what they do. The tides of history may ebb and flow from our collective souls or hearts, but on a moment-to-moment basis what we do comes from individual decisions we make in our *heads*. *Sirach* (one of the apocryphal books of the Old Testament) puts it well:

> A word is the source of every deed;
> a thought, of every act.
> The source of all conduct is the mind.

Several thousand years later sociologists Talcott Parsons and Edgar Shils in *Toward a General Theory of Human Action* said much the same, that before there is action, "a decision must always be made (explicitly or implicitly, consciously or unconsciously)." Or, if you prefer, existentialist philosopher Jose Ortega y Gasset: "At every moment of the day I must decide what I am going to do the next moment; and no one can make this decision for me, or take my place in this."

How do these decisions work? Starting in the mid-twentieth century, several branches of the social sciences addressed that question, each from its own point of view. The *behavioral psychologists* studied how animals (including people) learn to respond as a result of their histories of psychological reinforcement—rewards for doing the right thing, and punishments for doing the wrong thing. The *cognitive psychologists* studied how people learn and use information to solve problems. The *social psychologists*, believing that what we do is determined by our attitudes, researched how attitudes are formed and changed. *Transactional analysis psychologists* saw behavior and interactions as arising from a basic need for "strokes" (their term for the basic unit of human recognition), and looked at how we go about getting strokes.

Organization psychologists studied how we behave as workers, managers and executives. *Consumer psychologists* delved into the decision-making we do as buyers in the marketplace. *Economic game-theory* specialists examined how people make risky decisions, giving us familiar management concepts such as "expected values," "payoff matrix," and "decision tree."

You might think that, after all this effort by so many brilliant people, over so many centuries, we should by now understand persuasion, power and control. We don't. Each thinker, each school, each point of view has given us part of the answer, but all coming from their own particular assumptions, theories and interests; none went the final step of bringing everything together. Moreover, each viewpoint was kept from reaching that last summit by either *imprecision* or *incompleteness*. To fully understand persuasion, power and control, we need to comprehend how they pervade all areas of our lives, and we also need a handle on the precise mechanisms that make them work.

What do I mean by "imprecision" and "incompleteness"? Let's take up *imprecision* first. Study the Grand Theories, and you will notice that often they are founded on quicksilver concepts—imprecise terms such as "love" and "pleasure" and "will to power" that wriggle away in the face of hard-headed probing and questioning. These words float along at such a high level of abstraction that we cannot reliably tie them down to concrete referents in reality, although they are useful as long as we confine the discussion to generalities. Even concepts that appear scientific often turn out to have been defined so that they run around in circles, having no specific meaning beyond a definition that in effect repeats them in different terms. Take, for example, the economists' idea of "utility," and the behaviorists' concept of "reinforcement." Go into them very deeply, and you soon discover that while they seem to *explain* everything retrospectively, in real life they do not help us to *predict* very much.

Leo Tolstoy provides an excellent example of a complete theory that is imprecise. In *War and Peace* he says that history does not flow from the deeds of great men, but rather is a product of the totality of actions resulting from the moment-to-moment decisions of countless individuals. That is a very complete view of human behavior, one which the Gestalt psychologists might warmly embrace. Now . . . what determines the actions that individuals take as a result of these decisions? "A man's actions follow from his innate character and the motives acting on him," Tolstoy tells us.

So far, so good. Now . . . what is a man's "innate character?" Tolstoy didn't go into details, but presumably he meant something like "the kind of person he is." What about the "motives acting on him?" Again Tolstoy didn't get down to specifics, but he must have meant something like "what the man wants and what he doesn't want."

I agree with Tolstoy on this point, but there is a problem. How can we deduce from Tolstoy's theory any possible clue about what some specific person is going to do at some specific moment, that we couldn't have figured out without it?

To illustrate the problem of *incompleteness*, consider the work of B. F. Skinner, a great pioneer of modern behaviorism. Skinner and his behaviorist colleagues were relentlessly precise. Seeking to put psychology on a scientific footing equal with the physical sciences, they carefully measured behavior down to tiny detail. Pavlov, the grandfather of behavioral psychology, recorded exactly how many drops of saliva his famous dog let go in response to the stimulus of the bell.

Using these precise measurements and approaches, the behaviorists formulated the principles of "conditioned responses" and "operant conditioning," as well as other important psychological concepts. Skinner especially concentrated on operant conditioning, by which an animal's behavior can be shaped with "positive reinforcement" (giving the animal a reward when it does the right thing, or at least gets closer to doing the right thing).

So far, so good. Skinner demonstrated the power of these theories in many ways, perhaps the best known being the pigeons he taught to play a variation of the game of Ping-Pong, described in *A Matter of Consequences*. Operant conditioning has proved the most effective way known to train animals.

When we try to apply the behaviorists' theories to the grand sweep of history, there is a problem. Their experiments, precise though they may have been, were almost invariably done using caged, starved animals. From these experiments theories were built that Skinner and others have applied not only to animal behavior in experimental situations, but to all human behavior. Skinner went so far as to propose, in his books *Walden Two* and *Beyond Freedom and Dignity*, plans for redesigning society in order to produce a more favorable environment of positive reinforcements. But the actual research on which he based these ideas was limited to a few select species of animals in controlled laboratory conditions, and other researchers, observing animals in the wild, have found plenty of evidence that animals (let alone people) are able to think, to learn, to solve problems and to communicate with (and even teach) other animals (for example, Donald R. Griffin in *Animal Thinking*). As an analogy, consider this: How much could we discover about the normal behavior of psychologists by locking them up in solitary confinement, feeding them on short rations of bread and water, and then measuring their thinking ability by giving them simple tasks designed to measure how quickly they figure out how to get rewards of little tidbits of food?

Skinnerian psychology has been useful when applied to some aspects of learning and training—"programmed instruction" is based on principles set down by the behaviorists, for example. But in the real world people's ordinary social behavior is far too complex, and the human mind much too powerful, for Skinner's ideas to have application to very much of what people do in their normal, day-to-day lives. They account well for some of the processes by which organisms learn from direct physical experience, but they leave too many important questions unanswered to take us very far toward understanding how persuasion, power and control work.

We will approach people's actions at the operational level—what we can observe individuals doing from moment to moment—and will consider every action they take. However, in human affairs it is impossible to know exactly what is going on in anyone's mind, including our own. Mental processes work faster than we can track them. Ideas, thoughts, feelings, images, visions, sensations and perceptions come and go in split instants, and much goes on below the surface of our awareness. The psychological process I am proposing here seems to account for how people decide to do what they do. The process can be captured by the measuring instruments of the psychologists only crudely, because of the limitations of those methodologies. Nevertheless, this model appears to fit well with what psychologists, sociologists, political scientists and consumer researchers have found in their experiments and their surveys. It also seems consistent with what many thinkers have written through the ages; and it is the kind of thing you can confirm with your own observations.

Common Sense

Glancing through the newspapers, or just keeping your eyes open at home, on the job or out in public, one fact is indisputable: People do some *truly bizarre* things. Of course, they do far more things that are nothing but normal and ordinary. Still, how many times have you witnessed something that caused you to wonder why in the world someone would do it?

The short answer is that they did it because they *decided* to do it, but that only leads to the next question: Well, then why did they decide to do it?

Let's start with common sense, using a little introspection. Think of something you did recently—anything at all, big or little, important or trivial, private or public. Why did you do it? Why did you spend all day Saturday in the office? Why did you call a particular friend on the telephone? Why did you go to that specific restaurant for lunch yesterday? Why did you play your latest game of racquetball (or golf, or bridge, or tennis or poker)? Why did you buy that particular brand of beer (or soda pop, or breakfast cereal or lipstick)?

Commonsensically, the reasons why are probably in this list:

- You thought doing it would benefit you in some way.
- You figured no trouble or harm would result from it.
- You felt it was the right thing to do.
- Other people expected it of you.
- It was what you always do in that kind of situation.
- It was important that you do it right then.
- You were pretty sure how it would turn out.
- You really had no choice but to do it.

Now think of something that you *might* have done recently but did *not* do. Why didn't you tell your boss to take that job and shove it? Why didn't you answer the letter that has been sitting on your desk for months? Why didn't you pledge a contribution to the charity solicitor who called on the telephone? Why didn't you go over and introduce yourself to that attractive person you've been noticing lately in the cafeteria? Why didn't you look at the bum sitting on the grating along the sidewalk muttering "Spare change, spare change"? Why didn't you ask for that raise you know you deserve? The reasons why not are probably among these:

- You felt you had more to lose than you had to gain.
- You were uncertain of what the outcome would be.
- You felt it was the wrong thing to do.
- You didn't feel it was up to you to do something.
- The situation was so complicated that you felt you would be better off not doing anything just then.

There's nothing wrong with these commonsensical explanations, as far as they go, but we can do a lot better. Let's begin by being quite clear as to what we mean by "doing something." "Doing something" means:

A specific person
Doing a specific action
At a specific moment.

We're not talking about the human race, or about society, but about one specific individual at a particular moment in time. Jethro has just downed the last can in his last six-pack. He decides to run to the store for more beer. Then Molly, his wife, yells at him as he's getting into the car that dinner's on the table. So he postpones his trip and goes to the store after dinner. As far as we're concerned, there are two actions here—one Jethro did (going to the store after dinner) and one he didn't do (didn't go when he had first intended to).

Are we being too nitpicky here? Not if you want to understand how persuasion, power and control work. Isn't it going a bit far to worry about actions that people *don't* do? Actually, some of the most effective persuaders get their way by persuading people not to do things. So it's certainly worth our while to take into account that aspect of decision-making as well. Let's borrow an idea from the Gestalt psychologists here, specifically Kurt Lewin in *Field Theory in the Social Sciences*. Think of your life as a constant stream of doing things, big and little, immediate and far-reaching. One thing after another, every waking moment, and:

- Everything you do is preceded by a *decision* to do it.
- Every one of those decisions results from the same *decision process*.

Deciding on a new career, or a new place to live or whether to get married, may involve a long and complicated decision. Jerking your hand off a hot stove or dodging another car to avoid an accident may follow from a decision that took only an instant. You may be fully aware of making a decision, or it may occur outside of your conscious awareness. But no one does anything without having previously decided to do it—that is, making a mental commitment to take action.

The key to understanding persuasion, power and control lies in that decision process. Power is the ability to make effective decisions to do, or not to do, things. Persuasion is the ability to engineer other people's action decisions so that they do what you want. Power and control operate through the persuasion process, which in turn hinges on people's deciding what they are going to do. At the gut level, everybody already understands this. Seemingly by intuition we all know how to take action, and how to influence what other people do. With no formal instruction at all, even small children become masters of manipulation. Commonsensically people can account for why they and other people do things. The aim of this book is to help you to understand action, persuasion, power and control much better than you do right now. As our first and most important step, let's put those action decisions under the microscope and take them apart piece by piece.

The Action Decision Sequence*: Steps to Action

Figure 1 shows the Action Decision Sequence—the decision process everyone follows when he decides whether or not to do something. We go through it one step at a time, and at each step we make at least one choice, and possibly (depending upon how complicated the situation is) a large number.

Step 1: *Is there a need for action?*
Some sort of *stimulus* kicks off the decision process. It may be an *internal* stimulus—a hunger pang, a stab of pain, a feeling of apprehension, a wave of lusty desire or simply an urge to do something.

---

* The Action Decision Sequence is a "sequential decision model." For more information about this type of model, you might want to consult Engel and Blackwell (1982), Kahneman and Tversky (1979), and Janis and Mann (1977).

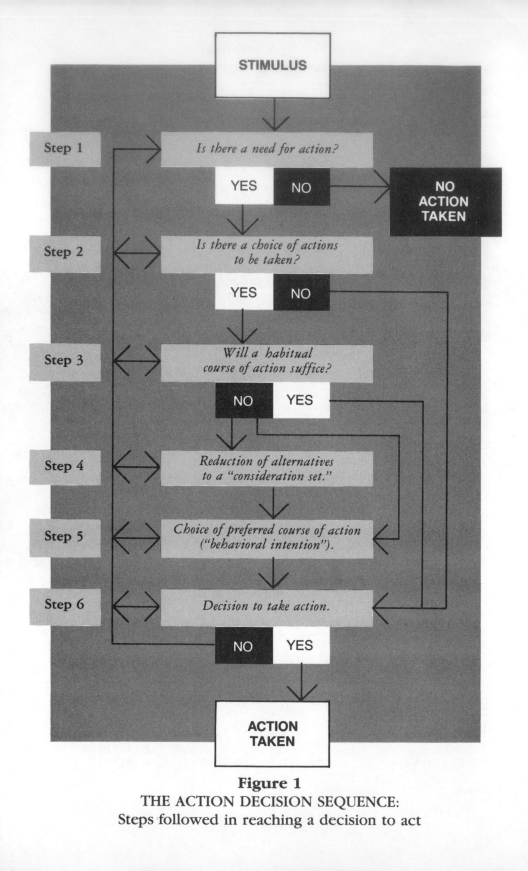

Figure 1
THE ACTION DECISION SEQUENCE:
Steps followed in reaching a decision to act

Or it may be an *external* stimulus, for example a letter from someone else's lawyer, or a catchy advertisement in the newspaper or a car in the next lane of traffic suddenly veering over across the line. One way or another, a stimulus gets the person's attention at some level of awareness, and the person has to make a choice:

- Am I better off doing something?
   or
- Am I better off ignoring this stimulus and not doing anything?

The fact is that we are constantly bombarded by stimuli, both internally and externally. Our bodies and our minds send us a constant stream of messages—thoughts, pangs, twinges, feelings, pains and pleasures. Externally, we are constantly awash with a chaos of sights, sounds, smells, tastes and touches. There is no escape. The stimulus bombardment flogs us even while we are asleep, and there is evidence that even people in comas are aware of external stimuli, though they may not show any response at the time.

For the vast majority of these stimuli, the decision process stops at Step 1, when we decide that *no action is needed*. We notice only the tiniest fraction of the stimuli in our environments. We constantly scan and filter information unconsciously, identifying and paying attention only to those stimuli that might make a difference. How do we know which stimuli might make a difference? Some of it—for example our reactions to loud noises—seems to be programmed into us. As another example, the sociobiologists tell us that human babies cry at the pitch absolutely most irritating to the adult human ear (which should be no surprise to any parent)—possibly a trait inherited because of its survival value for the species. (It certainly can stimulate parents to do something.)

But most of our reactions to stimuli have resulted from life-long learning processes. We come to know that when the traffic light turns red we step on the brakes, when the hometown team scores a touchdown we stand up and cheer and so forth. Eventually we get into routines of more or less automatic action/no action responses to the ordinary stimulus patterns in our lives, so we don't have to waste a lot of energy thinking about them. Still, when something unusual happens, we have to stop and think: Should I do something here, or not? Is this a practical joke, or is my life in danger? Is this a gas leak I smell here in the kitchen, or just week-old garbage?

If we decide no action is needed in response to a stimulus, the decision process stops right there, the case with about 99.9 percent of the stimuli impinging on us, and even the vast majority of the stimuli to which we pay conscious attention. But if we decide we would be better off taking action, we proceed to Step 2.

Step 2: *Is there a choice of actions to be taken?*

Once a person has decided some kind of action is needed, the next decision is whether or not there is a choice of action. It may not first appear that this a matter of decision—after all, if there is no choice, what is left to decide? But as long as there is a possibility, there is a choice, and the question to be resolved is this:

- Is there one action available so compelling I don't need to consider any others?
      or
- Am I better off considering more than one alternative here?

Ordinarily we decide there is no choice for one of these reasons:

1. We aren't aware of any other alternatives.
2. Compared to the one alternative, all the others look so bad that it's easy to reject them.
3. It suits our convenience to decide we have no choice.

Reason number 1 is often a matter of culture or upbringing. People are raised in certain ways, so that when situations come up, they "know" there is only one thing to do—any other response (if they are even aware of any) would be unthinkable. Ingrid burps in company, so she has no choice but to say "excuse me." Beauregard's boss tells him to be at a 10:00 meeting, so he has no choice but to be there.

A punk in a bar challenges Frankie's manhood, so Frankie has no choice but to punch him out.

The Godfather relies on reason number 2 when he makes an offer you can't refuse—something nice if you go along, and you get your brains blown out if you don't. Makes it pretty easy to decide that you have no choice (although note that many people throughout history have chosen death rather than do something dishonorable). Most of us are never going to be doing business with the Godfather and his associates, so that is an unlikely example. Here is the kind of "number-two no choice" that you are more likely to face. Imagine that you're in the market for a new car. You're sick to death of shopping. You know what car you want. You're ready to buy, burning with new-car fever. Checkbook in pocket, you're in the dealership that you have through an exhaustive search found will give you the best overall price, including trade-in. The exact car you want is sitting on the lot, ready to drive away, *but* it has air conditioning already installed, an extra $638.75. You don't want air conditioning, but you do want that car. The dealer has no other like it, nor does any other dealer in town. The next shipment of cars will arrive in a month, but there is no guarantee that this type of car, with or without air conditioning, will be in it. The dealer won't take out the air conditioning because he knows he can sell the car as is to someone else if you don't take it, then and there. Do you have a choice? No. If you want that car you take it with air conditioning.

"No choice" decisions result because of reason number 3 more often than you might imagine. Often people simply follow the path of least resistance. Yes, there are plenty of alternatives, but it's just too much trouble to think about it. We get an itch, so we scratch it. Nature calls, so we make a beeline for the bathroom. The telephone rings, so we go straight over and answer. We are Pavlov's dog—pure stimulus/response reactions, mostly out of lack of will to put out any effort.

Many people have discovered that "no choice" is a good excuse for doing what they want to do. They say "I can't," when they really mean "I don't wanna." Perhaps they truly believe they have no choice. Maybe they just believe that telling you they have no choice will make it easier for them to get away with doing what they want. That's for them to know and you to find out. You may decide that, given the trouble it would be to prove otherwise, you have no choice but to take their word for it. Also, "no choice" offers a convenient way for people to avoid taking responsibility for their actions.

If you are like most people, you are unaware of just how many things you do in the normal course of your life are based on no-choice decisions. The culture in which you were raised is a vast and subtle system of no-choice rules. Did you, for example, stop this morning to decide whether or not you would wear clothes today? The legal system is nothing but a host of no-choice directives—the law says thus-and-so, and we have no choice but to obey it. Etiquette books lay out no-choice actions so that we all can know in advance what is appropriate in "polite" social situations. In organizations, policy manuals set out the situations governed by no-choice actions. "I'm sorry, but it's not our policy to give cash refunds. I wish I could help you, but my hands are tied." As you may have figured out, structure power and agreement power both work because of Step 2. Each exists through no-choice decisions that direct the actions of those subject to them.

There is nothing wrong with all of these no-choice situations. In fact you should be grateful for them. If it weren't for culture, legal systems and organizational structures, people would literally go crazy—we just aren't equipped to make a lot of hard decisions on a continuous basis. Human societies have always been based on structures of no-choice behaviors that enable people to put as much of their lives as possible on automatic pilot. That was the point Dostoyevski made in his "Grand Inquisitor" chapter in *The Brothers Karamazov*—that most people really don't *want* to be too free. All it does is fill their lives with anxiety (see also *The Minimal Self* by Christopher Lasch). But even though laws, cultural mores, policy manuals and the like represent no-choice decisions, people often ignore them. "Rules are made to be broken," they say, as they decide in a specific situation that, for one reason or another, they do indeed have a choice as to what they might do, in spite of the no-choice confronting them.

Look at Figure 1. Deciding you have no choice at Step 2 is a liberating experience. It means you can skip Steps 3, 4 and 5, and go directly to Step 6. As we will see shortly, that is a good deal, if you can get away with it.

But let's assume we are in a situation in which we do have some choice—several actions we might take in response to the stimulus that initiated the decision process. So we decide that, yes, we do have a choice, and we move on to Step 3.

Step 3: *Will a habitual course of action suffice?*

People do many things just out of habit. They take the same route from one place to another, even though any number of other routes would do just as well. They go to the same stores, bars, lunch counters and dry cleaners. They watch the same television programs, on the same nights. They repeatedly buy the same brands of products— cigarettes, beer, shampoo or whatever. Year in and year out they eat the same kinds of food, wear the same kinds of clothes and hang out with the same people. They don't necessarily do the same thing *every* time, but more often than not, they will. Every so often they will do something different, just to break the monotony.

Why do people do things out of habit? For the very good reason that it sure does make life easier. Once we find a comfortable pattern of life, *we can make so many fewer decisions*.

But sometimes we find ourselves in a situation in which we don't have any habitual thing we can do. Sometimes, in spite of the comfort of our habits, other alternatives do look more attractive. Sometimes we'd like to relieve our boredom by doing something different. Sometimes we're with people who wouldn't approve of our usual habit, or we're in a setting in which our habit would be out of place.

At Step 3 we decide whether or not some habitual action will answer the need for action. The issue is this:

- Is what I ordinarily do in this situation going to be the best thing to do right now?

  or
- Will I be better off doing something else?

Think about buying hair shampoo. Very likely there is one brand that, all else being equal, you would buy without question, your habitual brand. So, with Brand X shampoo on your shopping list, you find in the store a special on Brand Z—50 percent off, half as much as your usual brand. If you have a very strong preference, or don't like making decisions, you'll probably ignore the special and buy your usual Brand X anyhow. If your preference isn't very strong, or if the savings make a difference to you, you may decide that your habit isn't good enough right now, that this is too good a deal to pass up.

That's how habits work. We usually go with them (otherwise they aren't habits, right?). But at various times, for various reasons, we choose to do something else.

If we can decide that once again, our habit will be good enough, we skip Steps 4 and 5, and save ourselves some mental effort by going directly to the last step in the sequence. If habit won't do this time, we must go either to Step 4 (if we have only a vague idea of what we might do) or to Step 5 (if it's a matter of choosing an action from among a small set of possibilities).

Step 4: *Reduction of alternatives to a "consideration set."*

As the Lovin' Spoonful song goes, "Did you ever have to make up your mind?" When I first moved to Philadelphia I was stymied for months by the problem of picking out a place to live. There was *too much choice*. Downtown close to where I worked looked attractive. The Main Line suburbs to the west were beautiful, but so were the suburbs to the north and the northwest. Should I live close in or further out? What about the schools? Did I want a manicured-looking area, or perhaps something more rural? An apartment, a house, a twin or a town house? What price range? For weeks I drove around (during one of the worst winters in the city's history), eliminating one area after another. Finally I settled on the northern suburbs, and the neighborhood was settled by which homes were on the market at the time. At last I got it down to three possibles, with one clear first choice. What a relief when the seller accepted the offer. The ordeal was over.

The point is that in deciding what to do in an unfamiliar and/or complicated situation, we usually have to narrow a large number of possibilities down to a manageable number that we will seriously consider—our "consideration set," as the consumer psychologists call it—because people can't comfortably pick one thing out of a large number. They must first winnow the alternatives down to a smaller number (rarely more than six) that they can handle psychologically. You probably did that the first time you bought a car or a house, selected a college or went on an expensive vacation—that is, unless you were in a "no choice" situation or were in a position to do something habitual.

When most people think about making decisions, they have Step 4 in mind. It definitely is the part of the process that sticks in our minds, because it usually takes the most effort and causes the most anxiety. That's why people so strongly prefer no-choice and habitual behaviors—they help us to skip Step 4.

Sometimes eliminating alternatives can be fun and exciting, for example picking out a movie, or a restaurant or a new article of clothing. But it can be exhausting and disorienting if it's a difficult decision that you'd rather not have to make in the first place. Imagine having to find a new place to live after your house burns down, or totaling your car and having to replace it over a weekend. Now we're talking Step 4.

At Step 4 people essentially decide what *not* to do. For every alternative confronting them, they must decide:

- Should I seriously consider this one?
     or
- Should I drop it?

Alternatives pop in and out of our minds. We strike off whole categories of possibilities at once. We seize excuses for tossing things out of further consideration. It can be nerve-wracking, especially if it has to do with something important and/or if we're under a lot of pressure. No wonder people try so hard to avoid Step 4. But one way or another we eventually get through it. We've got all of those alternatives narrowed down to a few serious contenders. Whew! Wow! Let's move on to Step 5 before any *more* possibilities come to mind.

Step 5: *Choice of preferred course of action.*

Whether we came out of Step 3 with a small number of possible actions, or whether we distilled a consideration set out of a large number in Step 4, we have now reached the step in the sequence at which we choose what we are going to do—as the psychologists would put it, we select our "behavioral intention." The decision-scientists, the game theorists, the consumer psychologists and just about everyone else who has studied decision-making have tended to concentrate on this aspect of it.

At Step 5 we have two or three, maybe as many as half a dozen possible actions in mind. Maybe one choice emerged in Step 4 as clearly the best, in which case we're through Step 5 like a knife through Jell-O. Otherwise, we find ourselves weighing one possibility, mentally setting it aside and weighing another, possibly looking at each one several times. For each alternative the issue at hand is:

- Is this what I ought to do?
     or
- Isn't it?

Eventually we pick one and reject the others, and on we progress to the final step in the Action Decision Sequence.

Step 6: *Decision to take action.*
The last step. We got here because:

- There was only one possible choice (Step 2).
- We thought some habitual action would be good enough (Step 3).
- Of several possibilities one seemed like the best idea at the time (Step 5).

Our final decision in the sequence comes down to a very basic issue:

- Should I actually *do* this?
     or
- Am I better off *not* doing this?

If we decide to do it, we do it. *Action taken!* It's over, we did it, and hopefully we chose our action wisely.

But "there's many a slip 'twixt the cup and the lip." How many times have you decided to do something and then backed out at the last moment? You were all primed to call somebody. You were all set to go somewhere. You had your hand on your money. Then you decided not to after all.

When this happens, we follow the path from the "No" box that leads toward the left of Figure 1 and takes us up the side of the diagram back into the previous boxes. After all, we decided that something must be done, didn't we? We have to lay the situation to rest. This can make good drama. Suppose a person has no choice, but he can't bring himself to do it, and finds himself caught in a loop between Steps 2 and 6. This was the problem Shakespeare posed for Hamlet. Early on he knew he had no choice but to kill his wicked stepfather, but he kept putting it off. "To be or not to be . . . that is the question!" Hamlet's conflict was resolved in a very bloody final scene, with corpses strewn up and down the hall; so it goes in real life. Suicides, murders and horrible atrocities have resulted when people could not bring themselves to follow through in no-choice situations.

For most of us, most of the time, things aren't nearly as desperate as Hamlet found them. We choose an action, then decide not to do it after all, so we rattle back up into the sequence:

- Back to Step 1—do we really have to do something?
- Back to Step 2—do we really have a choice?
- Back to Step 3—maybe our habit would (or wouldn't) be best after all.
- Back to Step 4—let's look again at some of those alternatives we eliminated, and maybe some others as well.
- Back to Step 5—let's take another look at our strong candidates and make sure we picked the best one.

Maybe *procrastination* is the answer: Jumping back to Step 1, we decided that no action is needed right now. Tomorrow is another day. Writing our will, or doing our income taxes, or starting to look for a job can wait.

We may bog down in *indecision* for a while, unable to decide what to do. We go bouncing from one step to another, rummaging through all the alternatives again and again, looking at them, sniffing them, shaking them to see how they sound, hoping that one will ring the right bell.

For big, complicated, scary decisions, people may combine indecision with procrastination. They can't decide what to do, mostly because they don't like the alternatives open to them, and they hope that given a little time the situation may change. Maybe the need for action will go away. Maybe a rich relative will die and leave them a million dollars. Maybe some better possibilities will appear. But these too are the result of decisions that people make. Essentially they are deciding they will be better off taking their chances on the future than by acting right now.

A few years ago a friend of mine living in New York City got a notice that her building was going condo, and that staying where she was would mean buying a very ordinary one-bedroom apartment, in a nothing special neighborhood, for about $70,000. She spun around in the Action Decision Sequence for months, not able to decide what to do and putting off doing anything definite for as long as she could. Every week or so she resolved to deal with the situation (after all, there was a deadline). She combed the classifieds, went and looked at a place worse than her own that cost twice as much money, and came home with renewed depression. Then one week she and her boyfriend both had their cars broken into, whereupon they got married and moved to Ho-Ho-Kus, New Jersey.

Let's sum up this section. Whenever people decide to do something, they make that decision following a simple sequence of only six steps. However, making these decisions is not necessarily a simple task. People like to pass their days in as serene and uncomplicated state as possible, and so they tend to make a lot of adjustments in their perceptions, their thinking and their patterns of living so that decision-making is minimized and things go as smoothly as possible. Hey, give them a break! They're only trying to minimize their effort (see Zipf, *Human Behavior and the Principle of Least Effort*) and keep from going nuts from too much decision-making.

If this discussion seemed a bit complicated to you, that's because it was. But we will never understand persuasion, power and control, unless we confront and learn to deal with the complexity. Figure 1 diagrams what you and everyone else do a thousand times every day of your lives, and it summarized the process more simply and straight-forwardly than you will find elsewhere. Test it out on your own—trace how you decide to do things. You'll find that you invariably follow Figure 1, one way or another. Figure 1 helps make the complexities of human action a little more understandable.

Of course, there is still another important question: When people make all those choices, how do they decide which alternatives to pick?

The Choice Evaluation Array*:
The Mechanism of Choice

General Macbeth was faced with a big decision: Three witches had made some prophecies to him, among them that he would be king. At the time the prophecies seemed unlikely, but in the course of events all save the last one had come true. The only obstacle remaining between him and the coveted throne was its current occupant, King Duncan. And here was Duncan, a guest in Macbeth's castle. What an opportunity!

If he murdered Duncan, he would have a fair shot at being king. But he knew that would be the wrong thing to do, for several reasons. Duncan was his kinsman. Duncan was his lord. Duncan was his guest. Duncan was a good man, an exemplary man and an innocent man. Also there was the matter of punishment, murder being then as now a heinous crime, particularly murder of the king. However, his wife, Lady Macbeth, urged him to screw his courage to the sticking place and proceed, as she had a plan for pinning the crime on the two chamberlains who were accompanying Duncan.

Well, it worked for a time (Macbeth did get to be "king for a day"), but justice ultimately prevailed. For our purposes, Macbeth's

---

* The Choice Evaluation Array is a type of "expectancy-value model." For more information about this type of model, and some of the ways in which the Choice Evaluation Array differs from the basic type, you might want to consult Hooper (1983), Tversky and Kahneman (1981), Wilkie and Pessemier (1973), Fishbein (1967) and Rosenberg (1956).

decision illustrates perfectly the principles of the Choice Evaluation Array. His choice (whether or not to do it, at Step 6 in the sequence), like all the choices we make, at all steps in the sequence, was the result of his answering the following four questions to his own satisfaction.

If I go through with this scheme . . .

- What do I have to gain? (the *rewards*)
- What do I have to lose? (the *penalties*)
- What says it's the right thing to do? (the *positive values*)
- What says it's the wrong thing to do? (the *negative values*)

It appears that in making a choice we must look into the future, trying to estimate what rewards and penalties will result from that choice; and also into the past, weighing the choice against the values we learned from our parents, our schools, our church and other sources that influenced our moral upbringing. However, it all takes place in the *present*—it is a matter of how we perceive the rewards, penalties and the values *at the time we make the choice*.

Note well that word, *perceive*. Our action decisions flow entirely from our perceptions of reality, not reality itself. The actions we take are in response to more or less accurate guesses as to their consequences and more or less certain beliefs about what is right and wrong.

For every reward and penalty we consider, we take into account two factors:

- How *important* is that particular reward or penalty to us at that moment?
- What is the *probability* of that particular reward or penalty resulting from our making that choice?

With the values we are considering, the factors are a little different:

- How *important* is this value to us?
- How *salient* is that value to the choice at hand?

Combining all these factors, we come up with a formula for the relative attractiveness of a choice:

Relative Attractiveness = Rewards (sum of the importances
                                    times the probabilities)
                        + Positive Values (sum of the importances
                                    times the saliences)
                        − Penalties (sum of the importances
                                    times the probabilities)
                        − Negative Values (sum of the importances
                                    times the saliences)

With some extremely constraining assumptions, this can be expressed as a formula suitable for quantitative operations*, but let's work with it on the *qualitative* level. In everyday life we make countless choices according to this logic without ever plugging a number into it, in fact usually without any awareness of using it.

The Choice Evaluation Array sheds some operational light on Tolstoy's model of human actions. He contended that men's actions are determined by their motives and their characters. The rewards and penalties in the Array important to a person represent his or her "motives." The important positive and negative values represent "character," or "soul" if you will. For what is a person's soul or character but his own particular complex of "rights" and "wrongs?" (Phrases such as "battles for the soul," and "soul searching" operationally have to do with these values—"what set of values a person will live by," and "evaluating values priorities," respectively.)

We can also now appreciate how the modern, specialized social sciences provide precise answers to only parts of the puzzle. For example, B. F. Skinner and the other behaviorists have concentrated on thoroughly answering the question of how organisms learn through direct physical experience which actions have high probabilities of rewards or penalties. Humanistic psychologists such as Abraham Maslow use the "needs hierarchy" to give some clues as to how certain rewards and penalties come to be more or less important. Social psy-

---

* For the mathematical expression of this formula, see page 229.

chologists such as Milton Rosenberg and Martin Fishbein provide "expectancy-value" models which prove to be simplifications of the Choice Evaluation Array that apply to selecting one alternative from a "consideration set" (Step 5) in situations in which values are not a factor. Consumer psychologists investigate how people make decisions in the context of purchasing goods and services. And so on.

Table 2 shows Macbeth's Choice Evaluation Array in more detail. There is only one reward for killing Duncan, but it is the biggie—being king clearly is Macbeth's hot button. And as far as Macbeth can tell, it is a highly probable outcome of that choice—after all, the witches had assured him of it, and haven't they been right so far? Add a big plus to the Relative Attractiveness.

The penalty he foresees is about as important as any penalty can

Table 2
Macbeth's Choice Evaluation Array

If I were to murder King Duncan . . .

	Importance	Probability
Rewards		
I would be king.	High	100%?
Penalties		
They would execute me for murdering Duncan.	High	0%?

	Importance	Salience
Positive Values		
None	—	—
Negative Values		
Shouldn't kill innocent people.	o	100%
Shouldn't betray your		
Lord	o	100%
Guest	o	100%
Kinsman	o	100%

be—being executed. But Lady Macbeth effectively wiped this one out of the Array. She had a plan, and it sounded to Macbeth like she knew what she was up to. So, as important as it might be, this penalty doesn't subtract much from the Relative Attractiveness.

As for the values—Macbeth can't come up with anything that says murdering Duncan would be the right thing to do, and he can think of several reasons why it would look pretty tacky, at the very least. And he has no doubts as to their salience to the choice at hand. But they pose no special problem here, because Macbeth is what we nowadays would call an amoral kind of guy—as salient as they are, those negative values have no special importance to him, or at least so he felt at that moment. According to Dante, going against those particular values would qualify Macbeth for a reserved seat in the nethermost reaches of Hell, but Macbeth's burning ambition was sufficient to set them aside for the time being.

Shakespeare had Macbeth add these factors up out loud so as to reveal the machinations of a depraved and soulless mind. At that moment, murdering Duncan seemed to Macbeth to be an alternative with a high Relative Attractiveness. He proceeded to act on his choice, with predictable (to moralistically-inclined members of the audience, at least) consequences.

Macbeth's story illustrates the essential principles of the Choice Evaluation Array, and George Orwell was of the opinion that Macbeth was "the story of any bank clerk who forges a cheque, any official who takes a bribe, any human being in fact who grabs at some mean advantage which will make him feel a little bigger and get a little ahead of his fellows." But most of the time we make more benign decisions in the course of our day-to-day lives. Here is a more commonplace scenario. Picture me in the showroom of a Ferrari dealership, spellbound by a two-seat, Italian racing red convertible. I'm caressing the leather bucket seats, visualizing myself drifting it through the corners on a winding mountain road, and drooling on the showroom carpet. Wow, I can feel it now! Then I leave off fantasizing and think about actually buying it. At that point I start flipping through the rewards, penalties and values, resulting in a Choice Evaluation Array something like the one in table 3 (see page 86).

On the face of it, that looks like a bad choice for me. To confirm it, let's plug some quick-and-dirty numbers into the equation. For each "high," put in a 2. Each "moderate" counts as 1, and each "low" is 0. Multiply the importances by the probabilities for the rewards and penalties. Multiply the importances by the saliences for the values. Add the scores for the rewards and positive values and subtract the scores for the penalties and the negative values. The Relative Attractiveness for me of buying that shiny red Ferrari at that moment is a resounding -15. No sale today. (Just for the fun of it, see if you can figure out from table 3 what kind of car I would be likely to buy.)

Table 3
Choice Evaluation Array for Shiny New Ferrari

If I were to buy this car . . .

	Importance	Probability
Rewards		
It would be good for towing my 14-ft sailboat.	high	low
It would be useful for errands.	high	low
It would be good transportation to the commute station.	high	low
I would have fun driving it.	moderate	high
I'd feel more important.	moderate	moderate
People on the street would be impressed.	low	high?
Penalties		
It would cost a lot of money.	high	high
Insurance would be out of sight.	high	high
Friends would resent me.	high	moderate?
It might be stolen and/or vandalized.	moderate	high?
I would have to put a lot of effort and expense into taking care of it.	high	high

	Importance	Salience
Positive Values		
I should treat myself well.	moderate	high
Negative Values		
I shouldn't spend money I don't have.	high	high

•

86

Most of our day-to-day choices are simple, with just a reward or two, no penalties to speak of, and no negative values to hold us back. But with something as important and involving as buying a new car, choosing a career, picking a husband or wife or deciding on a new place to live, we can find ourselves confronting some very complicated Choice Evaluation Arrays. And what about those "?" in figures 2 and 3? They indicate uncertainty. Many choices are plagued by uncertainty, as you well know from your own experience. Often the complexity and uncertainty inherent in our Choice Evaluation Arrays become important factors in the decision process.

Complexity

If after exploring the Action Decision Sequence and the Choice Evaluation Array you have concluded that this decision business can get pretty complicated—congratulations. Now you are getting the idea.

The very simplest decisions to take action involve at least three of the steps in the Action Decision Sequence—1, 2 and 6. At even the least complex steps a person has to decide between two alternatives. And for every choice, at every step, we must do the mental math for the Choice Evaluation Arrays for every alternative that we consider. The Arrays may be full of contradictory rewards, penalties and values. At each step the choices are qualitatively different from those at the other steps. From moment to moment new rewards, penalties and values may pop into our minds, and we find that their importances, probabilities and saliences keep shifting around.

Psychologists have found that people don't like making decisions, and it is easy to see why. Decisions take a lot of mental effort, and the more complicated the decision and the greater the pressure, the more effort it takes.

Therefore, complexity is an important factor in the decision process. The simpler the choice process, the more likely a person is to decide to act. The more complicated the choice process, the more likely people are to shy away from doing anything, or to find ways to simplify the process. Over the long term, people develop habits, become rigid in their outlooks or even become apathetic, to minimize the complexity in their lives. They may go out of their way to ignore things, or deny that things are happening, just so they can avoid having to make complicated decisions whether or not they should do something. They may see more and more situations as giving them "no choice." Thus the validity of the point made by Sartre, Dostoyevski and Fromm—most people are quite willing to trade away a lot of their freedom to choose in exchange for a life relieved of the burden of having to make hard decisions.

Uncertainty

In the vast majority of cases, we make decisions with only an estimate of what the outcome of the action will be. There are exceptions, of course. Jump off your front stoop and you are 100 percent certain to fall vertically to the first solid surface you meet. Slash your finger with an X-ACTO knife and it is 100 percent certain to bleed. But most things we decide to do come with no guarantees. Even people attempting suicide by shooting themselves in the head with a pistol have been known to survive.

We can't count on much of anything for sure, but rather operate on the basis of partial certainty. Getting into the car and starting off for work, we are pretty sure we aren't going to have an accident. We don't ask someone new for a date unless we estimate at least a fair chance of acceptance. We pick a lottery number with only a faint hope of winning. Just about all of the probabilities attached to the rewards and penalties in our Choice Evaluation Arrays are more or less uncertain. (We should distinguish between "risk" and "uncertainty." Strictly speaking, in a risk situation, one knows the possible outcomes and the odds. Betting on a spin of the roulette wheel or a roll of the dice is a *risk* situation. Under conditions of uncertainty, not all outcomes are known, nor are the odds of any outcome known. Choosing a career or a spouse or a stock involves *uncertainty*.)

The same holds true for the importances and the saliences. Generally we aren't any more sure of those than we are of the probabilities.

How important is it, really, that the guy at the next desk got a raise and you didn't, or that your son lost his first fistfight? It's important that we be charitable—but how salient is that value to someone whose boss is pressuring her to up her contribution to United Way so that he can win an award? Again, there are exceptions. Sitting here right now I am 100 percent certain that being killed would be an important penalty, and I wouldn't be surprised if you felt the same. I'm also 100 percent certain that it's important not to take food off strangers' plates in restaurants, not to drive on the wrong side of the road, and not to go into public restrooms that have WOMEN on the door. Would that I had that kind of certainty about the rest of my life.

Like complexity, uncertainty makes decision-making more difficult and more stressful. The less certain a person is about a choice, the less likely he is to go for it. People work hard at reducing uncertainty. They read *Consumer Reports*. They ask around, hoping to get better information from people who know more than they. They consult fortune tellers, cast horoscopes, deal out tarot cards and take up prayer. The ancient Romans used to seek clues to the future by studying birds in flight and by cutting open animals and studying their innards. Investors read Standard and Poors reports and make little marks on charts. Businesses survey their markets and keep tabs on the competition. Candidates take opinion polls. Nations set spy satellites into orbit over enemy territory. Husbands peep into diaries. Wives eavesdrop. Parents steam open letters.

Uncertainty is a curse. T. E. Lawrence (of Arabia) called moral doubt "our modern crown of thorns." Uncertainty creates such tensions that people will plunge ahead with actions, just to rid themselves of it. Executives hire yes-men. People avoid or even persecute others who cause them to doubt themselves. They join cults or clamp onto dogmatic beliefs. We can't bear uncertainty, and with good reason, for it paralyzes action. Couple it with urgency, and you have "panic"— the situation is crying out for action, but it isn't clear what is the best thing to do.

Uncertainty is a critical factor in persuasion, power and control. People who are able to deal with it make good corporate managers, military commanders, film producers, entrepreneurs and options floor traders.

Why People *Really* Do Things

Let's be realistic. People don't calculate out their every action, based on conscious estimates of rewards, penalties and values. That might happen in situations believed to involve measurable risks, such as investment portfolios or bets on draw poker hands, if the person is inclined to be rational in the first place. But most of the time we are dealing with uncertainty, not risk, and more often than not we act on intuition or "gut feelings." However, whether we are talking about conscious calculation, emotional whim or demonic urges, the same principles hold. Instead of estimating a high score on the rewards of an action, we feel a rush of anticipation. We perceive the penalties not by running them through a calculator, but by that queasy sensation in the pit of our stomachs. We make that wild plunge because we "know" that it's going to work. We balk at doing something because we have a feeling that it's just not the right thing to do. Often our guts are much more accurate than our brains—and how many times have *you* gotten "rational" about a decision only because you desperately wanted to do something contrary to what your intuition was telling you? Some people operate by calculation, carefully weighing the consequences and the rights and wrongs of everything they do. Others go on a seemingly instinctive cunning. Tolstoy caught it well in *War and Peace* in his description of Prince Vassily, a smooth operator in the court of Imperial Russia.

> Prince Vassily used not to think over his plans. Still less did he think of doing harm to others for the sake of his own interest. He was simply a man of the world, who had been successful in the world, and had formed a habit of being so. Various plans and calculations were continually forming in his mind, arising from circumstances and the persons he met, but he never deliberately considered them, though they constituted the whole interest of his life. . . . He never said to himself, for instance: 'That man is in power, I must secure his friendship and confidence, and through him obtain a grant from the Single Assistance Fund.' . . . But the man in power met him, and at the instant his instinct told him that the man might be of use, and Prince Vassily made friends

with him, and at the first opportunity by instinct, without previous consideration, flattered him, became intimate with him, and told him what he wanted. . . . If Prince Vassily had definitely reflected on his plans beforehand, he could not have been so natural in his behavior and so straightforward and familiar in his relations with everyone of higher and lower rank than himself. Something drew him infallibly towards men richer or more powerful than himself, and he was endowed with a rare instinct for hitting on precisely the moment when he should and could make use of such persons.

So some of us have it, and some of us don't. More accurately, some of us have more of it than others. Nor do we always do things for the nicest of reasons. Billy Bob may give Mary Jo a bouquet of flowers because he wants to brighten her day, or because the situation demands it or because he thinks the flowers may get her feeling obligated to give him a little loving in return. Melissa may pitch in and help Jennifer because she wants to be friends with her, because she's hoping it will get her some brownie points with the boss or because she sees it as a chance to sabotage Jennifer and get her into trouble.

Up to this point we have viewed the decision process as a neutral quantity—the logic we follow when we decide to do something, nothing more. Mastery of that process if the foundation of power. Power is the ability to make effective action decisions, and powerful people tend to make decisions that lead them toward their important life goals. However, as we have seen, not everyone is power-oriented. Some people use that same decision process not to accomplish anything positive, but to control other people. The distinction between power and control is crucial to making effective action decisions, as well as to dealing with other people in power situations. Power helps you win, and raw control helps you lose. Perhaps table 4 on page 92 can give you some clues as to why that might be.

Table 4
Power Motivations and Control Motivations

	Why Power People Do Things	*Why Control People Do Things*
Rewards: They want . . .	Achievement Fulfillment Esteem of others Salvation Contentment Love To make the world a better place	Control To get away with something Money Revenge To feel important Sex Self-gratification Envy
Penalties: They don't want . . .	Self-disapproval Disapproval by others Guilt Damnation To do less than their best	Loss of control Punishment Loneliness Loss of face Boredom Ridicule
Values: You should . . .	Be honest Be fair Be kind Be responsible Be generous Be courageous Be humble Be respectful Be open	Get all you can Not get caught Not be a sucker Look out for number one Take every advantage Make sure you're on top Always be in the right, never in the wrong Cover your ass Make an impression

5

HOW PERSUASION WORKS

The Keys to Persuasion

Having absorbed the ins and the outs of Action Decisions, you now know everything necessary for understanding persuasion, power and control. There are ten basic persuasion tactics, no more, no less. Each sentence below exemplifies a different one of them. See if you can figure out, from your knowledge of Action Decisions, what kind of persuasion is going on in each sentence.

1. A chicken for every pot. And a car in every backyard.
2. Oh, fiddle-dee-dee, Ashley!
3. Eat your vegetables. You should be grateful for them—think of all the starving children in China.
4. If whoever took my 1976 red Cadillac convertible with white top from Crabtree Mall parking lot August 9 will return my pet pregnant rattlesnake Cleopatra from under the seat, they can keep the car.
5. Don't think of it as spending a lot of money on these encyclopedias. Think of it as an investment in your children's future.

6. My opponent's religion will not be an issue in this election.
7. Call now! This once-in-a-lifetime offer ends at midnight tonight! That number again is 1-800– . . .
8. I didn't think you'd mind, so I just went ahead and bought it.
9. Don't worry about those other models—it's obvious that this one here is the right one for *you*.
10. This trail was made by Sand People—they walk in single file to conceal their numbers.

Did you figure them all out? On the surface they don't seem all that different from one another, but in a bit you'll see how each was well-crafted to accomplish a specific persuasion task, which none of the other tactics could have done as well.

The Persuasion Process

People do things because they decide to do them, and persuasion is engineering those decisions so they do what we want them to do. The ten persuasion tactics constitute the toolbox of the Madison Avenue copywriter, the trial lawyer, the supersalesman and the political propagandist. They also account for the mysterious powers of illusionists and "supernaturally powerful" people like Ted Bundy—for persuasion is part and parcel of their "magic."

Let's look at the overall persuasion process first. Figure 2 shows the three information flows a persuader must master: status information, persuasive messages and feedback. Most people believe persuasion is a one-way street—the advertiser, or the propagandist or the salesperson having his way with a hapless victim. Actually, persuasion is inherently a *two-way* process. Each party can have an effect on the other. Good negotiators know all about that. If the other guy *wants* something, that puts *them* in a good position to *get* something. People who invariably wind up as prey to one-way persuasion are victims only of their own naivety. The process is easier to understand if we think of it as working in one direction, as shown in the flowchart for "selling." Keep in mind that the flowchart for "bargaining or negotiating" is a more accurate map of reality.

Status Information

Status information is what you need to know about someone in order to be persuasive. What do you need to know?

- What decisions are on the person's mind.
- How he feels about the decision you want him to make:
  —Where he is in the Action Decision Sequence.
  —What rewards, penalties and values are influencing his choice.
  —What importances, probabilities and saliences they carry.

Sounds like a tall order? That depends. In many respects people aren't very different from one another, and a good working knowledge of human nature will take us far. Most often we are trying to persuade someone we know, or at least someone from a background similar to our own. Just by imagining yourself in the other person's place, you

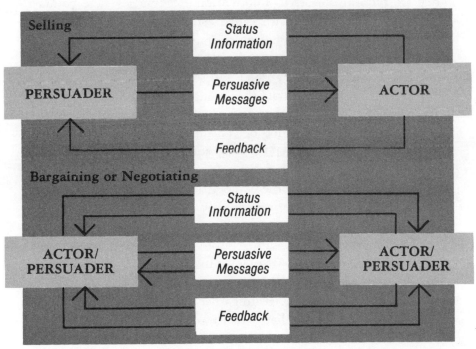

Figure 2
INFORMATION FLOWS IN THE PERSUASION PROCESS

may be able to home in on the most persuasive thing to say. If it's something you'd want, the other guy might want it too.

Dealing with strangers, we have to find out the key information for ourselves. Appearance can tell us a lot—how people groom themselves, how they dress, how they carry themselves. Sometimes we can tell at a glance whether we're in for a pleasant experience, or for big trouble. Successful hustlers, prostitutes and police officers have good antennae for sizing people up. Their intuition gives them an instant, accurate reading. The ones without this ability don't survive on the streets for very long.

Going beyond appearance, you can do a little probing. No doubt you've had the experience of salespeople striking up a friendly conversation by asking a few harmless personal questions: Where are you from? What kind of business are you in? Where do you live? What kind of car do you drive? How are your kids doing in school? Where does your husband or wife work? and so forth. It isn't friendliness. They are probing for status information, seeking leverage points to help them make that sale. It's called "sizing up your prospect," and people in sales read books and go to training programs to learn how to do it better. Real estate agents will sometimes offer "free financial counseling." In truth, they don't care whether the counseling does the prospect any good or not; they want to find out up front if he's a live one, or if he promises to be a waste of their time.

Companies that do a lot of consumer marketing (for example Procter and Gamble, General Foods, and Coca-Cola) have the same problem: What do we tell those people with our advertising so they'll buy from us and not from the competition? They can't come around and look us each over personally, so they do surveys and focus groups, getting status information from small samples that they hope represent the overall market. For the same reason, political candidates conduct polls around election time—they want to find out what kinds of issues, facts, images and promises the voters might respond to. America has the CIA, and Russia the KGB, to gather information about the status of the world at large. William Gladstone, prime minister of Britain at the height of the Empire, studied the Koran for information about the status of his enemies' souls.

We all understand this pretty well in our day-to-day lives. We understand it so well that we put a lot of effort into giving people the status information we want them to have. We get dressed having a pretty good idea of what effect we will have on others. For respect and good service we dress one way. If we want people to ignore us and leave us alone, we dress another. It's not for nothing that *Dress for Success* was on the best-seller lists for so long. Thousands of men and women, ambitious to become top managers in big corporations, understood very well that hiring and promotion decisions are to a large extent based on outward appearances. They wanted to ensure that they were sending the right status information to the people making those decisions.

You must have status information before you can persuade. Sometimes there isn't time but to take a quick look at your target, then go on the basis of first impression and intuition. On the other hand, if there's a lot on the line—say a megabuck contract for airliners or offshore oilwells—you can bet that plenty of research will be done on the people making the decision: how much money they have to spend; what their needs and requirements are; what they've been hearing from the competition; what their habits, likes and dislikes are; what their weaknesses are; who their friends are; what their situations are in their companies—*anything* for the edge that could bring home the bacon.

How are you at divining status information? Remember that Choice Evaluation Array in Chapter 4 having to do with my interest in the red Ferrari? That is the status information someone would need to sell me a car. (I wound up buying a Toyota Corolla liftback.)

Persuasive Messages

Okay, you've got your status information, and it's time to roll. Now you put together some persuasive messages and transmit them to your target. You can do it with words, but other methods can be just as effective. Instead of words you can use photographs or motion pictures. You can shake a fist or flip them half of the V for victory. Facial expressions may be just the ticket, perhaps a come-hither, or a withering glare calculated to melt the buttons off their shirts. There are all kinds of ways to transmit these messages—face-to-face, over the telephone, in magazines or newspapers, on television or radio, billboards, memos, notes under the door, notices on a bulletin board—persuaders are limited only by their own imaginations. Since this entire chapter is about how to put together persuasive messages, let's leave the details for later.

Feedback

You took your best persuasive shot. Now, keep your eyes open, watch closely. What happened? Did he like what you said? Does he seem to want to hear more? Did he turn white or step back when he heard your message? Maybe he said, "Sounds good to me—where do I sign up?" Those gratifying words are all too rare. More likely, you've got some more persuading ahead. Based on your feedback, you'll have a better idea of what to do. Maybe it'll take some clarifying. Maybe you'd be well advised to back off a little. You may have to excuse yourself, go away for a while, and think of some entirely new approach.

Expert persuaders know how to gather and use feedback. Oriental pearl traders carefully watch the buyer's eyes as they show him pearls. When his eye pupils grow larger, they take that as a sign of strong interest in that particular pearl, useful to know when they get down to haggling over the price.

Then there is the old story about the optometrist breaking in the new hire. "When they ask how much the glasses cost," he advised, "tell them it'll be thirty dollars. Watch their faces closely, and if they don't flinch, continue on and say '. . . for the frames. The lenses are thirty dollars . . .' and watch their faces again. If they still don't flinch, continue on and say '. . . each.' "

High technology is taking over. Nowadays people negotiating over the telephone use voice stress analyzers on the theory that it's stressful for people not to the tell the truth—for instance, whether the price they quoted *really* is their best and final offer. In expensive corporate trials, "shadow juries" are sometimes used—people hired to sit in the courtroom during the proceedings, then probed afterwards by the attorneys who hired them to find out how they reacted to both sides' arguments and evidence. One-way mirrors, hidden cameras, brainwave sensors and ultrasensitive listening devices also are useful for gathering both feedback and status information. All in the service of more effective persuasive messages.

To Do, or Not to Do

Most of us think of persuasion as getting people to do things, but that's only half the story. Truly, it's *less* than half the story, because the most effective persuaders, and the most effective persuasion, use the approach of persuading people *not* to do things. For one thing, it's easier—people don't like to make action decisions, remember? So, all else being equal, they'd prefer not to have to decide to do things. Also, people don't notice persuasion not to do things. Look at it this way: How many things did people persuade you *not* to do this week? You have no idea. But people trying to persuade you *to do* things are usually fairly obvious.

Think of the two attorneys in a criminal trial. In America we presume a defendant innocent until proved guilty. Therefore the burden is on the prosecuting attorney, who must present a persuasive, technically flawless case, demonstrating to the jury "beyond a shadow of a doubt" that they should unanimously agree to take the action of finding the defendant guilty. The defense attorney, on the other hand, doesn't have to prove anything, but can prevent the guilty verdict by finding a technical flaw in the prosecution's case, or by creating sufficient doubt or uncertainty in the mind of even just one of the twelve jurors.

Persuasion "not to" accounts for some of the "magical powers" of serial murderers like Ted Bundy and other will-o'-the-wisp operators. From the account given by Michaud and Aynesworth in *The Only Living Witness*, it is clear that Bundy had a remarkable talent for giving people no reason to do anything about him. Except for the few occasions when he seemed to be trying to give himself away, he simply blended into the vast American crowd of strangers. Once out of sight of others, anyone with the will and the skill can murder (or at least subdue) an unsuspecting victim in a matter of seconds. At all other times, Bundy made sure that nothing called attention to himself.

How did he do it? In a number of artful ways. At one time he owned a Volkswagen Beetle, from which he had removed the seat on the passenger side. One ploy he used was to put his arm in a sling, then ask girls by themselves if they would help him put his books in his car, or help him with his sailboat. Not every one he approached would do it, but these are after all reasonable requests. Many young girls have been brought up to be helpful, and Bundy was a good-looking guy. With the girl beside the car, and the passenger door open, it takes only a moment to knock her unconscious, handcuff her, pack her down on the floor and close her off out of sight. That done, the girls were calmly driven to an isolated spot in the nearby mountains, where the job was finished.

Having worked in politics and in law enforcement, Bundy knew something about avoiding detection. He knew that police jurisdictions do not cooperate with one another in sharing information about crimes. Therefore he operated in different police districts, away from where he lived. Thus each crime was treated as a puzzling, isolated instance, with no modus operandi, no pattern being established. In the meantime he lived an anonymous life. He had girlfriends but no close social ties. He worked at ordinary jobs, doing nothing to make himself noteworthy. He had a habit of changing his appearance, wearing a beard at times, a mustache at others, and trying different styles of haircut.

In Colorado he slipped up and was arrested. There a judge noted that he had a "changling face." His expression would so alter his whole appearance that some moments one couldn't be sure he was looking at the same person as he had been a half hour before. Or the day before. Or the morning before. In one police lineup, seeing the others with whom he would be appearing, Bundy combed the part in his hair to the other side of his head so as to blend in with them better. The day he escaped from jail in Colorado he wore two layers of clothing. Left alone for less than a minute, he jumped out of a second story window and took off, shedding the top layer of clothing to confuse pursuers. At one point during his escape he broke a window in a mountain cabin so he could hide out there. As always keenly aware of others' reactions, he put a note on it to keep passers-by from investigating: "Tom—sorry I broke the window—Amos."

During an escapade in Florida, Bundy was driving a stolen car, using stolen credit cards. He tried to check into a motel with one of them. The woman at the desk looked it up and told him it was listed as stolen. He replied that he had lost it but gotten it back, then went back out to the car and drove away. It takes a genuine instinct for manipulation to be able to produce, on the spur of the moment, an explanation plausible enough to throw off suspicion, or at least create enough doubt that someone is unlikely to call the police.

Bundy of course has no monopoly on these abilities. Josef Mengele, the notorious Nazi "Angel of Death," lived as a fugitive for nearly forty years by keeping a low profile. Bundy himself felt there were serial murderers running loose who were far more successful than he. As eighteenth-century writer Edmund Burke put it, "The only thing necessary for the triumph of evil is for good men to do nothing." Ted Bundy well illustrates some of the persuasive techniques for accomplishing just that result. Of course, not all persuasion "not to" is in the interests of evil, but his example does provide some fascinating demonstrations of the principle of "persuasion not to."

The Ten Basic Persuasion Tactics

Trying to persuade someone, you have two tactical options:

1. Change the relative attractiveness of the choices.
2. Manipulate the decision process itself.

What's the difference? Picture two little kids standing in grocery store checkout lines with their mothers. One tells his mom that he wants a candy bar, that he hasn't had one for a whole week, that the one he wants is full of vitamins and quick energy, and that all of his friends' mothers get them candy bars when *they* go shopping. This kid is trying to make buying the candy bar a relatively attractive choice for his mother.

Over in the next line, the kid sneaks the candy bar off the rack and in among the frozen dinners and the hamburger buns on the checkout conveyor belt, then stands back and affects studying the covers of the *Star*, the *National Enquirer* and *Cosmopolitan*. This one is trying to put his mother into a situation in which buying the candy bar is the path of least resistance, even though the last thing she wants is to buy a candy bar right then.

According to current popular belief, persuasion is a matter of making choices seem more attractive. But the real experts manipulate the decision situation itself, and the amateurs don't even notice what's going on. We can sum it all up in ten basic tactics.

Changing the Relative Attractiveness of Choices

Tactic Number 1: *Work on the probabilities.*

This is the one most advice books concentrate on: trying to convince people that doing what you want will be in their own best interests. So, you figure out what rewards are important to them, and then you show them how doing what you are pushing for will result in their reaping those important rewards.

This is the essence of the classic political campaign promise, for example "A chicken for every pot. And a car in every backyard." This was a Republican slogan in 1928, and it helped Herbert Hoover beat Al Smith in the presidential election that year. Prosperity was important to the voters, and the Republicans were telling them that a vote for Hoover would bring them prosperity. Too bad about the Great Depression that started a year later, but the slogan does illustrate Tactic Number 1—find out what rewards they want, and tell them that your option has a high probability of delivering them.

It also is the principle behind Henry Kaiser's marketing dictum: "Find a need and fill it." Advertisements for products often employ this same tactic. You want more dates? Buy our toothpaste, and you'll have them. You want to be in style? With our designer jeans, you will be. You want a million dollars? Buy a lottery ticket, and you just might win it. You're after this reward? Fork over your money and it's yours.

With rewards, you try to increase your target's probabilities. But

.

sometimes people foresee penalties that make a choice seem less attractive. No problem. With *penalties* you work on *decreasing* their perceived probabilities. Worried that too much coffee will keep you awake? Not our decaffeinated brand. Pain relievers upset your stomach? Not ours. You think drinking beer gives you a fat gut? Try our new low-cal light beer.

Salespeople are in a good position to use this tactic, because they can find out exactly what is on your mind and then tailor their pitch to suit it. You want a car that gives good mileage? Out come the favorable EPA mileage ratings. You think the car ought to go fast? Out comes the car's record in the stockcar races.

So to make the choice more attractive, increase the probabilities for the rewards and decrease the probabilities for the penalties. It works around the house ("Good children get a treat"), and also at work ("Good employees get a raise"). But what about things you *don't* want people to do?

For persuading people not to, do exactly the opposite. Decrease the perceived probabilities of rewards, and increase the probabilities of penalties, making the choice seem less attractive. "You can buy from the competition if you want, but it's only decent to tell you that their stuff doesn't do the job, and furthermore it breaks down within a month after the warranty expires." "WARNING TO SHOPLIFTERS: You won't get away with it. We will catch you and prosecute to the fullest extent of the law."

On the negative side, Tactic 1 is the principle behind *intimidation* and *coercion*. "Intimidation" means suggesting that important penalties will result if your target doesn't do what you want. A former Mafia boss in Philadelphia had a reputation for being uncommonly persuasive, which he achieved by using punchlines such as: "I'll pull your eyes right out of your head." This approach is known in management circles as "The Hammer"—some bosses know of no other way to supervise than to bully their workers into compliance. Control People like this method, but whether used on the job, around the house, or anywhere else, it ultimately is ineffective. The usual result is that everybody loses in the long run. Morale erodes and so does performance.

To "coerce" someone, you raise the level of threat and make it appear not only probable but inevitable that terrible penalties will result if he doesn't comply, thus giving him no choice. Imagine some doped-up punk pointing a sawed-off, double-barreled shotgun straight at your nose. His eyes are glazed, his hand is shaking, you can see the tips of the shells sitting down there at the bottoms of the barrels, and he's telling you to move, *right now!* Got it? Now you understand coercion. It can get people to make some very accommodating action decisions.

Tactic 1 is tried, true and familiar to us all. There are many variations on the basic principle—knowing what is important to the person, change the relative attractiveness of his choices by working on his perceived probabilities of rewards and penalties.

Tactic Number 2: *Work on the importances.*

Sometimes outcomes of actions are 100 percent probable. If you do *this, that* is bound to happen. And sometimes it's clear that there is no chance at all a particular reward or penalty will result from an action—0 percent probability. Sometimes whether or not a value is salient to an action is perfectly obvious. In cases like these, one way to change the relative attractiveness of a choice is to work on the importances your target attaches to rewards, penalties or values.

If you buy a Cabbage Patch Kid, a Cadillac, a pair of Calvin Klein jeans or a diamond ring, what are the only outcomes that have 100 percent probabilities? All you can be sure of is that if you buy those items, you *have* those items. But it's important to many people to have those items, isn't it? Guess why. Give Coleco Corporation, the Cadillac division of General Motors, Calvin Klein and the international diamond cartel credit for successfully increasing the importance, to millions of people, of owning their products. These items became, through skillful advertising and public relations, very important rewards. And, of course, 100 percent probable outcomes for anyone who bought them.

So "brand image" is a special case of a more general principle: If it's sure to happen, try to convince the target that it's an important reward.

"You'll love the feel of our expanded vinyl upholstery."

"Coke is it!"

"I know you'll like the view from the office we've assigned you to."

"Won't it be nice to see all your friends at daycare this morning."

On the other hand, some inevitable outcomes are seen as penalties. Does it have a high price tag? "Costs only pennies per day!" Pennies don't seem so important, but of course ninety of them per day total to about $300 over the course of a year. Is the target going to have to spend some time at it? "It takes only a few minutes!" Minutes aren't very long, and it takes only a few. Doesn't seem so important at all. "That's no big deal." "It happens to everybody."

Values also influence the attractiveness of choices, and the more important they are, the more influence they have. You can jack those importances up: "Yeah, stick to your guns!" Or you can move those importances down: "Hey, a hundred years from now, who will care?"

As for persuading people *not* to do things—usually, people want to do something because it is important to them. Therefore, knock down those importances. Scarlett O'Hara, manipulator par excellence in *Gone With the Wind*, used this tactic (among many others). When somebody else wanted something, she brushed it off with a breezy "fiddle-de-dee!" Convincing them that what they wanted wasn't important made it that much easier for her to persuade them to go along with what *she* wanted.

What are put-downs but chunks knocked out of someone's importance? ("And this is Phillip, my daughter's little friend.") When Freud said that wit was aggression, he must have had this very principle in mind. The same holds for laughter and ridicule—they deflate the importance of whatever they are directed at. No wonder the Soviet Union keeps its satirists and comedians on a tight leash. No wonder Control People can't stand to be the butt of a joke. They know the score.

There are many ways to influence how people view the importances of things, some of them rather subtle. Job titles communicate the importance of people, and so do nicknames ("Tiger," "Duke," and "Big Louie" project a lot more importance than "Shorty," "Stinky," or "Skeeter"). Trademarks and brand names can attach greater or lesser importance to products. One restaurant chain advertised on a standup table display its "Great Awakening® Breakfast Special" for $2.25, with a photograph showing two ordinary fried eggs, three strips of bacon, two ordinary slices of toast, and a cup of coffee (presumably the title justified the thirty-cent premium over what other restaurants charged for the same, untitled breakfast). "Status symbols" such as European sports cars, private secretaries, first-class airline travel, imported silk suits and Gucci accessories usually are attempts to hype the importance that others attach to the bearer. Even maps may shape the importance unconsciously given to countries, with the ones positioned in the center, and the larger ones, seeming to be more important than the smaller ones and the ones off to the side.

I'll bet you've used Tactic 2 once or twice yourself. It's one of the most popular tools in the persuader's kit: Make little adjustments in the importances that people attach to their rewards, penalties and values.

Tactic Number 3: *Work on the saliences.*

Values are partly personal and partly a matter of social expectation. So we don't always know just how salient a value might be to an action we're considering taking. Sometimes there's no doubt: A faithful Mormon or Muslim will be 100 percent certain that his religion's values apply to his tossing back a shot of Jack Daniels, and an Orthodox Jew will be 100 percent certain about the salience of his religious values to his eating a ham sandwich. But many situations we face are not so certain, and often we have to estimate how salient our values are to some action at a particular moment. We don't know for sure, and that gives a persuader something to work with.

What does patriotism have to do with automobiles? Patriotism—love of country—is a very important value to many Americans. In the late 1970s some of our car companies did their best to convince us all that it applies when we decide to get a new car: "Buy American!"

What does fairness have to do with hamburgers? Fairness is a very important value to Americans, and one fast-food chain spent multimillions trying to convince us that it applies to burgers, shakes and fries: "You deserve a break today!"

Tactic 3 is a major thrust of rhetoric, the type of persuasion held in such high esteem by the ancient Greeks and Romans. They saw the goal of rhetoric to be logically demonstrating that the advocated action is the Right Thing to Do. "As we have agreed, Justice is the Highest Good, and therefore . . . and furthermore . . . and let me also point out . . . and so we may conclude that kings should be philosophers." Translating this to our terminology here, it means that Justice has an overwhelmingly high importance, and that the value, Justice, is 100 percent salient to having kings with a philosophical approach to their duties.

This tactic also represents the central issue in American legal proceedings—does the court reach a just verdict? Both sides try to persuade the judge or the jury that the supreme value of justice is 100 percent salient to their side, and 0 percent salient to the other side. "In summation, the evidence clearly proves that justice will be served only by finding the defendant guilty."

One of the classic household scams rests on linking the highly important value of *gratitude* to the act of eating vegetables: "Think of all the starving children in China. You should be glad to have those brussels sprouts." I can't believe that any kid ever really bought this masterpiece of illogic, although eating a few bites did at least get my parents off my case. ("If those Chinese children are so hungry, why don't we send these brussels sprouts to *them*?" "Shut up, kid.")

Confidence games hinge on this tactic. Many people can easily be convinced that the highly important value of honesty doesn't apply to situations already tainted by dishonesty. What's wrong with stealing from a crook, right? They find out what's wrong with it after they've been "stung." Sure they were conned—but they were doing something illegal themselves, so who are they going to complain to? You may have noticed that Control People use Tactic 3 to justify their actions, especially to themselves—they tend to believe that standard notions of right and wrong are 0 percent salient to what *they* do.

Surprisingly often people are not sure how their values—the "rights" and the "wrongs"—apply to a decision. The nimble persuader will be ever alert to these opportunities, ready to move in and use Tactic 3 where it will do the most good. One of the most common versions of Tactic 3 is "You are being childish," a phrase useful for talking people out of whatever it is *they* want.

Tactic Number 4: *Bring in new rewards,*
penalties or values.

There are many, many potential rewards, penalties and values for just about any action—certainly more than most people would be likely to think of. So "sweetening the pot" may help persuade them to do it. "Souring the pot," on the other hand, may encourage them to reconsider.

It doesn't necessarily have to cost anything. Just point out a feature of The Appliance they hadn't noticed, or a use for The Product they hadn't realized. Going the other way, mention a drawback they weren't aware of, or a cost or inconvenience they had overlooked. Salespeople make out well with this tactic, because they almost invariably know more about their product, and their competitors' products, than their customers do.

You may have to go a little further, throwing in some kind of extras, or making some concessions, to persuade them: free delivery, gift wrapping, monogramming, "batteries included," or whatever. Going further yet, bribes or threats (that is, rewards or penalties that hadn't previously been in the picture) may tilt the action decision in your favor. Or they may push your target the other way, and get you in trouble besides (that's the point of status information—know what's likely to happen before you try it).

I recall meeting a computer timeshare salesman, who greeted me with a very strange handshake. I was puzzled. Then it dawned on me that he was giving me his old fraternity grip. No doubt you have had people whom you barely knew at all start calling you as "pal," "buddy" or "friend." These are examples of Tactic Number 4. The salesman was looking for an edge, and figured that if by odd chance I happened to be a "brother," I might feel a little obligated because of loyalty to the house. Strangers who get quickly familiar are trying to obligate their target to the bonds of friendship (it's a good tip-off that you should keep an eye on your wallet).

Everyone plays a number of social roles (for example, fraternity brother, friend), and if a target isn't succumbing to persuasion, appealing to him in a different role just might do the trick. Implore them as a fellow American, Christian, veteran, Democrat, parent or anything else that will bring in some new leverage points. A variation on this is to try to stick labels on others that bring in rewards, penalties or values automatically putting them in the right or the wrong in the eyes of others—"highly respected ally," "bloodthirsty barbarian," etc.

An expert persuader will always have some extra bargaining chips in reserve, in case a situation arises that cries out for Tactic Number 4. That's what the fellow whose Cadillac was stolen was trying to do. He was adding the penalty of a possible rattlesnake bite on the ankle into the thinking of anyone who might want to drive his car around. I have no idea what his ad accomplished, but certainly he rates an "A" for creativity.

Tactic Number 5: *Change the natures of the rewards, penalties or values.*

There you are, selling new cars at a reputable dealership. Seeing a new customer come in the door, you stroll over and ask if you can be of help. "Yeah," he says, "I want a fast car."

"Ah," you intone conspiratorially, "you've come to the right place! Our cars go fast!"

Then he whips out his copy of the latest issue of *Road and Track*. "Izzat so?" he challenges. "According to these tests in here, these other cars go faster than anything *you* got." There it is in black and white. Are you dead in the water? Come on now, you're a persuader. You can't let this commission walk. Use your imagination. This guy has "fast" on his mind. Go to work on that.

"Yes," you agree, "on a straightaway test track, with an expert driver at the wheel, that car will do 137 miles per hour, while ours will only do about 130 (actually 127.6, but hey, all you're doing is rounding it up). Of course, there isn't a highway in the country where it is safe to a drive a car faster than 110 miles per hour, even if you'd want to. But that's not the important thing anyhow. Why do you want the car to go fast? Because that's fun, right? (The guy thinks for a second, and you can tell he bought it.) Sure. I like a car that's fun to drive too—everybody does. Now, what those tests don't account for is how the cars handle on the curves, where the fun really comes in. Our sports model, due to its high-tech suspension and its state-of-the-art weight distribution, handles like a dream. Fun? You'd better believe it! Come on, I've got one out on the lot, and I know a road that winds up into the hills, never any traffic on it. You'll see what I mean."

Did you follow that? He was thinking "fast," and you switched him over to thinking about "fun." "Fast" you couldn't offer him, but with "fun" you've got a chance. (Did you notice you also knocked down the importance of "fast" and hyped up the importance of "fun.")

The same has been happening lately with golf balls. Amateur golfers equate "quality" with "distance off the tee." One brand of golf ball didn't test out quite as far off the tee as the competition did, so the manufacturer redefined the notion of "distance"—*total* distance, tee shot plus fairway shot. That way their brand had better distance and therefore higher quality in the eyes of the market.

Is the prospect balking at signing the contract? Don't call it a "contract": refer to it as "filling out the paperwork." Is the prospect having trouble over the amount of money he's spending? Follow the lead of the encyclopedia salesman in the examples: It's not "an expense." It's an "investment."

People sometimes get hung up on words and concepts that seem to give a choice the wrong kind of attractiveness. A few changes in the way they see the rewards, penalties and values can give them a whole new perspective. It's not a "war department," but a "defense department." They're the "disadvantaged," not "poor people." We're talking about "youthful offenders," not "teenaged hoodlums." A little creative wordsmithing can help persuasion along. You didn't think all that weasel-wording was to make the people involved feel better, did you? No indeed. The purpose is to get people like us to go along with those government programs. It's nothing new. It was one of Big Brother's tactics in Orwell's *1984*. Nearly two thousand years ago Plutarch commented: "The way the Athenians have of softening the badness of a thing by ingeniously giving it some pretty and innocent appellation, calling harlots for example mistresses, tributes customs, a garrison a guard, and the jail a chamber, seems originally to have been Solon's contrivance, who called cancelling debts a relief or disencumbrance." Now our politicians are discussing "tax reform" programs that will most likely wind up costing the average taxpayer more money.

Advertising agencies and the federal government have elevated

Tactic Number 5 to an art form. A few little changes in how people look at the rewards, penalties and values can make a choice seem considerably more, or less, attractive.

Manipulating the Decision Process

The first five tactics help make an alternative seem more or less attractive. But what if there's nothing you can do to change your target's views on the attractiveness of the choices? What if you don't want him to realize you are trying to persuade him? Working on the attractiveness of the choices is, after all, a little obvious, and people don't like to think they're being persuaded.

Tactics 1 through 5 covered the basics—what amateurs think constitutes "persuasion." Now it's time to move up to the expert level. Here is how we persuade people to do or not do things, not by working on their choices, but by manipulating the decision process itself.

Tactic Number 6: *Stimulate their thinking.*

To use this tactic, you have to know what makes your target tick—which buttons are the hot ones. What is the person naturally inclined to do, and what kinds of stimuli will set it off? Then you push the button, and they do the rest. The stimulus leads them to decide that they have to do something; they choose the alternative you knew they would, and they do it. Some examples:

- A woman in a bar, wanting to meet the hunk at the next table, brushes by him on her way to the ladies' room, making sure that their eyes meet. Next thing you know, he's offering to buy her a drink.
- A politician, knowing that the voters have some strong feelings about religion, forthrightly states that his opponent's religion should not be an issue. This just happens to remind the voters that his opponent's religion is one they don't much care for.
- The three witches whom Macbeth meets give him the idea that he will be king, which his ambition and lack of scruples quickly convert to a chain of heinous crimes.

It doesn't take a lot to stimulate someone's thinking. Mention who you saw going into whose office. Mention where (and with whom) you saw their girlfriend or boyfriend with last Saturday night. Put your best goods out on display in the window. Wear a tight red satin skirt slit all the way to the hip. It's all a matter of capitalizing on people's hopes, fears and desires.

Tactic Number 6 is a favorite with manipulators of all varieties—not only Macbeth's witches, but real life witches as well. Using it, one isn't really persuading anyone to do anything at all, but only planting an idea. The target's own character and inclinations do all the work. If things should happen to turn out badly, well, what the heck, *you* weren't responsible—*they* made the decision, didn't they?

Tactic Number 7: *Move them along* the Action Decision Sequence.

As any good salesperson will warn you, be careful not to talk yourself out of a sale. When you sense the customer has decided what to buy, immediately start working on moving him toward Step 6—getting him to do it. This is what they call "moving to close the sale." In his mind, the customer has bought the item, but you still have to get him to commit—to sign the contract, pay you the money and cart the goods away.

In general, if the decision process is going the way you want it to, try to move it to the next step in the Decision Sequence, working them down toward deciding to *take that action*. Sometimes a little urgency helps. "This one-time offer ends at midnight tonight." "It's now or never." "We are giving a special premium to the first five hundred people who call."

On the other hand, if they seem to be heading toward doing something you *don't* want them to do, try to run them back up the Decision Sequence, *away* from taking action. Get them to go back and reconsider the alternatives. Maybe you can convince them that their habit really isn't (or really is) good enough this time, or that they really do (or don't) have a choice. Take them all the way back to Step 1, and see about having them decide to put it off to another day. Anything to prevent them from deciding to do the wrong (from your point of view) thing.

Using Tactic Number 7, the choice is all theirs. By moving them up or down the Action Decision Sequence, you are only trying to ensure that their choice also is *your* choice.

Tactic Number 8: *Change the nature of the decision.*

Some decisions are harder for people to make than others. Never forget it, because you may find giving a target a different decision to make will help you achieve your persuasion objective. Let's say you want to buy a new outboard motor (or a new party dress), but you are afraid that if you bring it up with wife (or hubby), it will be vetoed. No problem. Go down to the store and buy it. Pay cash. Lose the receipt. Then innocently tell her (or him): "I didn't think you'd mind, so I just went ahead and bought it."

This is the principle behind the old saying: "It's easier to get forgiveness than it is to get permission." You see, it's very little trouble to decide not to do something before the fact. After it's happened, deciding to undo it means a lot more effort and hassle. This is the tactic a child uses who slips a candy bar in among mommy's groceries. Mommy isn't motivated to let me have a candy bar, so let's see if she's motivated to say that she doesn't want it, when she notices the clerk ringing it up.

This variation on Tactic 8, the *preemptive strike*, is a favorite with bullies of all stripes—not only schoolyard bullies, but social bullies, courtroom bullies, road bullies, moral bullies and all the others who, realizing full well that they are violating others' rights, plunge ahead on the assumption (usually accurate) that most people will let them get away with it rather than suffer the embarrassment of a confrontation. It works in households. It works in politics. It works in business. Book and record clubs long ago discovered they can sell a lot more books and records if, rather than having members decide whether or not to order the monthly selections, they arrange it so that members have to *refuse* the monthly selections. Seems it's easier for many people just to let it slide. Consumer advocate Ralph Nader used the same tactic with his "Public Interest Research Groups." He raised funds for these groups on many college campuses by having the school include the student contributions as part of their regular fees. Students who preferred not to contribute could apply for refunds. Nader did

■

it that way (until the Supreme Court put a stop to it) because he found he could get about ten times as much money that way, compared with relying on voluntary contributions.

Another variation on Tactic 8 is to *change the description* of the action, so that it sounds more appealing to the target. For example, instead of asking for a "contribution to charity," ask if the prospective donor would like to make "an investment in the community." Advocates of pro-choice tell us that an abortion is "nothing more than removing a clump of tissue"—a neutral or even healthful action. Contrarily, pro-life advocates call abortion an act of murder—a terrible thing to do.

Another variation is to create a *chain of actions*—"one thing just led to another." By getting someone to do one thing, it may make it that much easier to persuade him to do what you want him ultimately to do. Get someone up on the high dive, and he is that much closer to deciding to jump off. Put a weapon in someone's hand, and she is that much closer to using it. First get the girl up to the apartment; give her a glass of wine; invite her to take her shoes off and make herself comfortable; . . . well, one thing led to another (of course, she might have been doing a bit of leading herself).

If you want to keep someone from doing something, *distraction* is a useful variation on Tactic 8. Take their mind off it by giving them something else to think about. Drop something. Stir up some kind of ruckus. Point at something out the window. Scream insults or nasty names at them. Spill hot coffee in their lap. Suggest something else to do. If a traffic policeman stops you, come up with some urgent problem you need help with, just to get his mind off writing up that ticket. Witches (again, the real-life kind, not fictional supernatural creations) make good use of distraction, creating little doubts, obstacles and problems that keep their victims from focusing their attention on their true objectives. Borrow a page from the witchdoctors' manual. In the African bush, lions are a commonplace item with which people deal as a matter of routine. But when someone is cursed by a witchdoctor to "die by lion" within a year, he suddenly has a new problem weighing on his mind. This makes him nervous around lions, and sooner or later he makes a false move which disturbs one. Roar! Chomp! The curse comes true. Distraction is a traditional tactic of pickpockets, and during the onslaught of American tourists in France during the summer of 1985, one popular technique involved gangs of children. An adult mentor (usually a woman) would point out a victim, and the children would surround him or her, poking, darting to and fro, chattering and tugging, while the adult came up on the blind side and rifled the victim's purse or pocket. A variation had the woman handing the tourist a baby, with the children lifting the money while the tourist's hands and attention were thus occupied.

Putting people on the defensive is one more way of distracting them and thus keeping them from doing something. Attacking them, you sidetrack them into defending themselves, which serves to deflect them from their own objectives. Answering a question with another question is a gentle variation of this—a target who falls for it finds himself continuously giving, rather than getting, answers. "Why do you always answer questions by asking questions?" "Huh, doesn't everybody?"

Tactic Number 8 requires a little flexibility. Keep your own primary objective in mind, of course. But remember that many different kinds of decisions can lead your target to it. Pick the decisions that are easiest for him to make, and your chances of success will be that much better.

Tactic Number 9: *Work on the complexity.*

When trying to persuade someone *to do* something, complexity is *bad*. It only confuses things, and when things are confused, people hesitate to decide. Therefore, Keep It Simple. Make your points clearly, directly and simply. Brush aside issues, facts or questions that might complicate things. Keep the alternatives, rewards, penalties and values to a minimum. Concentrate your efforts on your persuasion objective, and don't let your target's attention stray unless it's to your advantage. For example, if a prospect seems to have a strong interest in buying some particular item, a good salesperson will work on getting him to buy that item, rather than bringing in others for him to consider.

But if you are trying to keep someone *from doing* something, complexity is *good*. Bring in as many facts, questions, possibilities, alternatives, objections, statistics, witnesses, or whatever, as you can conjure up. Standard purchase contracts and insurance policies are good examples of strategic complexity. If they were simple, prospects might read them, have second thoughts, and then not sign them. So the companies make them too complicated for the average person to understand. The prospect takes one look, decides the heck with it, accepts the salesperson's assurances that everything will be all right ("It's only paperwork—I hate it too, but the company requires it"), and goes ahead and signs.

Tactic Number 9 is not easy for everyone at first, because many of us have poor instincts for simplifying things. But it is an invaluable persuasion tool, so work at it until you can control the complexity.

Tactic Number 10: *Work on the uncertainty.*

Arthur Andersen & Co., one of America's major accounting and consulting firms, has been described as being "occasionally wrong but never uncertain." This is proof they know their business. They help decision-makers make decisions—and decisions don't get made when uncertainty prevails. Pay close attention to business executives, politicians and other "movers and shakers." They invariably are certain about what they want, where they are going, and what is going to happen. Salespeople always have an air of certainty about them. This gets to be downright amusing in the case of stockbrokers and financial analysts, whose forecasts and recommendations taken as a group are no better than anyone could do by throwing darts at the stock listings. But let's give them their due. Any good persuader is going to be certain about the outcomes of what he is trying to persuade you to do. Shoot—otherwise you wouldn't be very likely to decide to do it.

Like complexity, uncertainty is easier to use on the "not do" side. Most people don't have that flair for appearing certain, that aura of self-confidence—face it, most people aren't very self-confident. But just about anybody can use uncertainty to *prevent* people from taking actions they don't want them to take. If it looks like they're going to do it, and you don't want them to, why, pile on the uncertainty. "Are you sure that's a good plan?" "You have no idea how that might turn out." "Those figures are pure and simple B.S." "The other side's case rests on the testimony of convicted felons, psychopathic liars, admitted perjurers, discredited attorneys and union-busting employer consultants."

This tactic is popular in both business and international politics. The less sure others are about your objectives, your motives and your capabilities, the more difficult it is for them to interfere with what you want to do. The Soviet KGB is acknowledged to be the world's expert at sowing uncertainty through propaganda and disinformation. Recall the first *Star Wars* movie. Obi-Wan Kenobi points out a trail in the desert and says to Luke Skywalker: "Sand People—they walk in single file to conceal their numbers." This is tactical uncertainty. If enemies don't know their numbers, how can they optimize their forces against them?

Tactic Number 10 takes advantage of a key principle of decision-making: uncertainty stops decisions. Minimize uncertainty if you want someone to do something. Maximize it if you want them not to.

There you have them: ten tactics that summarize how people persuade other people to do, or not do, things. You have been using them all your life, although you may not have been aware of all of them until now. A lot of seemingly innocent and incidental things we say and actions we take are actually persuasive messages, consciously or unconsciously designed to influence what other people do. And they work. Now that you know them, keep your eyes open. They happen all around you—all of them, all of the time.

Watch Out for the Steps

The ten persuasion tactics work at every step of the Action Decision Sequence, but always keep in mind that at each step a person has a different type of choice to make. Be sure your tactics are the right ones for the steps.

At *Step 1* the decision is whether or not action is needed. To get someone to decide something must be done, call his attention to a situation that cries out for action. Or convince him that taking action is a good idea. Circus barkers and street peddlers shout to call attention to their wares. Waiters are trained to plant suggestions in their customers' heads. ("A California chablis would go nicely with that entree, sir.") Displays in stores stimulate us to take a closer look. Babies cry to get some service out of their parents. Conversely, to prevent action, keep a low profile. Be a calmative. "There's no need to get excited." "There's nothing to be concerned about." "Be cool." "Be nice." "Trust me." Distraction may be just the thing here—direct their attention elsewhere, and they may completely forget the matter at hand.

A good approach at *Step 2* is to persuade the target he is in a "no choice" situation. Values come in handy here: "Tell the truth." "Keep your word." "Don't be selfish." "Obey the rules." "Be courteous." "Do what the boss says." Work on the importances and saliences of carefully selected values so that the target concludes he has no choice but to do (or not do) what you want. You may want him to decide that he *has* a choice. In that case, make him aware of new alternatives (i.e., the one you favor). Appeal to variety, adventure, independence or even the thrill of "getting away with something." This latter is a favorite of manipulative children (of all ages) who enjoy getting other people into trouble.

The *Step 3* choice is between habit or other alternatives. Often persuaders like habits. Manufacturers want brand-loyal customers. Merchants like to have a loyal clientele. People delight in reliable spouses and dependable children. Employers prefer workers they can count on. Getting someone to do something several times may be enough to establish it as a habit. Telling someone that he's done something before may get him to decide to do it again, just to be consistent with his habit. A lot of persuasion goes toward encouraging habitual behavior, and people usually are happy enough to go along: Habits make for a simpler life and greater peace of mind. To get someone to do something *non*-habitual, try to make it seem like a relatively attractive choice. "Live a little!" "Variety is the spice of life!" "Get out of your rut!" "Do something different for a change." "Don't be such a stick in the mud!"

People at *Step 4* have a real problem—too many things to choose from. As a persuader, your mission at Step 4 is: Don't let your alternative be eliminated. Give good reasons for considering it seriously at the next step, and give no reasons for tossing it out. This can be delicate. Get too pushy at this step, and your target may decide you are too much trouble to deal with, a good excuse for dropping you from consideration. This is the situation a person faces in sending a résumé in response to a job want ad; or in a "cattle call" audition for actors or dancers; or in a preliminary, qualifying stage of bidding for a contract. The main thing is to give your target good reason to come back and take a serious look. Present your case in the best light possible, and try to intrigue them. Don't give them *any* reason to toss you into the circular file. Dealing with large bureaucracies, make sure that every form, procedure and directive is followed to the letter.

Step 5 is the only step at which you sell your alternative *on its own merits*. Here is where working on the rewards, penalties and values associated with the action you want them to take will help the most. Your target is trying to decide which of several alternatives has the greatest relative attractiveness. Your job is to raise the relative attractiveness of your alternative, and lower it for all the other alternatives. Let Tactics 1 through 5 be your guides.

Steer them through *Step 6*, and you've got it. Stress the rewards of quick action ("Chance of a lifetime if you act *now!*"). Point out the penalties of delay ("If *you* don't do it now, *I* may not feel like doing it later"). Make some important values more salient: *consistency* ("You said you were going to do it, so you really ought to"); *obligation* ("Please don't let me down"); *decisiveness* ("What's the matter, can't you even make up your mind?"). If it's something they wanted to do anyhow, this step shouldn't be difficult ("Come on, you know you want to"). The real challenge is to get someone to do something he never really intended to do in the first place. If you want to experience firsthand what *that* kind of persuasion is like, take up some timeshared resort's offer of a free weekend and gifts. But have a little dramamine first— you may need a strong stomach.

Combination Punches and MIRVs

These persuasion tactics are effective enough in their own right, as your own experience should attest. But we have been looking at them as one-shots, aimed at specific audiences. Used in combinations, and aimed at multiple audiences, these tactics can be downright devastating.

.

For example, consider "the razzle," a carnival game described by Darwin Ortiz in his book, *Gambling Scams*. This game is played with a board having 130 holes, each with a number from one through six. The player rolls eight marbles onto the board, and the total of the holes they land in is his "score." Some scores result in "points," some qualify him for "extra prizes," and the others yield nothing. The player picks out a prize (these games offer TV sets, stereos, microwave ovens and other expensive items) and rolls the marbles, betting a dollar per prize on each roll. When the player reaches twenty points, he wins all the prizes he is rolling for.

If played fairly, this game is virtually impossible to win. One FBI study estimated that over six thousand rolls are necessary for an average player to reach twenty points. So the operators of these games cheat—in the *player's* favor! They do that not out of the goodness of their hearts, but to keep him putting down bets and rolling the marbles until his wallet has been thoroughly flushed out. Often players who have busted run home and get more money, which they promptly bring back and lose. What accounts for the magical power of "the razzle?" Nothing more than a clever combination of a few persuasion tactics.

It starts with Tactic 6—stimulating the sucker's thinking. The guy operating the game calls him over and offers him a free try "to show him how the game works." Miscounting the score, the operator tells him that the first roll was good for, say four points. "That's a great start," the operator remarks. "Want to pick out a prize and try again for a dollar?"

Now the sucker is interested. As far as he can tell, the prizes are valuable (Tactic 2: winning is important), the dollar at risk is insignificant in comparison (also Tactic 2: losing is not important), and the game seems to be easy to win (Tactic 1: high probability of rewards).

So the sucker pulls out his wallet, providing the operator with status information by revealing how much money he is carrying. He decides on a TV set, bets a dollar and scores another point. His next dollar bet scores nothing, but that's to be expected—after all, the operator reminds him, you can't expect to win on every roll. Of the next few bets, some get points and some don't. Now the sucker has nine points, and he rolls a number that indicates an "extra prize." This entitles him to add another prize, so now he is rolling for a TV set and a food processor. But, he is informed as he puts down his dollar, rolling for two prizes means the bet is now *two* dollars. No problem—after all, winning will be just that much more rewarding (Tactic 4: bring in new rewards, plus Tactic 2: increase the importance of winning).

As the game progresses toward the end of the sucker's bankroll, the operator through a variety of maneuvers controls the scores to keep adding on points and creeping relentlessly toward the magical twenty points. Thus Tactic 1 (increase the probability of rewards) is operating with a vengeance. Just a couple more points! Almost home! And after a time the sucker begins to realize that now he has to consider two decisions at each roll (Tactic 8: change the nature of the decisions). *Should he play again?* He is going for important rewards, and the closer to twenty points, the more probable they seem. The amount he is risking on the *next roll*—only a couple dollars—seems insignificant by comparison. Or, *should he quit and walk away?* This gets him no rewards at all, but some very important penalties—losing all the money he has bet so far with nothing to show for it; having to admit to himself he was a sucker; and having to explain to his wife how he lost all the vacation money in less than a half hour—are 100 percent certain if he does that.

All along, complexity (Tactic 9) has been working in favor of the operator. He reveals the rules of the game to the sucker only when it is to his own advantage, and the board itself is too complicated for the sucker to quickly figure out (the numbering system is heavily weighted in favor of the operator). Furthermore, the operator totals up the eight marbles faster than the sucker can follow, and if the board is held so that the numbers are backwards to the player, it isn't easy to tell what the actual scores are anyhow. Each player is in a booth, positioned so he can't see what is happening to other players; and onlookers are discouraged from giving players advice or wising them up. Thus the information reaching the sucker is kept pretty much under the control of the operator.

According to Darwin Ortiz, nobody *ever* gets that last point. The best strategy for "the razzle" is to run like heck the second somebody offers to show you for free how a carnival game works. For once the operater hooks a sucker into playing this game, he draws him ineluctably toward going broke, much like a psychologist leading a starving rat through an experiment. Magical powers? Heavens no—just an exquisitely designed combination of the persuasion tactics we covered. Study cons and hustles, and you'll find that they all are based on these same ten tactics, coupled with a control-person motivation to cheat the unsuspecting out of their money. The best defense against all of them, Ortiz tells us, is honesty. For they all depend on the sucker trying to get something for nothing.

Only a hick or a hayseed would fall for a carnival game like "the razzle," right? Consider the chain of decision-making that led to RCA's launching its videodisc player, Selectavision, in 1981. Originally RCA forecasted an $8-billion market and projected selling 200,000 units the first year at $500 each. By October 1981, 40,000 units had been sold; but RCA, still hoping to reach 200,000 by year end, spent $20 million in promotions for the Christmas rush. Even with retailers discounting the videoplayers down to $350, only about 25,000 additional units were sold by year end (meaning that each sale cost RCA about $800 in advertising alone). Finally, in April 1984, RCA discontinued making Selectavision, writing off a total loss of $580 million. All the elements of "the razzle" were there: the Big Score, the optimistic forecasts, upping the bet, the big penalties for throwing in the towel. Were the RCA decision-makers any more sophisticated than the rubes on the midway? They conned themselves, without even an operator to lead them on. At least we can credit them with being more efficient than the hicks—for it would take a lot of suckers a lot of hours at the razzle board to blow away $580 million.

Combination punches needn't be as elaborate as the razzle or the Selectavision decision. Here is a statement made in answer to questions raised after two CBS cameramen were killed by an Israeli tank in Lebanon, in 1985. "Many journalists have been killed in different parts of the world, and never has CBS or any other network reacted in such a prejudiced and hysterical manner." This single sentence raises the following issues:

- What is so important about these particular journalists being killed?
- Why is CBS acting non-habitually in this instance?
- What makes CBS so special?
- Why pick on us?
- Being prejudiced is a no-no.
- Being hysterical is a no-no.

The intent is to close off debate, and the statement is effective. Anyone foolish enough to respond to it would find himself in a quagmire of self-defending and explaining, having to publicly deal with some very complicated and touchy issues.

A "combination punch" brings together several persuasion tactics or messages. A "MIRV" is a persuasive statement aimed at several audiences (like the nuclear missile containing several warheads each aimed at a different target; MIRV—Multiple Independently targeted Re-entry Vehicle). MIRVs can be quite simple—a number of targets can be hit with very few words. For example, during the 1985 flap over President Reagan's visit to the cemetery in Bittburg, Germany, which was found to contain several graves of SS personnel, the following statement was quoted in the press: "Any honest German would admit these soldiers fought for the Third Reich and believed in it." The statement hits two audiences. It raises uncertainties in the minds of the general audience about any rebuttal that might come forth; and it puts any German who might want to disagree in the position of having to defend his own honesty.

The Soviet Union, with the world's most effective propaganda apparatus, are masters of the MIRV technique. When questions were raised in the early 1980s about communist forces using bacteriological warfare in Indochina and Afghanistan (the "yellow rain" controversy), a torrent of propaganda issued forth whose arguments could be summarized as follows:

1. It never happened.
2. It wasn't us and them, but two other guys.
3. They were the aggressors, so they had it coming.
4. You did the same thing yourselves in Vietnam.
5. What about how you exterminated all those Native Americans?

■

Rhetoricians will be quick to point out that these arguments are totally without logic. But rhetorical logic is not the point. The Russians aren't interested in convincing us of the rightness of their position or their actions, but in dissuading others from interfering with them. What they (and other propagandists, for example the Nazis) do is raise so many doubts, uncertainties and complexities in the minds of everyone who might want to object, that it is easy to find an excuse not to take action. It is part of the "bully approach" on an international scale, and the Soviet Union is not the only nation that uses it.

Self-Persuasion

So far we've looked at persuasion as something one person does to another, but people also persuade themselves to do things. If a person wants to do (or not do) something badly enough, he can talk himself into it or out of it with very little trouble. The same persuasion tactics apply.

One approach to self-persuasion is to concentrate on Tactics 1 through 5, working on the attractiveness of the choice. Someone who desperately wants to do something but is blocked by contrary rewards, penalties and values, will inflate the importance of the rewards and manufacture evidence that they are highly probable. Likewise he will deflate the importances and the probabilities of the penalties, and will make whatever adjustments are needed to bring the values into line. Thus we pay attention to ads, facts, advice and opinions supporting what we want to do, and ignore whatever suggests otherwise.

Faith healers, magnetizers, purveyors of patent medicines and witch doctors have since time immemorial utilized self-persuasion to facilitate their "magic." This is the principle of "the power of suggestion." Call attention to what is certain to happen, and help the person interpret it by giving it a positive or negative importance. If the underlying hope or fear is sufficiently compelling, people can talk themselves into just about any mental or physical state. Voodoo spells and placebos work on those who believe they work. They convince

·

124

themselves that they are having an effect, and the belief becomes a reality.

Laughter directed at others can serve to minimize their importance, a commonly used weapon of persuasion. Turned inward, laughter can be a powerfully positive persuasive force. Having a sense of humor, being able to laugh at ourselves, helps keep things in a healthy perspective, knocking down the importances of conflicted hopes, fears and values so that they don't tax our systems with unnecessary stress. Editor Norman Cousins claims that he was cured of a mysterious paralysis by the will to live, huge doses of vitamin C, and a lot of what he calls "laughter therapy."

Often we use self-persuasion to simplify our decision-making, especially in complicated or uncertain situations. Rebecca desperately wants to get married, and Claude is the only available prospect. He doesn't like to bathe, and he does drink a wee bit too much. She finds herself deciding that those aren't really so important, that he'll probably outgrow them, and that anyhow she can do something about them after they get married. Pete wants to go out drinking with the gang, but he's just about broke, and he has a final exam coming up. He finds himself building up the probabilities of fun, excitement and good times, and downgrading the importance of the money it will cost and the studying he won't be able to do. Some RCA managers, their career advancement riding on the introduction of Selectavision, paid attention only to the most optimistic forecasts of the market, placed a lot of faith in the power of advertising, and convinced themselves that once the public saw the product, they'd go for it in a big way.

For persuading oneself *not* to do something, *complexity* and *denial* can be handy tools. Complexity is easy. Keep thinking of new penalties and negative values. Carefully consider every option. Dwell on how much more you will need to know before you'll be *sure*. With very little effort you can complicate yourself right out of having to make a decision, at least for the time being.

Denial is another common way of talking ourselves out of having to do things. Denial stops the decision process right at Step 1. Simply reject all evidence that action is needed. This works especially well for people faced with deciding whether or not to do something that

·

125

will entail a lot of trouble, inconvenience or pain. Perhaps the most notorious example of denial in this century was the reaction to the Nazi holocaust during World War II by most people (including many of the Jews themselves). The horror and the implications of it were such that people chose to ignore the rumors, and even the evidence, they heard. Of course the Nazi propagandists made denial easier, by creating confusion and uncertainty. At the present time there is a lot of denial about Soviet bacteriological warfare, for the same reasons. The implications of doing something about it are rather grim.

On the personal level, denial is a frequently used tactic. People "stuck" in rotten jobs deny there is anything wrong with their situation. Husbands or wives, dreading divorce, disregard the most obvious evidence that they are in destructive marriages. Parents, reluctant to face up to their responsibilities, ignore blatant indications that their children are on drugs, are sleeping around, are troublemakers at school or are criminals. Alcoholics and drug addicts staunchly deny that they are hooked.

Self-persuasion often occurs when a person feels he has no choice, or when he has committed to doing something, only to realize that choices at the previous steps don't really justify doing it. Self-persuasion rests on the same tactics as any other kind of persuasion. It is a fact of life, and it isn't necessarily bad. If you are interested in using power wisely, recognize it for what it is, and use it to your own advantage.

The Strategy for Successful Persuasion

Let's sum up how persuasion works with the strategy steps for persuading some specific person to do some specific thing.

1. Decide on your persuasion objective—the specific person, the specific action you want him to take, and the time frame you are aiming for.
2. Collect your status information for that person and that action.
3. Select the appropriate step(s) in the Action Decision Sequence.
4. Select the appropriate persuasion tactics.

5. Transmit your persuasive message(s) to your target.
6. Gather feedback on your target's reaction.
7, Design and transmit additional messages as indicated by feedback and status information.
8. (Hopefully) achieve persuasion objective.

Listed as these eight steps, persuasion strategy looks like a very complicated and demanding process requiring a lot of time and effort. For someone in charge of planning the advertising for a major corporation, or managing the election campaign for a candidate for president of the United States, that is correct. It takes months of time and millions of dollars to persuade people to buy your product or vote for your candidate.

On the other hand, ordinary practical persuaders such as husbands, wives, children, managers, salespeople, street hustlers and even yourself, can do the whole thing in a second. They can cover every step, from picking an objective, to getting the target to do it, faster than anyone can follow what is going on. Maybe that is why persuasion seems so mysterious—sometimes it happens very, very quickly.

Warding off Persuasion

People generally don't like being persuaded or influenced by other people. If you want to repel unwanted persuasive intrusions, here are some tried-and-true techniques.

Put on the blinders. Pay no attention at all to them. Don't notice them, and don't hear what they are saying to you. Do not acknowledge the situation if it would require that you do something you don't want to do. After all, with no stimulus, you have no reason to have to decide whether or not to take action.

Be stupid strategically. It pays to be ignorant. If you don't understand what the other person is trying to get you to do, you can't very well be expected to do it. "I don't get what the problem is." "No spikka da English."

Avoid clear definitions. If you are in a situation in which certain conditions demand action, take care not to let anything be defined as those conditions. For example, if someone breaks an agreement, and that demands a response that you don't want to make, define it as being a "misunderstanding." Diplomats and administrators live by this principle.

Give an unassailable excuse. Have a reason handy that no one can argue with:

"Sorry, doctor's orders."

"Sorry, but that's our policy."

"Sorry, but I've already made plans."

"Sorry, but my (wife) (husband) (boss) would kill me if I did that."

"Sorry, but I have a terrible (migraine) (stomach ache) (venereal disease) (war injury)."

Control the information flow. Don't give away any information that a would-be persuader could use against you. Button your lip. Keep your cards close to your vest. Act erratically. Tell him to mind his own business.

In a word, *stonewall*. Refuse to go along. The experts do it all the time. Here is a gorgeous example, from the *Wall Street Journal*,* of corporate raider Carl Icahn in action during a deposition:

TWA LAWYER: What is written below the phrase "28,000 employees"?

MR. ICAHN: It says—I'm not so sure I can read it, either.

TWA: "Let 2,000 employees go," is that what it says?

MR. I: I think it's discussing [something else].

TWA: Immediately below the phrase "28,000 employees," in the box on the left there is some writing. What does that say?

MR. I: I'm not sure. I don't think it means the 2,000 employees. I see how you are reading it, but I don't think that is that. I'm not sure what it says. It says something 2,000 employees. It

---

* "Carl Icahn's Strategies in His Quest for TWA Are a Model for Raiders," by William M. Carley, June 30, 1985.

might be let go, 7 percent reduction. It might not be "go."
It's silly to argue over it. I'm not sure.

TWA: The words are, are they not, "Let 2,000 employees go"?

MR. I: I'm not even sure that says "go."

TWA: G-O spells go, doesn't it?

In the end, the exasperated TWA lawyer gave up.

Final Exam: The St. Thomas Hustle

Okay, we've surveyed all the ways people persuade one another to
do things. How well did you get it? See if you can figure out what
is going on in the following episode:

The scene is the small municipal parking lot adjoining the shopping district of Charlotte Amalie, St. Thomas, U.S. Virgin Islands.
Brilliant reds and oranges explode out of bougainvillaea and frangi-
pangi blossoms in the bright tropical sun. The blue harbor sparkles
out beyond the low tangle of stuccoed buildings, and the earlier cool
of the July morning has given way to a sultry cover of heat starting
to settle down over the town.

Ray F. wheels the weathered, rented Datsun into a parking space.
He and his new wife have just survived his first try at driving on the
left side of the road, no small feat on the rutted ribbon of pavement
that winds erratically through the hills from the other side of the
island. On their honeymoon, they arrived two days ago, the first
Caribbean trip for either of them. Now they are ready for some serious
exploring. They climb out of the car and pause a moment to look
around, get their bearings, collect themselves and figure out what to
do next.

Suddenly a willowy young girl with long, straight dishwater blonde
hair and wearing a trim tropical-weight cotton dress materializes beside
them. She moves in close to Ray F., pins a flaming red hibiscus flower
on his shirt and says, "Good morning. Would you please contribute
to help feed the starving children?" Then she flashes an official-looking
identification card with a lot of fine print on it. "Most people give a
dollar," she adds helpfully.

·

129

Ray F. pulls out his wallet, locates a dollar bill and dutifully hands it over. She gives him a cheery "Thank you" and floats away.

Is Ray F. just a good-natured, charitable kind of guy? Or what?

What kind of guy Ray F. is, is irrelevant. The fact is that he never had a chance to think about it. He was very expertly hustled out of a dollar.

Let's run that scene again on instant replay, in super-slow motion.

First, why did the dishwater blonde pick on Ray F.? He obviously was an American tourist. He looked confused. He had a woman with him. American tourists nearly always have money. Confused is good. What about the woman? She was the insurance that he wouldn't likely try any troublesome flirtations, but even more important, Ray F. would be concerned about what *she* thought.

Why the flower? That is the key to the hustle. Had the girl simply asked if he would like to contribute, Ray F. probably would have ignored her or said something like, "Thanks, but I gave at the resort." The flower changed the picture completely. By pinning it on his shirt she forced him to pay attention to her. It also gave him a different decision to make. No longer was he deciding whether or not to contribute, but rather, what do I do about this flower? Take it off and give it back (might make me look cheap)? Walk away with it without giving her any money (might start a ruckus—who needs it)? For someone fresh off the boat, it was a very uncertain situation.

While Ray F. was pondering these troublesome questions, the girl told him most people give a dollar. Why did she do that? (1) A dollar isn't much money. (2) Most American tourists have one. (3) It clears up a lot of uncertainty, i.e. how much to give. So, she gave Ray F. a very simple and attractive alternative. For just one dollar he could get rid of an embarrassing situation. What a bargain!

So that dollar "contribution" had very little to do with feeding hungry children. Granted, it was a better reason for her to give than that she wanted the dollar to buy a bottle of cheap muscatel. On the way home Ray F. and his wife saw her working the airport in San Juan, Puerto Rico, reinforcing their suspicion that the "hungry child" that dollar went to feed was the girl's parents' own offspring.

As Ray F. thought about it, the beauty of it struck him. What a perfectly designed and executed hustle, and it all took less than a minute. He now uses it as an example when he teaches courses about communication and persuasion. Had he realized at the time how much mileage he would get out of that little episode, he would gladly have given her . . . why, at least *twice* as much.

There you have them—the ten persuasion tactics, and some examples of how people use them to get other people to do things, in situations where neither structure power nor agreement power hold sway. Apply these principles to your own experience and you will soon find yourself able to recognize and understand all the persuasions that go on in your life. When you get really good at it you will be able to figure them out while they are in process. At that point, only the *real* experts will be able to get the advantage on you. Don't feel bad if that happens every now and then. No one is totally immune to persuasion; and sometimes it isn't even a bad thing to be persuaded. After all, not all persuaders have evil intentions. As P. T. Barnum discovered, people sometimes even enjoy being conned.

Let's move on to using persuasion, power and control wisely. In the next section we will take a practical look at how they work in the marketplace and on the job. The processes of structure power and agreement power will become clearer when we apply them to organizations. We will see what it *really* means to have power.

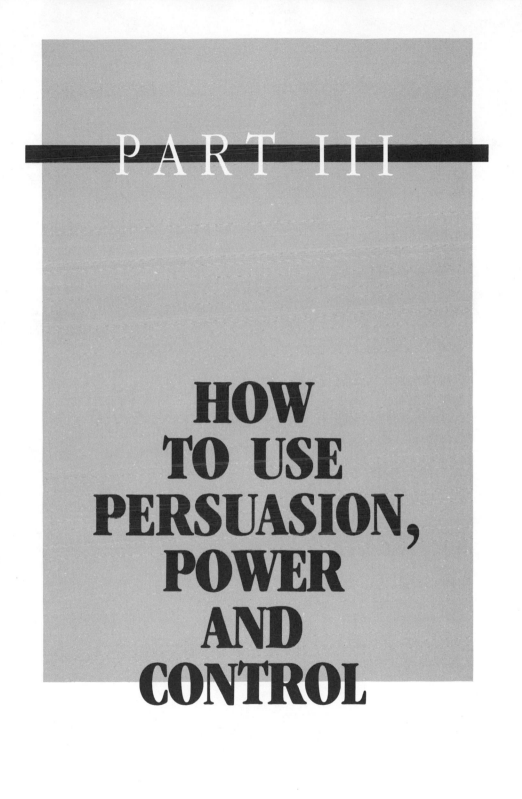

PART III

HOW TO USE PERSUASION, POWER AND CONTROL

6

POWER IN THE MARKETPLACE

Marketing Warfare

Out in the marketplace it's a jungle as savage as any jungle could be. High in their skyscraping, glass-walled lairs, some of the world's smartest, sharpest, shrewdest minds plot and scheme relentlessly around the clock. Their objective: to separate as much money from as many consumers as quickly as possible.

They concoct intricate, meticulously drawn strategies. They devise finely tuned tactics and the subtlest of manipulations. They probe, and test, and survey, and measure and observe. They hire psychologists to plumb the furthest reaches of our psyches, searching for advantages in deeply-buried secrets, fears, desires and vulnerabilities. They feed endless tapes of data into the most powerful computers money can buy. Whatever it takes to entice, cajole or trick the market into buying, they are prepared to do it.

Some have characterized the process as "marketing warfare," and the metaphor is apt, for titanic corporations wage continuous, bitter, Olympian struggles over the dollars in the public's pockets. Coke versus Pepsi. McDonald's against Burger King. Budweiser and Miller.

National rollouts. Media blitzes. Hand-to-hand fighting in the trenches. Scratching and clawing for megabillions in sales and profits.

Ah, who among us can ever forget the Great Coffee War of '77, when General Foods and Procter and Gamble duked it out over the $4.8 billion that Americans spend each year on coffee? General Foods held the high ground, its Maxwell House and Sanka brands commanding 42 percent of the market. Procter and Gamble marched easterly from their Cincinnati stronghold and unleashed a massive assault with their Folgers and Highpoint brands. Attacking General Foods head-on, they salvoed an advertising onslaught borne on a $100 million budget and saturated the market with a monsoon of cents-off coupons. General Foods answered back by doubling the advertising ante and disgorging its own cornucopia of seductive cents-off specials.

The two corporate juggernauts stood toe-to-toe for four furious years, trading staggering marketing punches, tilting and jousting, slugging and elbowing. When the smoke finally cleared, and the dust settled, General Foods stood victorious. It had repelled the upstart, its 42 percent lock on the coffee market still intact. Procter and Gamble withdrew from the field of battle to patch up the wounded and regroup, having managed to seize only 21 percent of the nation's coffee sales. An ignominious defeat for a proud company with the reputation of taking no prisoners in its devastating marketing campaigns.

What, you *had* forgotten the Great Coffee War? Worse than that, you never even noticed it when it was going on? Come on, you must have—all those sappy family coffee-drinking vignettes on television—all those heart-tugging "tender moment" commercials—all those fifty-cents-off coffee coupons in the Sunday paper inserts—all that money they spent (would you believe a half-billion in total?), and you weren't even paying attention?

Most amazing of all—during four years of intensive marketing competition by two of the world's most powerful corporations, coffee-drinking in America changed hardly at all. The peak year for American coffee consumption was 1962, and since then the percentage of coffee drinkers has fallen by 17 percent (mostly because young people are drinking soft drinks instead). From 1977 through 1980, while the average number of cups per drinker per day did rise by a smidgen (from 3.51 cups in 1977 to 3.57 cups in 1980), the percentage of coffee drinkers declined from 57.9 percent of the population to 56.6 percent. What happened to the $500 million that General Foods and Procter and Gamble spent trying to sell us coffee?

So much for another popular American myth. Most of us fancy that the Madison Avenue mindwarpers have us over a barrel, and many authors, journalists and social critics have built lucrative careers out of sounding the tocsin and viewing the situation with alarm. Certainly marketing is one of the most conspicuous features of the American landscape. On a typical day the average citizen is exposed to well over a thousand advertisements. We can hardly turn around without having somebody trying to sell us something or other. Marketers will try to sell us *anything*—during 1985 several enterprising fellows even mounted campaigns to sell us Halley's Comet (in the forms of "official" T-shirts, trinkets and memorabilia). As you will soon see, there is even more marketing going on than you probably realize. The big marketing battles are for real, and the corporations take them very, very seriously. (In 1984 Pepsi Cola spent $1 million just *producing* one ad featuring Michael Jackson, on top of which they paid the Jackson brothers a record-shattering fee of $5.5 million.) This year, on the average, more than one thousand dollars will be spent for every man, woman and child in America to get us to buy things.

The truth is that the marketing people are *desperate* to find out what consumers want, and what makes them tick. They spend billions of dollars each year on consumer research. They pour over report after report, peep through one-way mirrors and peer hopefully into computer displays. The consumer seemingly only grows more elusive with each passing year. All the money that marketers spend on advertising and selling has very little direct impact. If an advertising campaign gets one person in a hundred to buy the brand, it is a stunning success. Salespeople beat their chests and scream victory cries if as many as one out of ten of their attempts results in an order.

In the marketplace only persuasive power is allowed to operate. The huge corporations, the giant grocery and department store chains, the Madison Avenue pitchmen and the silken-tongued salespeople, can't *make* anybody do anything. Marketplace persuasion is not a compelling force. The contest is strongly weighted in the consumer's favor.

Despite that easily demonstrated fact, many people dislike, distrust and even fear marketing and advertising. Why?

- People don't like being manipulated, and ads and salespitches try to manipulate us.
- Everybody has been burned at one time or another by some ad or salesperson, and we don't easily forget those little defeats.
- A lot of ads and salespeople strike us as being tasteless, obnoxious, insulting and offensive.
- Many don't like the constant pressure to buy, buy, buy. It is the privilege and glory of being Americans that we get more of that than can be found anywhere else in the world.

Look at your own situation. For most of the things you buy, you make up your own mind. You have your own needs and responsibilities, and you have your own lifestyle, largely habit. Your own tastes and preferences have developed over the years, shaped by your experiences, your family, your friends, your acquaintances and the people you work with. Ads and salespeople can't do much to change your mind if you know what you want. And as a rule you do.

The fact is that consumers are in the driver's seat. It's their money and their decisions. The marketing giants do their best to influence those decisions, but for all their money and resources they have no more power over any person than that person *wants to give them*. For anyone who wants to keep full control over how he or she spends money, *it's easy*.

- Know exactly what you want.
- Know everything necessary for satisfying those wants—all the products, all the brands, differences in quality, where they are available, who has the best prices, the best times to buy, how the people in your life will react to what you buy, how the styles are changing, what your needs in the future will be, etc.

Marketplace Leverage Points

Well, actually, it's not so easy. People don't always know exactly what they want. We can't foretell the future, and we can't always estimate other people's reactions. Who has the time or the energy to find out everything they need to know to shop wisely? No one can cover every possible base, and so we leave a lot of opportunities that the marketers can exploit to gain an advantage. If they are clever enough, they can put any of a number of leverage points to work:

- *Marketplace complexity*, works against the consumer. With so many products and services, and so many places to get them, no one can possibly know very much about anything anymore.
- We are pulled in so many directions at once that we often are *uncertain about what is important to us*. Life is complicated, and it's difficult to know what we really want. A scrumptuous hot fudge sundae, or keep our weight down so we can't pinch an inch? Spend our two weeks vacation in Florida, or use it to repaint the family room? Do what we would enjoy, or do what the kids have been pestering us to do?
- Most people have a *poor sense of value*. Only an expert can accurately judge a thing's worth, and who has the time to be an expert about everything?
- Americans are very *equality-minded*. We feel we ought to be as well-off as the next person.
- We are subject to *social confusion*. With common standards of taste and behavior dissolving all around us, we are uncertain about what is acceptable to, or expected by, other people.
- We are *self-indulgent*. We deserve it, we're worth it, we want it and we're going to have it.
- We want it right now. Our *impatience* is unequalled. We demand quick solutions to our problems. Once we make up our minds, we don't want to wait.
- We have *too little time* to be smart shoppers. Jobs, families, obligations of all kinds soak up the few hours we have each day.
- When we do get some extra time, we don't know what to do with ourselves. We have trouble *structuring our time*.
- Many of us are unhappy with who we are or how we live. We long for ways to *make ourselves better and our lives more interesting*.

This list of leverage points leaves plenty of rewards, penalties and values for marketers to operate with, and you bet they do. Look around. You'll have no trouble finding all ten persuasion tactics at work. The classic marketing tactic is Number 1: Figure out what rewards, penalties and values are important to consumers, then convince them you can deliver. It is the essence of the old marketing motto—"Find a need and fill it."

It works. One of the surest pathways to marketplace success is to have the product that provides the most important benefits, with the fewest penalties, at the lowest price. Let people know about it, get them to try it, and from that point onward the product sells itself. Unfortunately for many marketers, some competitor occupies that position, not them. That's why all the other approaches to persuasion are so prevalent.

Marketplace power relies on pure persuasion. Let's look at the persuasion tools the marketers use. Advertising and selling are the two best known, but they have some other, often more powerful, tricks in their bag as well.

How Advertising Works

On the average, about two cents of every dollar you spend goes to cover the cost of the advertising that tried to get you to buy it. This varies from product to product, of course. Items like automobiles, gasoline and airline tickets don't have a very high percentage of advertising folded into their prices. As a rule, the more a produce relies on "image" to sell it, the more advertising you pay for. Buying expensive cosmetics or perfumes, you can pay more than thirty cents of every dollar for image and advertising—fancies and fantasies, mirrors and blue smoke.

Advertising comes to us mostly through the mass media—newspapers, television, magazines and radio. You may not like to hear this, but the *only* reason those mass media exist is to deliver your heart, mind and pocketbook up to the advertisers. That's why the TV networks worry so much about their ratings—not because they love us, but because the better the ratings (i.e., the bigger the audience), the more they can charge for their advertising time. The same is true for newspapers, magazines and radio.

There are many other ways besides mass media that advertising reaches us—matchbooks, billboards, point-of-sale displays, skywriting, promotional gimmicks like pens and calendars, signs, wrappers, shopping bags, junk mail—the list is endless. In fact, advertisers seem a little desperate these days. They scramble to put their messages before our eyes in every conceivable way. The horde of hucksters clamoring to sponsor sports events so outnumbers the available events, that in recent years a boodle of races, contests and tournaments has been perpetrated to provide more advertising opportunities (you thought all those athletes were competing just for the fun of it?). Supermarkets sell space for ads on shopping carts, on the faces of clocks, on the aisle directories, and mixed in among the Muzak on the public address system. It is as though another article has been added to the Bill of Rights: "Any advertiser has the inalienable right to impose his pitch on as many souls as possible, any way he can."

Advertisers pay good money, and plenty of it, for the opportunity to hawk their wares. They pick up the entire cost of television and radio broadcasting, and most of the cost of magazines and newspapers. Many magazines and newspapers are profitably given away for nothing. The prices of the others often are a fraction of their production costs. The theory is that if you pay for them it shows you are interested in the contents. Therefore you will be more likely to pay attention to the ads, and this increased "audience quality" justifies charging a higher rate for space. As far as the marketers are concerned, the programs, newscasts, stories and articles are there to lure you into position for exposure to the selling messages. Media content carries its own subtle selling messages as well. It is no accident that most of the people you see in the programs on television obviously are big-spending consumers themselves. Just about any article in the food, sports, travel or entertainment section of a newspaper is selling something, one way or another. Any branded item you see in a movie almost certainly paid a lot of money to appear there. Ever since the end of World War I the American mass media have been the vehicle of a vast program to sell our entire society on a consumption-based way of life.

What kinds of effects can advertising have? What can it actually do to people? There are six essential ways that advertising can impact someone's buying decisions.

1. Advertisements bring things to our attention.

"Advertising" stems from a Latin root, *advertere*, "to turn toward." For many years that was the aim of advertising—to get the buyer's attention. It still is the most common, and potentially the most effective, use of advertising. If you have something you want a lot of people to know about quickly, advertising is without a doubt the best way to spread the word. The advertiser controls what the message says, when and where it appears and who is exposed to it.

Are you putting on a play, a concert, or a charity event? Are you opening a new store, or having a Presidents Weekend Sale? Are you coming out with a new product, or with a "new and improved" version of an old one? Have you discovered a new use for The Product? Perhaps it has some benefit that many people haven't realized? You want the public to know about these things, and the more and quicker the better. Maybe they'll pass by and see your sign. Maybe they'll hear about it from a friend. Maybe they'll notice it on the shelf in the store. Most likely they won't, and even if they do, count on it happening later rather than sooner.

If you want to bring information to the attention of the marketplace, advertising is the quickest, surest and most effective way to do it.

2. Advertisements get people to try things.

No advertising campaign can keep people buying a product they don't like. But an ad can persuade them to try it once, at least. The ad can promise new benefits, or arouse their curiosity, or make trying The Product seem like a low-risk proposition. Pepsodent toothpaste was launched as a new product around 1920 with one of the most successful advertising campaigns of all time. What was the magic ingredient of the ads? They featured a coupon offer of a free sample of Pepsodent, sufficient for ten days of normal toothbrushing. Applying the stuff to their own precious pearlies, enough were convinced it was a superior product that consumer demand forced retailers to stock it, and in spite of being priced at a premium to other toothpastes on the market it soon became one of the leading brands worldwide. The copywriter, Claude C. Hopkins, took pains in his autobiography to point out that never once in any of the ads in the campaign were people asked to buy the product.

Ah, you are thinking . . . but what if the product is lousy, and those tricky ad guys dupe us into trying it? You'd never buy the product again, right? And if the rest of the market feels the same way, the product goes down the toilet. That happened to Pringle's potato chips (the ones in the tennisball cans). When they first came out they spurted to sales leadership, while everybody gave this novel approach to potato chips a try. Then most people decided they didn't like them, and sales collapsed. Not many people know it, but Procter and Gamble shot nearly as much money on Pringle's chips as Ford Motor Company blew away on its ill-fated Edsel (although P & G continues to support Pringle's, hoping to breathe some life into it).

Product trial is an objective well-suited to advertising's capabilities. Promise valuable benefits, and make trial a low-risk proposition. If the product is a good one, every advertising dollar comes back manyfold. If not, well, advertising experts claim that the fastest way to kill a bad product is to advertise it heavily.

3. Advertising makes us believe that a product is acceptable to, or even expected by, other people.

A hundred years ago life was simple. People didn't move around much. They stayed in one locality where they got to be very familiar with others that lived there. There weren't very many consumer goods, and few branded products indeed. So knowing other people's tastes and expectations was no great problem. People intimately knew everybody that counted, and they weren't all that different from one another in matters of taste anyhow.

How different things are today. We have to deal with scores, maybe hundreds, of people in our lives, few of whom we know very well. There are thousands of products, multiplied by all the brands and versions of each product. This creates some problems. What if you have to buy a gift for someone? What should you serve to guests who come to your home for dinner, or for a party? In a bar or restaurant with people you want to impress, what should you order? We all want to be in style. We're anxious to fit in, wherever we go. We want others to think well of us, and we certainly don't want to offend.

Everywhere we are surrounded by more or less strangers. And we can't help but suspect that our own tastes are (let's be truthful) rather ordinary. Say that your boss, or your prospective in-laws, are coming to your home for dinner. What kind of drinks do you serve? Not just any beer . . . the *best* beer! Not just any scotch whiskey . . . a scotch that will show your guests how highly you think of them! Now, it is a fact that most people, even knowledgeable people, have a hard time telling the taste of one beer, or one scotch whiskey, from another. So taste is no sure guide in helping to ensure that you serve only the very best.

What to do?

Advertising has the answer you are seeking. Ads have helped millions to avoid the discomfort of social embarassment. They can do the same for you. Look to the television commercials for "super premium beers," brands of beer expressly for special people and special occasions. Look to the elegant full-page ads in "sophisticated" magazines for expensive brands of scotch sipped by suave ladies and gentlemen as they recline on the afterdecks of their yachts, relaxing from an exhilarating sail and contentedly watching the flaming red sun slide below the distant horizon.

Forget the fact that none of your guests can really tell one brand from another by taste, and that it costs little more to manufacture the classy brands than it does the others. Ads tell us, and everyone else, what is upscale and what isn't. Serve something that has been heavily advertised and you can be sure that everyone else has seen the same ads you've seen. If "super premium" beer isn't necessarily better, for just a few pennies more you can at least be assured that it is *safe*.

Are you worried about what kind of running shoes, or sportshirt, or jeans, or bathing suit to buy? Ads to the rescue! Working at their best, advertising campaigns capitalize on Tactic Number 2—take what is highly probable and convince people that it is important. If ads can convince the public that it is important to be seen wearing Calvin Klein jeans, or drinking Heineken beer, or parking a Cadillac in their driveways, anyone (and especially *you*) has a 100 percent probability of achieving those important rewards, through the simple act of buying those particular brands.

Advertising can go a step further and make things seem to be *expected* by other people. Mother's Day and Father's Day have been so effectively promoted by advertisers (mostly greeting card companies) that we now dutifully send gifts and cards out of fear of hurting or disappointing our parents (and lately Grandparent's Day has reared its head). Retailers have ballyhooed Christmas into a frenzied national buying orgy—we have been made to feel positively obligated to give extravagant gifts a-plenty. A few years ago the nation's florists invented National Secretary's Week. The campaign was so successful that I now pity the fool who doesn't do something for his secretary when The Week rolls around. After all, it's obvious that everybody else does. You can see that in the ads.

The diamond engagement ring is a classic case of expectation-building by advertising. Thanks to a superb advertising campaign ("A Diamond is Forever"), coupled with skillfully managed public relations, every American girl now devoutly believes that at the precise moment she receives a proposal of marriage, somebody owes her a diamond. Thanks to monopoly control by the DeBeers Company over the world's supply of diamonds, the belief has been maintained that diamonds are valuable. Prior to 1938, when the campaign was begun, very few diamond engagement rings were given. This strategy would never have succeeded, of course, without the willing collusion of American women.

4. Advertisements make things seem familiar.

Would you rather buy a brand that's familiar to you, or one you've never heard of before? Sure, and I would do the same. Better the devil you know than the devil you don't. Of course, the best way to become familiar with a brand is to use it. But what about products you don't buy very often? What if there is no way to tell whether one brand is really better than another?

Think of cold remedy pills. Most people buy them, if at all, maybe once or twice a year. Every cold is a little different, and each eventually goes away no matter what brand of pill a person takes, or even if the person takes no pills at all. Most cold pills claim only to relieve symptoms . . . but who knows what would have happened to the symptoms if they hadn't used the pills? So, why buy one brand of cold pills instead of another?

That's why you see so many ads for cold remedy pills during "cold season." Because when most consumers finally get to the shelf in the pharmacy with the cold pills on it, chances are that if they don't already have a habitual brand, they'll reach for one whose name seems most familiar (advertisers call this "top-of-mind awareness"). The same principle can push any type of product for which it doesn't really make much difference (except to the manufacturer) which brand you buy— bath soap, detergents, cereals, toothpaste, pain relievers, margarine, potato chips, facial tissue, fast food hamburgers, cola beverages, dog food and the like.

So run the ad over and over. Repeat the brand name endlessly. Put it in a catchy jingle or slogan. Show the package clearly in the ad. *Anything* to make the brand familiar to the person standing at the shelf, puzzling over which of a half-dozen nearly equivalent brands to buy. This approach to advertising uses Tactics 9 and 10: It helps save consumers the trouble of thinking by reducing their uncertainty and/ or complexity.

5. Advertisements connect mental images with brands or products.

When you think of Marlboro cigarettes, you think of _____. But _____ don't grow tobacco. And _____ don't pick tobacco. They don't manufacture cigarettes. There aren't many _____ at all these days, and when there were a lot more of them (about one hundred years ago), there weren't many manufactured cigarettes (which didn't become stylish until the 1920s, and at first were popular primarily in the cities). Some _____ smoke Marlboro cigarettes, I'm sure; but I'm also sure that you've personally never seen one do it.

Why, then, do we all think of *cowboys* when we think of Marlboro cigarettes? Credit a skillful advertising campaign with creating "the Marlboro image" out of absolutely nothing.

Think of Sunkist orange soda, and you picture surfers and beach-bunnies frolicking in the California sun. Chanel and Revlon bring to mind visions of glamorous women, English Leather and Ralph Lauren of suave men. Image-building through advertising doesn't always work, but when it does, it creates a new reward for buying the brand (Tactic Number 4)—it provides a pleasant fantasy to indulge in while using it. Lighting up a Marlboro the fellow fancies himself a bit of a cowboy ("sort of rugged and independent, like"). Dabbing on Cover Girl makeup, the girl feels suddenly possessed of alluring beauty. ("Gee, I wonder if my cheekbones are high enough to get me into modeling?")

It works not only for specific brands, but for whole categories of products. Would people have the same feeling of fun and companionship when they break out the beer, were it not for all those fun-filled beer commercials? The real truth is that most beer is drunk by lonely, downscale men, not those hyperhealthy college frat types, those hearty working men or those jocular ex-jocks. Of course, most smokers aren't exactly Marlboro men either (check out the smoking section of an airplane, or the smoking car of a commuter train).

6. Advertising makes us dissatisfied with who we are and what we have.

Sometimes the whole point of an ad is to make you unhappy. It dangles something desirable before you—a sleek new car, or a shiny new appliance or a fun-filled vacation in the Caribbean. You don't have one, and darn but it looks like it would be a fine thing to have. Well, of course, all you need do is go out and buy one, and then you will be happy again.

The real impact comes from the cumulative impact of all the ads and commercials taken together. Look closely at the people in the television ads. You will notice this:

Except for the problem they have that only The Product can solve, they are *perfect*.

With very few exceptions they are better looking, better groomed, more articulate, more self-confident, richer and have happier marriages and cuter children, than *you* do. They are nothing short of saintly in their relations with everyone else.* They also have vastly more fun in their lives than you do. *Nobody* has as good a time as the folks in the beer and soft drink ads.

To me, this is the most sinister thing anyone can pin on advertising. Who can feel good about him or herself in the face of such an incessant bombardment of perfection and fulfillment? As socially isolated as many of us are, it is easy to get the impression that just about everybody lives the way the people in the ads do. (How can we be sure they don't?) Since we all are equality-minded, the natural reaction is to start thinking that our lives ought to be that way too, and then to get frustrated—because there is no way in the world that is ever going to happen. In real life we can't afford all the things that surround the "beautiful people" in the ads (some of their kitchens look bigger than many people's entire houses). Nor do we have makeup artists or people with airbrushes correcting our every blemish. We don't have experts writing scintillating material for us, arranging every scene we appear in, rehearsing us and retaking each segment until we finally get it perfect. Yet more and more we take our cues about living from television and other mass media that are driven 100 percent by the agenda of persuading us to buy more things.

How effective is advertising in persuading people to do things? That depends on what you mean by "effective." Advertising must overcome some big disadvantages in trying to persuade people. An ad may have to reach millions of individuals, who are at different stages in their thinking about buying The Product, and who have different rewards, penalties and values on their minds. It has to deliver an average, non-offensive, convincing message. It has to get through all the competition for audience attention and reach a public that resolutely does its best to tune advertising out of their lives. All things considered, that one out of a hundred response—1 percent of the

---

* Claude Steiner, in *Scripts People Live* (p. 239), notes the discrepancy between images of women presented in the media and reality. The media use feminine allure to sell products and attract audiences for programs. Men who fall for this portrayal of women may have expectations impossible for real-life women to fulfill, and also can find themselves sadly unprepared for the angry, demanding women whom they inevitably sooner or later encounter in their lives.

audience—isn't so surprising. That's not a very impressive hit-ratio, is it?

It seems more impressive when you realize what 1 percent of American consumption adds up to. If an advertiser can get just 1 *percent* of consumers to switch to his brand from other brands, that means his company will each year have additional sales of about:

- $270 million if they are in the soft drink business.
- $100 million if they are hawking cigarettes or beer.
- $48 milion if their product is coffee.
- $30 million if they are peddling dog food.
- $12 million if hair shampoo is their game.

This means an ad campaign can turn off a lot of people and still pay the freight, as long as it gets its one or two percent. People don't have to *like* the ad, as long as they buy what it's pushing. The "ring around the collar" ads are nobody's favorites, but they do move the goods. On the other hand, "Try it, you'll like it" and "I can't believe I ate the whole thing" were on everyone's lips a few years ago, and the agency that created the campaign was fired because sales didn't improve.

So that clears up a mystery that puzzles many people. We tune out ads. We ignore them. We scurry out of the room to grab a snack or hit the john. We slam the junk mail into the wastebasket. When a slug of commercials interrupt our favorite movie just as it's getting exciting we mutter crude remarks at the TV set. Nearly everybody does, nearly all of the time. Then why is there so much advertising, when the public so steadfastly works at disregarding it? The answer is that, in spite of what we think of it, advertising still manages to create enough extra sales that the advertisers find it well worth the billions they spend on it.

Incidentally, if particular ads you see don't seem to conform very well to what I've said here, consider the possibility that the people who made them didn't know what they were doing (yes, that can happen). It takes a very effective ad to score even one hit in a hundred.

.

Most aren't that successful, and some campaigns are downright disasters.

How Personal Selling Works

When people think about good persuaders, they usually have in mind *salesmen*—fast-talking operators who seduce the unwary into buying encyclopedias, lemon used cars, self-destructing investments and underwater real estate. Most salespeople really aren't like that, but in truth good salespeople are very persuasive. This is because they enjoy some important advantages over advertisements:

- Usually, by the time you talk to a salesperson you have all but made up your mind to buy the item from somebody.
- Salespeople are in a position to shape their pitch to the specific rewards, penalties and values that are on your mind at that moment.
- They also are able to tell by direct feedback which appeals are working and which aren't.
- They have your attention all to themselves, without the competition and distractions that advertising must overcome.
- They can take advantage of your common courtesy and feelings of obligation to other people. You may scream the F-word at TV ads, but you'll nod politely when a salesperson says the same thing. You may change the TV channel in disgust at an ad, but you won't throw a salesperson out of your front room.

How do the good ones do it? First and foremost, they are good listeners, and very knowledgeable about human nature. They are sensitive to other people. They find out what is important to you, what you are looking for. They learn your concerns, your hopes, your fears and your uncertainties. They probe your feelings toward their offerings, and toward the competition. They know their own products (and those of their competitors) absolutely cold. They probably have been trained intensively and thoroughly by their companies. (IBM, the world's premier high-tech marketing company, gives its sales

.

people 15 months of training before it turns them loose.) There are few questions you can ask, or objections you can raise, that they cannot answer in a way that is to their own advantage. What you may think of them, and whether you turn them down, is not going to hurt their feelings, for they have learned not to take it personally. If there is one stumbling block that an aspiring salesperson must overcome, it is learning to deal with the constant rejection that is the salesman's lot (even the best day in and day out have to absorb about seven no's for every yes).

Salespeople are able to use every persuasion tactic, at any step in the Action Decision Sequence. They are very certain, very positive, very easy to listen to. Some develop a tone of voice and a delivery style verging on hypnosis. Contrary to popular stereotype, the best salespeople are not necessarily outgoing, hearty backslappers who stick cigars in everybody's mouth. A few may be like that, if their customers expect it, but most are just earnest, sincere, hardworking people. The customer's schedule is *their* schedule, and they are constantly running to keep their current customers happy while at the same time developing new ones.

Nurturance—the impulse to take care of people—is a valuable trait in a salesperson, and many women (as a rule more naturally inclined than men to be nurturant) are using this to good advantage in sales careers. Although salespeople may not come across as especially brainy (an undiplomatic thing to do: Always try to make the customer feel smart), the successful ones are likely to be at least as intelligent as you are, and certainly know more about the goods, the competition and the situation, than you do. Once you get into dealing with a salesperson, he or she will try to control the process to keep you heading toward closing the deal. The ones to watch out for are those who don't seem to be trying to sell you anything at all. At least you can usually tell what the loudmouthed ones are up to.

Salespeople can be effective at every step of the Action Decision Sequence, and they are in a position to figure out exactly at which one to operate. At *Step 1* (Is there a need for action?), they can show you a careful and thorough analysis proving that you need whatever it is they are trying to sell you—and maybe you really do. Ripoff artists go even further. Out West along the lonely desert highways some service station attendents squirt oil on tourists' shock absorbers, then point it out as evidence of dangerous leakage. One burglar alarm salesman would rob the homes of people who turned him down, then go back and sell them an alarm system now that they were alerted to the need. (He won the company Salesman of the Month Award several times before the police took him away.)

Sales tactics at *Step 2* (Is there any choice?) and *Step 3* (Will habit be good enough?) depend upon whether the prospect is already buying from the salesperson, or from some competitor. A good salesperson will make it as easy as possible for his customers to continue doing business with him, keeping them supplied with order forms and staying alert to needs he can satisfy. Salesclerks learn the tastes and preferences of their clientele so that they can let their best customers know when something comes in that they might like. This also provides a pretext for keeping in touch, so that the customer doesn't forget where he or she has shopped in the past. Car dealers try to handle their customers' financing and insurance, partly because it means extra profit, and also so they can keep track of the situation (when loans are paid off, and when people have accidents, they often are good prospects for another car). But equally important, these extra services help habituate customers to doing business there and make it seem that much more complicated for them to take their business elsewhere. In industrial sales a favorite trick is to get one's own material or component written into the buyer's specifications, leaving the purchasing agent with no choice of where to buy it. On the other hand, a salesperson trying to break into an established habitual or no-choice buying situation will be prepared with myriad reasons for trying something new or different, just to make one small initial sale and "get a foot in the door." Hopefully that first order can be nurtured into bigger and bigger ones, turning into a habit as the buyer becomes used to dealing with the new supplier.

At *Step 4* (Narrowing the possibilities), salespeople can give out loads of information, brochures, samples and spec sheets, as well as cards, gadgets and gimmicks with the company name on them, so that prospects will have them in mind as they winnow the alternatives down to a final few serious contenders. A good salesperson will be nothing but friendly and helpful at this point, providing no reasons to drop him or his offerings from further consideration. A poor salesperson might make the mistake of prematurely putting on the pressure, leaving the prospect with the impression that there must be more congenial places to do business.

Salespeople come into their own at *Step 5* (Making the choice). Trying to portray The Product as the very best choice you could possibly make, the salesperson may use any or all of the following:

- Convincing you that The Product best delivers the rewards you feel are the most important.
- Persuading you that the unique features of The Product are compellingly important to you.
- Showing you how buying The Product will not result in any important penalties, or that the penalties it will result in (e.g., the price) are not important. One ploy is to talk only about the monthly payment, not the total price. Another is to avoid mentioning add-on fees, charges and other "extras" until the last possible moment. Another is to make the price seem small by using some kind of comparison: "It will cost you less than it would cost you to smoke just one pack of cigarettes per day for only one year," is a pitch that can make a $300 set of encyclopedias seem a little less expensive to a hesitant buyer.
- Keeping the selling situation simple:
  - –Focusing on selling you one specific item, rather than presenting you with a large, confusing assortment.
  - –Figuring out who the family decision-maker is, and shaping the pitch to that person (while not ignoring the other, of course).
- Creating doubts and uncertainties about competing products or dealers.

Step 6 (Do you buy it, or don't you) is the make-it-or-break-it for salespeople, and the good ones are ever alert for that magic moment when the prospect (perhaps even unknowingly) makes his choice. They then promptly quit selling The Product and move to close the deal, for they are all too well aware of the danger of talking themselves out of the sale. The tone of the conversation subtly shifts. They begin referring to the prospect as "the owner." Out comes the contract (or

153

"the paperwork"), the E-Z terms, arrangements for delivery, etc. Having sold The Product, the salesperson now works on the purchase situation itself, using tactics like these:

- Appealing to the values of *consistency* or *decisiveness* ("You said you liked all those features, didn't you? And you know that you can't beat the price I'm giving you here. So what is keeping you from buying it?")
- Emphasizing the *penalties of delay* ("Another family was in here looking at this same one earlier, and they seemed pretty serious." Or: "The manager on duty okayed this deal, but he's going on vacation tomorrow, and the regular manager will kill it for sure, because I'm really giving away too much here.")
- Tugging on your *impatience* ("Sign right here, and we'll have it all ready for you to drive it home in less than an hour.")
- Downplaying the *penalties of commitment* ("Trust me, you'll never regret it.")

At this point the prospect may be weary of shopping, and just putting an end to the whole ordeal may in itself be an important reward. One salesman in southern California did very well selling tract houses with this pitch: "I'll bet you've looked at a lot of houses that are pretty much like these?" (Numb nod of agreement.) "And after you leave here you're going to look at more houses pretty much like these?" (Another numb nod of agreement.) "These are nice homes, as you've seen. The location is good, and for what you're getting here, nobody is going to beat our price. Why not just buy one of these, and you'll have it all taken care of." Many house-hunting families found the proposition irresistible.

The salesperson's situation determines his tactics. People who sell big-ticket items (cars, homes, investments) for reputable firms or dealerships, and who work in a specific community, can succeed only if they get a lot of repeat business and good word-of-mouth recommendations from satisfied customers. If they stick a few prominent citizens with lemons, they are finished. Therefore people who sell neighborhood real estate, new cars from dealerships, stocks and bonds to a steady clientele or other expensive things to customers that they have to live with, will tend to go easy on the pressure and instead strive to deliver the goods and create goodwill. Joe Girard, the world's most successful car salesman, mails out about thirteen thousand greeting cards *every month* to his customers, just so they will keep him in mind. That kind of visibility works only because they are happy with the deals he gives them.

At the other extreme, people who sell used cars, or undeveloped boondocks lots, or precious metals investments over the telephone, or home repairs door-to-door, have to make that sale right then and there, take the money and run like a thief. It's a numbers game— talk to as many people as possible, flush out the pigeons and clip them good. In the early days of time-shared vacation condominiums one high-pressure artist made millions of dollars in a matter of months. He had sales gangs out combing the streets, rounding up tourists by the score (one Waikiki "OPC"—"outside public contact" person— jokingly deemed his work "openly pimping customers"). They lured vacationers to the condos with promises of gift Cross Pen sets (actually seventy-nine-cent imitations) or with complimentary TV show tickets (which studios give away so as to fill out their audiences). Brought to the condo site, the marks were turned over to the "hammers," whose job it was to close the sale. Under the pretext of "checking their credit ratings," someone took their credit cards and disappeared for a couple of hours, trapping them there. They then were subjected to a "grind session," a high pressure barrage of exaggerations, lies and outright bullying ("We gave you these gifts in good faith, and we've spent a lot of valuable time with you. How about being a little bit fair with *us?*") This fellow had to flee several states just a step ahead of the federal marshalls, so I wouldn't exactly call him a "success." But he does illustrate the kinds of tactics used in "hit and run" sales situations.

What about salespeople's recommendations? If a prospect knows what he wants to buy, no sane salesperson is going to argue with him. But never forget that people in many walks of life, for example stockbrokers, waiters, bankers, beauticians, consultants, building contractors, lawyers, automobile repairmen and doctors, have to be good at selling if they are going to prosper. Anyone who asks for *any* seller's advice should count on the recommendation being whatever is to the seller's advantage. His management may be offering "push money," netting him a bonus if he sells some specific item. A supplier may be behind a sales contest, a bonus program or a kickback (this is standard operating procedure in the travel business). Some items may bring a higher commission or a bigger profit than others (term insurance is usually the best buy from the consumer's point of view, but insurance agents rarely recommend it because they get a much bigger commission from whole life policies). The clerk may see it as an opportunity to move some item that has been cluttering up the stockroom. It may simply be the option that saves the salesperson some time or inconvenience. Of course there is a chance that the salesperson will see it as an opportunity to demonstrate superior service, and will strive to satisfy the customer's own best interests in the hope that this will help build a loyal clientele. Unfortunately, the odds favor the other possibilities.

Salespeople are a diminishing band, having seen their heyday around the turn of the century (when all the "traveling salesman jokes" originated). Personal selling is an expensive way to move the goods, and Americans have for years exhibited a growing preference for self-service. But whenever close customer contact, and/or ongoing service and support, are necessary, a business will live or die on the strength of its salespeople. Companies such as Xerox and IBM put a lot of effort into training and maintaining their sales forces. But even the best corporate training and management cannot solve all the problems. Not everyone in sales is blessed with the ability to compose the perfect, tailormade pitch to suit each customer. As products and product lines become more complex and faster-changing, the mountains of detail can bury the best of memories and filing systems. Letters, greeting cards and other friendly client contacts can be invaluable, but they do eat up valuable selling time. Time management itself is a problem—being only human, salespeople tend to gravitate toward spending more time than necessary with friendly, established customers, rather than going out among strangers and creating new business.

As with so many other activities, high technology—in the form of microcomputers and custom-designed software—have jumped in to fill these needs. Some programs feed the salesperson instant customer information, or a psychological profile of the purchasing agent to help with designing the pitch, or even produce sales scripts right on the spot. Computers spew out letters, greeting cards and other routine paperwork, and can monitor the status of client needs (for example, noting when a contract is about to expire or when the previous goods delivered are about to run out). Sales managers are tracking the way their people spend their time, enabling them to lean on those who aren't making enough calls on new prospects.

None of this creates any new weapons in the salesperson's arsenal, but only extends the time-proven skills yet a little further. The number of bytes in the central processor, the scope of the information system, and the sophistication of the training program, are not the decisive factors. It all finally comes down to the same timeless persuasion process, and the determination and ability of the individual using it to make that sale. And that requires much, much more than Willy Loman's smile and a shoeshine.

Other Marketplace Power Tools

Human engineering is an exquisite way of getting people to do things, because people aren't even aware of it. The "human engineers" design the situation to capitalize on people's natural inclinations, creating painless no-choice or habitual behavioral pathways for them to follow. It can be done on the Grand Scale—Disney's Epcot facility is superbly engineered to present people with gentle but compelling options which channel the crowd into going with the intended flow. The two Disney Worlds have set the standards for "user-friendly" crowd control.

Human engineering does the job on the modest scale as well. Take the problem of the New York City lunch counter. It has to make all its money in the short space of a few hours during the workday. That means turning over customers as fast as possible, so that the maximum number comes in and buys lunch. But workers aren't in any hurry to get back to the office. They'll linger over coffee, smoke a cigarette, yak with their friends . . . anything to prolong the escape from their jobs. How to move them along as soon as they finish their food— that's the problem. A sign (PLEASE MOVE YOUR BUTT/OTHERS ARE

WAITING) would be ignored. Have a bouncer throw their butt out, and they'd never come back again. Human engineering solved this problem by installing hard, uncomfortable seats. No pleasure to sit on, the seats irritate the customers' butts enough that they tolerate them only as long as it takes to scarf down their soup and sandwich, then are happy to move along voluntarily.

Human engineering is an important factor in designing stores. Not by accident, the typical shopper's necessities are spread from one end to the other of the typical supermarket. That way shoppers are exposed to just about every item in the store as they wander around hunting down the items on their lists. Impulse items like candy, gum and magazines are positioned by the checkout counters so that bored shoppers (and especially their bored children) are tempted to buy them while waiting in line. The lighting, carefully chosen, makes the meat look redder and the vegetables greener. Upbeat music puts the shoppers in a buying mood. Bakeries are located near the front door so that their enticing smells will activate dormant tastebuds. Popular, fast-moving items go on the shelves in the easy-to-notice spots: center sections of the aisles, at eye level. Manufacturers wage a continuous battle for these prized shelf positions, one of the popular tactics being to proliferate as many different brands, versions and sizes as possible so as to command more space in front of the shopper.

Elsewhere in the stores, enormous stacks of goods, and exposed ceiling joists and girders, suggest subliminally that massive buying (and therefore tremendous savings) are going on. Stores trying for a high volume, discount image strive to project a "horn-of-plenty" atmosphere by piling the goods high, using cheap-looking colors (bright yellow is a proven winner) and having cut-price specials strewn through the store. Some designers have their own pet theories. One insists on putting toys in the same aisle as breakfast cereals to ensure exposure to children ("If the kid wants a rubber ball, it makes it that much harder for the mother to say no"). Another believes that putting milk near the front of the store forces shoppers to take a cart, "and if they get a cart, they'll fill it up." Many stores are arranged to commence the shoppers' trek in the high-profit produce section, to have them there before their enthusiasm wanes.

Displays are intended to stimulate more buying. Stores set the goods out where shoppers can see and touch them, making them seem more accessible and attractive (once you have the item in hand, it's that much easier to carry it to the register clerk). Done expertly throughout an entire store or shopping mall, displays create an exciting atmosphere which makes people want to buy things just to be part of it. If you have ever shopped in a Bloomingdale's department store, you know what I'm saying. Interior designers plan gambling casinos on the same principles. The gambling areas come *alive*: glitter, flash, color, noise, *action*! Things Are Happening! The hotel rooms are drab, dull and boring. The point is, they want people to get out there and Bet Big, not sit on the bed watching TV. As a rule, that is what people will do. One casino architect puts it this way: "Your objective is to make people part with their money—a much larger sum of money than they would normally think of doing."

Packaging conveys some of the most subtle and effective persuasive messages in the marketplace. You thought the package was just supposed to keep the stuff contained in one place and protect it from rust, rot and corrosion? Wise up—the whole point is to *sell*. Packages play games with our perceptions. They can make the product look enticing (for instance, those photos on the frozen dinner boxes of some gourmet treat that doesn't look anything like what you find in the box when you open it up at home). Packages change our impressions of the amounts we are buying. Who can forget those stirring words: "Contents may have settled during shipping." Some shapes of containers just look bigger than others that hold exactly the same amount (if in doubt, check the ounces). More subtly, sizes of women's clothing vary from one type of store to another. In the more expensive stores the sizes tend to run a little larger, providing yet another reward for shopping there. ("Well, thank goodness I can still get into a size 8.")

Pricing gives marketers another power tool to use. Having a low price helps, of course—everybody loves a bargain. But the lower the price, the lower the profit margin, so no seller follows that path unless he has to. Besides, people often would *rather* pay a high price. Strange but true. Look at it this way: With all the products, brands, and services on the market, and new ones popping up every day, we can't always be sure of what we are getting. One thing we have learned, because it is by and large accurate, is: You get what you pay for.

Therefore in uncertain situations many people opt for a higher priced item as an assurance of higher quality (if you had to hire a criminal lawyer, or a brain surgeon, would you search out the cheapest one in town?).

Most people can't tell by taste the difference between an expensive brand of liquor and a cheap one, and more than one liquor marketer has found it very profitable indeed to raise the price and change the package a little. They make a much bigger profit per bottle, but even better than that, many have found themselves selling more bottles, presumably to people who fancy themselves "high quality kinds of guys." In some cases higher price translates directly to higher quality. Are $30-per-pound chocolates really six times better than $5-per-pound chocolates? They may be if you are giving a gift and you want to impress the recipient with your generosity.

Another pricing game sellers play is starting high and letting the buyer beat them down. No doubt this originated five thousand years ago in the bazaars of the Middle East; it still makes for a lively negotiating exercise in marketplaces around the world today. It also is one of the time-honored tricks of the car selling trade. Manufacturers and dealers inflate the asking prices to begin with, and savvy sales-people know enough to fight the customer all the way down to the predetermined selling price of the car. As one of them put it, "Anyone can give a car away; but you want the customer to think he has won a battle." So a lot of play-acting goes on, leading to an important (if illusory) reward for the buyer—"It took some doing, but, by jing, I was sharp enough to get that salesman down four hundred bucks." Going the other way, some sellers give what seems to be a good deal but then have a number of little add-ons magically appear on the bill after the price has been settled—a few bucks here, a few there, for "handling," "supplies," "preparation," "servicing," whatever. The theory, accurate often enough, is that the average person won't quibble over a few bucks at that point. Hotels sometimes tack on "telephone fees," which most people will routinely pay without question even if they never once touched the telephone in their room.

Well, how much *are* things supposed to cost? Supposedly prices are determined by the market. But if the market isn't cooperating, marketers have their little ploys. A major art world scandal broke in

1985. It seems that fine art had not been moving very well back in 1981. Fearful that prices might drop were that known, the eminent art auction house, Christie's, falsely reported that several paintings (including a Gaugin and a Van Gogh) had sold in the $1 to $2 million range. Apparently it worked, although when it finally came to light the director at the time was forced to resign, and the auctioneer responsible lost his New York auctioneer's license.

Hidden selling messages are more common than most people realize. "Subliminal advertising," which received a brief spate of publicity in the 1950s and has disturbed Americans ever since, has never been proved to work. But other ways of hiding messages, even in plain sight, can be very effective. If you see a branded product being used in a movie or a television program, count on it that the manufacturer paid dearly to have it appear there. (One noteworthy exception to this involved Reese's Pieces, which were used to lure "E.T." out of its hiding place. Initially turned down for a promo deal by M&M/Mars, the movie's producers offered to use Reese's Pieces for *free*. The film's runaway success resulted in a smashing marketing coup for Hershey Foods Corp.) Many children's television programs are based entirely on marketed products. Star athletes, even entire sports teams, are given free equipment so that sports fans will see them using it. Various lobbies and pressure groups feed story lines and plot ideas to television producers, thus getting their own propaganda enfolded into prominent soap operas or prime-time dramas.

Then there are the million and one *reminders* all around us. Walking through the glass door of the drugstore, you notice that the "PUSH" and "PULL" signs are sponsored by a cigarette company. You go to the grocery and there you see little ads on the shopping carts, on the shopping bags, taped to the windows out front, hanging in the air above the aisles and even on the bar that you put between your stuff and the next person's on the checkout belt. Pulling up to the booth on the toll road, you notice that the ticket machine has been festooned with little brand-logo stickers by passing salespeople. Everywhere you look you are pelted by ads—on signs, billboards, cars, trucks, license plate holders, bus stops, streetcars, menus, even on the clothing that people wear. It finally gets to you. Desperate, you take refuge in your neighborhood bar, hoping to find a quiet, salespitch-free sanctuary;

but to your horror you realize that the place is a kaleidoscope of neon signs and animated beer displays. You close your eyes to shut it all out, ease back to relax and listen to the music—and you notice that the band is playing "Wastin' Away in Margaritaville," followed by "Just Another Tequilla Sunrise," followed by "Scotch and Soda, Jigger of Gin," Oh, didn't you know? Groups that play in bars are supposed to do what they can to keep the booze flowing freely.

Customer Power

So far this discussion has been very one-sided: What do the marketers do to the consumer? Let's turn it around. What do *consumers* do to the *marketers*?

Consumers have all the power, if they only realize it and have the nerve to use it. They decide what, where, when, and from whom to buy. The only leverage the marketers have is their ability to persuade, to engineer the consumers' decisions by using the tactics I've described here. They have no weapons to use against any consumer who knows what he wants and knows how to get it. In that case all they can do is offer him what he wants, at the best price, in a convenient location, from a friendly and helpful salesperson.

In America the consumer is king. So act like royalty. If they give you guff, take your business elsewhere. If they try any fast ones, there are plenty of laws to protect your interests, and many corporations have hotlines or customer relations offices that will listen to your complaints. Of course it's not always that simple. Sometimes exactly what you want isn't available. Sometimes it's available, but at too high a price, or at a place miles out of your way, or from someone you'd rather not do business with. Then you're going to have to make some tradeoffs. Fair enough, as long as you know what you are doing and have the situation under control. Remember, as long as you can walk away from the deal, you are the boss, not them.

It's possible to go further than that, if you want to. Companies and salespeople are trying to do business, after all. There's no such thing as a "fixed price," and a little shrewd bargaining may get you a discount or some kind of extras. They want to sell their goods. Find out how badly they want to make that sale. One fellow I know claims to buy his new cars by breezing right past the salespeople on the showroom floor and going straight to the boss's office. He tells the boss: "I didn't talk to any salesman, so I'm not going to pay any commission. I want such-and-such a car, and I'll pay you X dollars for it. I have the cash in my pocket. Do you want to sell it to me for that much, or not?" Sometimes it works, and if it doesn't, what has he lost? But you have to know what you're doing, and you have to have the stomach for it. Most people don't—the typical American doesn't like hard bargaining, but rather prefers fixed prices and self-service (the guy that does this is a Bulgarian refugee).

Going even further, consumers can be downright scoundrels, cheats, crooks and liars. Some people make careers out of stiffing department stores. Party dresses and shoes "bought" on Friday before the prom are returned on Monday. Products wrecked by misuse are brought back for refunds. Grocery shoppers change their minds and leave items they decide not to buy—including ice cream and fresh meat—wherever in the store they happen to be. They knock over displays of cans or cereal boxes, roll apples and tomatoes all over the floor, or watch their kids play bombardier with jars of pickle relish, then walk away from their mess. Some make a hobby of picking on clerks, waitresses, airline flight attendants or other service personnel, who are forced to stand there and take it with a smile on their faces, victims of the bullying customer. Some industrial and government purchasing agents routinely extort wining and dining, kickbacks or temporary female companionship out of their suppliers.

And businesses put up with it. "The customer is always right," they say, fearful of offending people, causing a scene or driving away trade. This kind of thing seems to be on the increase, and the marketers have brought much of it on themselves. All the Buy, Buy, Buy pressure does get tiresome. The over-built expectations fostered by all the commercials can't but create frustrations. Many consumers with disappointed hopes see nothing wrong with striking back or "getting even."

Petty retaliation is an important factor in the impulse toward shoplifting, which in America now totals annually into multibillions of dollars. Many shoplifters pick on stores and merchants which they feel failed to live up to their end of the bargain—they in one way or another didn't deliver the satisfaction the vengeful customer felt he had been promised. That being the case, all bets are off. Values such as honesty and fairness go out the window when you're dealing with a cheater. Among many Americans there seems to be a pervasive sentiment that business in general is screwing them, making just about any store or business fair game for "revenge" of one kind or another.

I'm not advocating that anyone do any of this. Jerking the marketers around may be an amusing recreation for Control People. It may provide an outlet for Victims who want to vent their frustrations. That's their problem. It is certainly a waste of time for Power People. If dissatisfied they will try to get the merchant to straighten the matter out—more often than not problems in the marketplace result from honest mistakes. They may quit doing business there. They realize that the nastiest thing they can do is not give the real reason for their dissatisfaction. That way the marketer keeps right on doing to other customers what irritated them, causing himself the most damage in the long run.

The vast majority of people in marketing, advertising and sales are honest and hardworking, doing their best within the rules of the game to offer products and services that meet people's needs. The problem is not that marketplace persuaders lie to consumers. Most of them tell the truth, most of the time. The problem in the marketplace is that too many tell the truth without being accurate. The version of the truth the consumer hears is carefully selected and edited, giving only the portion that serves the marketer's own agendas. They leave to the consumer the task of digging out the rest of the truth, which one must have to make effective buying decisions. In the marketplace especially, knowledge is power.

One closing thought on power in the marketplace:

> Wouldn't life be swell if everybody were as nice
> as the fellow who is trying to skin you.

7

POWER IN ORGANIZATIONS

Tremulous Times at HugeCo, Inc.

To an outsider the company seems calm enough. Snow-white cumulus clouds coursing above the industrial park reflect gloriously off the mirror facade of the ten story headquarters building. Out front regal swans glide to and fro across the glassy surface of a wide blue pool centered in a verdant golf course of a lawn. As we enter the foyer, crisp highlights dance off the chrome appointments to titillate our eyes, and the sea of impeccable burgundy carpeting yields to our feet with a satisfying springiness. The rubber tree and the bank of African violets broadcast a healthy, deep green glow, in counterpoint to the tastefully striking acrylic painting behind them. Rosewood paneling backdropping the receptionist's workstation exudes a luxurious, muted gleam. Neatly fanned out on the big round oak table in the visitors' waiting area, four copies of the monthly employee magazine proclaim good news, progress and warm family feeling.

The portrait of corporate contentment. Don't be fooled.

Beyond the portals to the main hallway and the elevator banks, HugeCo is a bubbling, boiling, frothy cauldron of trouble. The stock-

·

165

holders (that is, managers of the pension and mutual funds that own the bulk of the company's shares) are up in arms. Sales have stagnated. Profits are down. The last time the Board voted a dividend increase was eight quarters ago. The competition is surging ahead. The stock price is in a tailspin.

Around the table in the Board Room, implicit fingers point at marketing. Why are they sitting on their duffs? The new product GreatBigCo introduced last July is selling like gangbusters. Last month GiantCo announced they'd bought out BrightCo, thereby adding some of the hottest items on the market to their own already formidable line.

B. F. ("Bigelow") Deal, vice-president of marketing, is clearly the man on the hot seat. Though no one in the room would state it so bluntly, nevertheless one weighty question silently reverberates through the tense room: "How do you intend to correct this situation, B.F.?"

At the center of the storm, B. F. Deal looks calm, concerned and thoughtful. He's been working on it. Three months ago the results of the big marketing survey came in, and consumer opinion about HugeCo's product line rang out loud and clear: BOR–ING! So Mr. Deal has stepped up the pressure on his director of product development, Hardy Charger. The guy hasn't been doing the job. He's proposed a few ideas so off-the-wall that the Review Committee had to shoot them down, but mostly it's been the same old stuff. Change the color. Change the shape. Change the size. Put it in a twin-pack. Nothing that's going to take the market by storm. Nothing that's going to jerk the consumer up by the lapels and shout "buy me!" in his face. What does it take, Mr. Deal wonders, to light a fire under that man?

Meanwhile, Hardy Charger, the director of product development, is down in his office entertaining the distinct possibility that invisible aliens from outer space have swaddled him up in a mile of Ace bandage and are slowly tightening a large vise around his head. His boss, Mr. Deal, is on his case to get some new product ideas going. Lord knows he's been spending his days, evenings and weekends trying to do just that. But he can't get anything through the Review Committee. They'll pass the plain vanilla, safe bets every time. But those won't make a dent in the competition, and every time he floats something out with a chance of shaking things up, they give it thumbs down. And he can't get the support he needs from his people. It's like doing the breast stroke through cold molasses. Just the other day he gave a crash report to his secretary, Rosemary, in the middle of the afternoon, and it wasn't until nearly lunchtime the next day that she had it typed. What does it take, Hardy wonders, to light a fire under that woman?

What Organizations Are

We'll get back to B. F. Deal, Hardy Charger and Rosemary in a moment. They have some big problems to solve, but we can't help them until we understand their situation better. Common to all three is that they work in a big organization. Organizations are power structures. Their problems are power problems.

Looking at the organization chart in figure 3, HugeCo seems neat and tidy. Each little box stands for a particular job, and that brings up an important point—the boxes represent *jobs*, not people. Were we to go down to the personnel office and dig out the policy manuals, we would find that each job is defined by a job description—the duties, responsibilities, etc. The lines between the boxes indicate which jobs report to which other jobs, or in other words, which tells which others what to do. The boxes, the reporting lines and the job descriptions portray the organizational structure. HugeCo's was designed by a team of executives and management consultants who learned when they got their MBA degrees that executives and managers make the decisions. Top managers and executives decide on corporate policy and strategy and allocate resources. Using those resources, middle managers make operational decisions about the details of implementing those policies and strategies. Corporate staff departments provide information, advice and support to help the decision-makers. One staff department at HugeCo even uses mathematical models and computer simulations to help management optimize its decisions ("optimize" being another thing they teach in MBA school—"get the biggest bang for your buck").

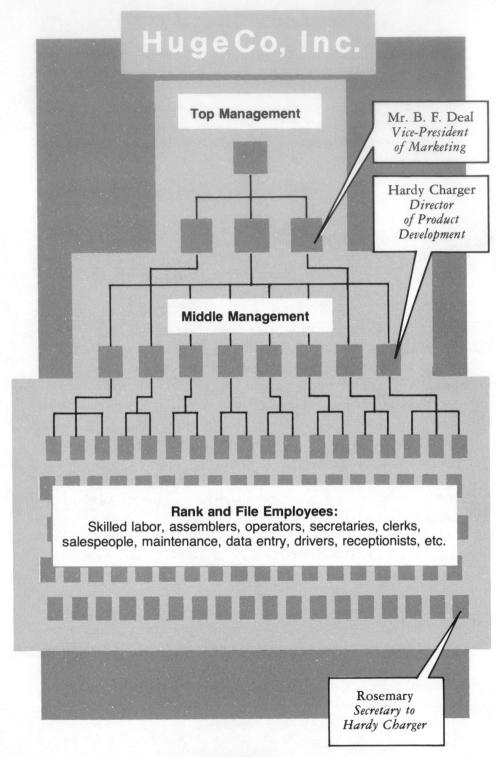

Figure 3
ORGANIZATION CHART FOR HUGECO, INC.

According to the business school professors, business is a "rational enterprise." A company tries to make the most profit possible in a competitive marketplace. Top management monitors the market, the competition and the business environment, making well-informed policy decisions as the need arises. They communicate those decisions down the "chain of command" to the people who report to them. Those people do their jobs and make other decisions that they communicate to the people who report to *them*. Who do their jobs, make some more decisions, and communicate *their* decisions . . . all the way down the line to the people who actually do the work: make the parts, assemble the product, put it in boxes, load the trucks, sell the goods, type the invoices, open the mail, count the money, send it to the bank. They do their jobs, and the company prospers.

You know better than that.

Anyone who has worked in any organization for more than one week knows better than that. Crazy, stupid, unbelievable things go on in organizations. Some top level decisions not only are not "optimized," but make no sense at all. Orders and instructions communicated to underlings are often misunderstood, botched, ignored or even sabotaged. Earnest, hardworking employees sometimes get the shaft, while cheats and malingerers prosper. Some people do everything at work except work—sleep, talk to their friends on the phone, romance each other, daydream, do their night school homework.

- One 1984 study estimated that time wasted at work costs American business $150 billion a year, mostly through employees habitually getting to work late or leaving early, making personal telephone calls, reading and socializing. The report cited one Texas company where employees made more than ten thousand long distance calls a month to listen to erotic recorded messages.
- Another study, done in 1980, estimated that the federal government *deliberately* wastes $2 billion every year because of the way its budgeting procedures operate (the amount similarly wasted by state and local governments was not mentioned).
- Also in 1980 a major scandal broke concerning the General Services Administration, which works as the federal government's business

manager. Employees were discovered to be accepting bribes from contractors, conspiring with them to defraud the government, and stealing and then reselling millions of dollars' worth of supplies. One GSA supervisor had managed to acquire eleven racehorses and twenty-five bank accounts (total balance of $294,000) on a $33,000 yearly salary.

■ The *Wall Street Journal* in 1985 estimated that office football pools accounted for $1-$2 billion of bets *on the Super Bowl Game alone.*

■ Business fraud and employee theft annually run into the multibillions of dollars, with several embezzlements in recent years of more than $200 million.

■ In the late 1970s drugs and alcohol on the job emerged as a serious workplace problem. Drunken operators caused several major train wrecks, and cocaine became prevalent among numerous occupational groups, including the entertainment industry, professional athletes and Wall Street traders and money managers. In 1985 it was estimated that more than one third of the workers assembling American automobiles were high on drugs or drunk on the job, and that illicit drug use by workers was costing the construction industry billions of dollars.

What is going on? Why does organization theory as taught in the textbooks and business schools so often seem contrary to reality?

The problem is that organizations are structures of human behavior designed to accomplish organizational goals. In fact, most organizations do a fairly good job of that. All of civilization depends on organizational structuring, and the more complex the civilization, the more structuring necessary.

But anyone who tries to structure other people's behavior quickly discovers that people are very slippery characters. No matter how neat the organization chart, no matter how expertly designed the job descriptions, and no matter how optimized the reporting network, there can be a lot of space between what the people in the organization on paper are *supposed* to do, and what they *actually* do at their workstations.

Let's go back to our first and most basic assumption: *Everybody is continually making decisions to do, or not do, things.* They make these decisions at work as well as elsewhere. Those strange, non-businesslike things that people do on the job . . . well, after all, they do decide to do them. They go through the Action Decision Sequence; and at each step they pick the choice with the greatest relative attractiveness—the best balance of rewards, penalties and values.

Trace out the key decision choices in table 5 on page 172. It is quite different from how the sequence would go were you in a store deciding whether or not to buy something. You don't usually *have to* buy things, but in any organization you are going to come up against a lot of "have to's." For instance, at work you have to do your job.

Look closely also at the workplace motivators in table 6. Yes, we work for money (reward). We should do our duty (value). Otherwise we might get fired (penalty). But so many other rewards, penalties and values influence our decisions on the job, including many not listed that have nothing at all to do with the job but come in from other areas of our lives.

One key to understanding power in organizations lies in realizing that individual, genuine *people* occupy those boxes in the organization chart. Job descriptions and reporting networks tell us how an organization of robots, managed by rational computerized decision models, would behave. What *people actually do* goes right back to the Action Decision Sequence, the Choice Evaluation Array and the ten persuasion tactics.

Also, recognize the importance of understanding the person's situation at the time the action decision is made. More often than not in organizations, if you understand the situation, you have a pretty good idea of what any reasonable person would do.

Not everyone is reasonable, you say? How right you are. We'll take that up presently. First, let's see how reasonable people operate on the job. Like the Horatio Alger heroes, we will start at the bottom of the organization and work our way to the top.

Power at the Bottom

Rosemary has been a-tingle all day, looking forward to quitting time. Because tonight is her first date with that handsome hunk of an engineer she met last week. She worked especially hard to get

.

Table 5
Key Choices in Organizational Action Decisions

Step 1: Is There a Need to Take Action?
Do I *have* to do something?
—Is it in my job description?
—Did someone in authority tell me to?
—Do I owe it to someone?
Should I do something?
—Would it somehow benefit me, my boss, my group or the company?
What will happen if I *don't* do anything?
—Will it be to my advantage?
—Will it get me into trouble?
—Will anybody notice?

Step 2: Is There a Choice of Action?
Is there a specific action I *have to* take in this situation (because of my job description, company policy, instructions from the boss, etc)?
What will happen if I do something else?

Step 3: Will a Habitual Course of Action be Good Enough?
Will I be best off to do what I usually do in this situation?
Should I do what everybody here usually does?
Is it worthwhile to consider doing something different?

Steps 4 and 5: Weighing the Alternatives and Choosing an Action
For each option considered—
—Am I able to do this (do I have the ability and the resources)?
—What do I have to gain (rewards)?
—What do I have to lose (penalties)?
—What says it's the right thing to do (positive values)?
—What says it's the wrong thing to do (negative values)?

Step 6: Decision to Take the Chosen Course of Action
Do I *have to* do this?
Is it to my advantage to do it?
Would I be better off delaying or declining to act?

Table 6
Workplace Motivators

	Rewards	Penalties
Material	Money Benefits Vacation Pleasant environment	Loss of job Loss of compensation

Social	Status or prestige
	Participation in
	    activity
	Social interaction
	Meeting new people
	Approval of others
		Ostracism
		Disapproval
		
		Having to spend time with
		    people you don't like
		Rejection

Personal	Self-esteem
	Power
	Fulfillment
	Enjoyment
	
	Advancement
	Achievement
	Worthwhile
	    accomplishment
	Control
	Getting even
	Getting away with
	    something
		Embarrassment
		Humiliation
		Getting in trouble
		Giving too much
		    effort
		Failure
		Inconvenience
		Loss of power
		
		Boredom
		Injury or disability
		Lack of advancement

Positive Values: You should:	*Negative Values:* You should not:
Do your duty Do what the boss says Make something of yourself Support your family Be honest Be fair Be competent or skillful Be loyal Be important Be well-mannered	Sell your soul Waste your time Disturb other workers Be taken advantage of Be dishonest Be lazy Shirk your duty Go against your group Go against your friends Let people push you around

everything taken care of by 5:00, which will leave her just enough time to freshen up and get to the restaurant where they have arranged to rendezvous.

Then, at precisely 4:46, her boss, Hardy Charger, drops a stack of paper on top of her typewriter, mumbles, "Here's some letters and a last minute report," and bustles out the door. Thumbing through it, Rosemary estimates two hours' worth of typing, minimum. Decision time! Rosemary is about to traverse the Action Decision Sequence in table 5.

Step 1: *Is there a need for action?*
Rosemary could settle the whole issue right here by deciding that the typing can wait until tomorrow. She has to decide *something* about it, that's for sure.

Step 2: *Does she have any choice?*
Does her job description require this sort of last-minute overtime, or must secretarial overtime be previously scheduled? If her job includes "uncompensated overtime work when necessary," then strictly speaking she has no choice. But if the job description doesn't clearly spell this situation out, Rosemary might conclude that she does indeed have a choice here. Deciding she has no choice but to stay and do the typing is a very unattractive alternative right now. (However, note that "no choice" might look a lot better if her date tonight were with some nerd her cousin fixed her up with.)

Step 3: *Will her habitual course of action be good enough?*
What does she customarily do when Mr. Charger dumps last-minute work on her? If she usually stays and does it, then if she doesn't do it tonight, she at least better have a good story for him in the morning, because he'll be expecting to see it done when he comes in.

Steps 4 *and* **5:** *Choosing a course of action.*
Rosemary may have been in this situation before, and therefore she may know several possible ways to handle it. Or she may be

frantically running one idea after another through her mind, searching for the way to get out of the office on time that will cause her the least amount of trouble. Finally she decides that the typing can wait until the morning. After all, he didn't *say* it had to be done right then, did he?

Step 6: *Decision to do it.*
At precisely 5:00 Rosemary rises from her chair, sticks her tongue out at the stack of papers, and heads for the powder room to put on her evening face.

So much for Hardy Charger's crash report. Well, to him 4:46 may seem like the middle of the afternoon. But he knew what was going on, and he even felt a little guilty about it. He could have given her that report hours earlier, but with all the recent distractions it had slipped his mind. He finally noticed it hiding under his copy of the *Wall Street Journal* when he picked it up to stuff it into his briefcase on his way out the door. That's why he pulled a "dump and run," rather than working it out with Rosemary. He was hoping to get the report typed by morning without the embarrassment of explaining to her why it came so late in the day.

It happens in organizations every day. A janitor is told to clean up some mess outside his normal work area. A supervisor presses his assembly workers to speed up the line way beyond the standard rate. A truck driver, looking over the dispatcher's schedule, calculates there's no way he can meet it without long hours at twenty miles over the speed limit. A desk-jockey lieutenant orders one of his sergeants to take his men on a mission which the sergeant knows is highly dangerous and completely pointless. What power principles apply?

Structure power A person has a job, reporting to some other job. If the job that gives the orders tells the other job to do something, as long as the order is in the bounds of both job descriptions, it is a no-choice decision. If a person's job description stipulates certain actions to be taken when certain situations arise, those are no-choice decisions too. Organizations essentially are structures of no-choice decisions. These no-choices may be formally spelled out in constitutions, policy manuals, or codes of rules or laws, but even if unwritten or informal they are nonetheless binding. You do this. You do not do that. This is true of corporations, small businesses, governments, clubs and associations, and also of families, nations and cultures. Fortunately for Rosemary, Hardy Charger didn't have a no-choice working in favor of getting his report typed after hours.

Agreement power   Joining any organization, we make an agreement to abide by its rules and to support its values. This may be formalized by a contract, an oath of office or signing a dotted line on the employment application. Just by *being* in an organization we implicitly agree to go along with it. In centuries past people didn't choose to be born under particular royal houses, but nevertheless felt they should be loyal to the king. In any society or culture, the point of raising children to be "good citizens" is that they grow up with a sense of commitment to their country and/or their cultural group. An organization needs committed, loyal members in order to function and endure, and that means securing and maintaining agreements from all members to support its policies, objectives and actions. Similarly, when someone goes to work for a particular boss, he is agreeing to do, within reason, what the boss says.

While these agreements may commence at a definite point in time, they are not fully formed right away, and are ever changing. It takes time for people to find out what they can expect from one another, and from an organization. *Fairness* is the key to keeping these agreements (or "commitment," if you will) alive and healthy. If the boss, the company or the government stabs us in the back, we change our notions of what *we* owe *them*, and the result can range from bare minimum compliance to mutiny, sabotage, treason or revolution. On the other hand, if some person, or some organization, goes that extra mile for us, we may feel we owe them more than the minimum spelled out in the job description.

If a member fails to live up to *his* side of the agreement the organization will usually try to bring him around, but may ultimately have to show him the door in the interest of the integrity of the group as a whole. This may be done through such devices as a pink slip, a divorce, ostracism or "shunning," or at the extreme a firing squad or an all-expenses trip to Siberia.

Hardy Charger blew it on this one, because he has never put much effort into building a good working relationship with Rosemary. He didn't hire her in the first place, you see. When he got promoted to a position that came with a secretary, there she was. Hardy's sights are trained up the corporate ladder, not down; and he figures that as long as she gets the work done, why pay a lot of attention to her? For her part, Rosemary likes to work with people on a friendly basis. Mr. Charger's attitude doesn't really upset her, but it sure doesn't motivate her to go out of her way for him, either. Like, for instance, breaking her date to type his stupid report.

Persuasive power   Human behavior, as infinitely complex as it is, is impossible to structure completely. No matter how meticulously we draw the job descriptions, define relationships among all the positions and scope out company policy and procedures, situations inevitably will arise that are not clearly governed by either structure or agreement power. Every individual brings his or her own perceptions, experiences and arrays of rewards, penalties and values to bear on the situations in which they find themselves. Many situations fall outside the range of structure power and agreement power, and when that happens people must apply persuasion (which includes, of course, bribes, threats and intimidation) to get the desired results. Persuasion may be necessary to get more productivity out of people, as well as to keep them from doing non-work kinds of things on the job. In deteriorated, low-morale organizations persuasion may be the only way to get people to move at all. Threat of punishment is about the least effective way to motivate an organization, but sometimes is unavoidable. The Soviet Union would no doubt prefer its citizens to extend their best efforts out of heartfelt duty to the motherland and the Communist Party, but alas finds it still necessary to keep wayward souls in line with secret police and sojourns in slave labor camps or mental hospitals, at the same time guarding its borders so that the entire workforce doesn't jump ship. Nor does bribery build the kind of commitment on which organizations thrive. Anyone who can be bribed into joining one outfit will likely leave it for the first better offer that comes along.

Hardy Charger could possibly have persuaded Rosemary to do the report, had he appealed to her sense of loyalty, offered her an extra day off or threatened to fire her. It's just as well that he was too embarrassed to try it. It only would have made things worse in the long run.

Performance power   As a rule, people want to do a good job. In organizations as elsewhere, performance finally comes down to being able to make effective action decisions. Part of that lies in experience, knowledge and good judgment. When a situation arises, the top performer knows what actions will best achieve the proper objectives. In an organization good performance takes more than simply one's own abilities and judgment. Resources (money, equipment, other people) may also be necessary, because the whole idea of an organization is to accomplish objectives that individuals cannot accomplish without it. Hence the jockeying around in organizations over budgets, personnel, and equipment. The better the resources available, the more effectively and efficiently people can perform.

Ultimately, power in the workplace comes down to performance power—the individual's ability, in the context of a network of structure, agreement and persuasive power, to make action decisions that achieve the organization's primary objectives, as well as his or her own *personal* objectives.

That's part of Hardy's problem with Rosemary. She's no shirker—she wants to do a good job as a secretary. But she really is much more interested in getting married. Her decision-making at HugeCo is aimed at achieving those objectives, in that order. Let's look at the rewards, penalties and values on Rosemary's mind while she sorted out what to do about the last-minute pile of typing:

- Should she stay and do it?
  —Rewards:
      none (that jerk won't even thank me)
  —Penalties:
      inconvenience

late for date (or might even have to break it)

loss of new boyfriend

—Values:

should do your duty (is this really my duty?)

should be treated fairly (which this isn't)

shouldn't be taken advantage of (which this is)

- Should she leave them until tomorrow morning?

—Rewards:

on time for date

get away with something (he thought I'd just stay and do his dumb letters, did he?)

—Penalties:

disapproval of boss (who cares?)

—Values:

should live up to agreements (I made that date *days* ago!)

should be treated fairly

shouldn't let people walk on you

No wonder she left the typing—nothing in it for her if she does it, and no trouble she can't handle if she doesn't. Plus it *just wasn't fair*—she gets no extra pay for spur-of-the-moment overtime, and Mr. Charger didn't even give her a chance to rearrange her plans. He doesn't deserve it. If he says anything about it, she can innocently reply that she hadn't realized he wanted them done right then. After all, he didn't *say* so, did he?

The point is that like everything else we do, what people do on the job results from action decisions they make arising from the immediate situation. Here is the situation of rank-and-file people in most organizations, businesses and government offices alike:

- They feel they should put in a fair day's work (as *they* perceive it—problems can arise when workers and bosses don't have the same perceptions of "fairness").
- They see little reward for doing much more than that because:
  —They aren't strongly interested in being promoted to supervision or management. That would only get them a lot more hassle and not much more money.

—The work itself is generally pretty uninspiring.

—Unless they are on piece rate or an incentive plan, it won't put any more money in their pay envelope.

■ They see few penalties for doing no more than "a fair day's work," or for asserting their rights occasionally, because:

—That job is not all that important to them (Rosemary could easily find another job—good secretaries are scarce).

—It may be impossible to fire them, especially if they are in a union or protected by civil service.

—They have no particular relationship with their boss, so his or her disapproval makes no special difference to them.

—Pay rates are standardized and based on seniority or job classification, not individual merit or performance.

Not everyone at the bottom of the chart is this secure, of course. For many, keeping that paycheck coming in is all-important, and jobs as good as theirs are hard to find. That gives their bosses some leverage over them. And many rank-and-file employees are motivated, hardworking people, simply because they were raised to feel that they owe it to their employer. But workers (at all levels) may take full advantage of a secure spot. A few years ago certain categories of federal government employees became virtually immune to any sort of punishment or threat, no matter what they did on the job. Enough seized the opportunity to malinger and cause trouble that eventually some agencies in Washington took to assigning them to "turkey farms"—sections that isolated them and kept them at least from disrupting other employees who were trying to get their own work done.

How, then, can Hardy Charger "light a fire under Rosemary"? He could get bursts of extra effort (like staying late to type his report) out of her by using threats or bribes, or by appealing to her sense of obligation or duty. But managing people by lighting fires under them goes only so far. Do it too often and they become burned out, demoralized by the disappointments and resentments that usually follow each such conflagration.

Hardy would be far better off trying to build a good working relationship, based on treating Rosemary as a *person* rather than as a job. The pay, the benefits, the vacation and sick days, and even the red rose for National Secretary's Week, are for the *job*, not for the person. He needn't go prying into her personal life, or fawn all over her with flattery, empty praise and phony fellowship. First and foremost, he should treat her *fairly*, recognizing her legitimate needs and rights both on and off the job. Dumping work on her desk that his own ineptitude delayed until the last minute wasn't fair, for example.

Beyond that, he should try to provide her with the non-material rewards that truly motivate people to put out their best efforts: respect, self-esteem, a feeling of accomplishment and a sense of participating in an important activity. He should do his best to help her do her job. Not that he should pitch in with the typing. Rather, one of his top priorities should be to ensure that his staff has the best equipment and supplies possible, and that they are all able to plan, schedule and control their own work to the greatest extent possible. This will keep distractions and frustrations at a minimum, and morale and effectiveness at a maximum. Especially, he should always make sure Rosemary (and everyone else who works for him) understands exactly what he expects. Few things are more frustrating than wasting valuable hours botching an assignment because the boss's instructions were unclear.

Finally, he should try to give her a sense of working *with* him, not for him. He should keep her informed as to what the whole group is working at, what it means, and how it fits into the bigger picture at HugeCo. It's a matter of helping her appreciate how her work contributes to an important activity. He should share the group's victories with her, not just its problems.

So, Hardy, knock off the dump-and-run, and stop leaving the stacks of work with the urgent note for Rosemary to find in the morning, and drop all the other gutless little manipulations you use to avoid having to deal with her. You ought to know you can't win that way (it sure isn't working *now*, is it?). Treat Rosemary like a human being, and you'll be amazed what she will do for you. Keep in mind that, the more successful you make the people who work for you, the more successful *you* will be.

■

181

Leadership

What we are talking about here is *leadership*, that elusive ability to get people to follow. A leader can take followers only where *they* want to go. People follow because they decide to, and material rewards rarely are sufficient to do the trick. The greatest leaders have not been business people, but religious or military leaders. The former offered nothing tangible, and following the latter could get you killed. What did they offer, then? History's great leaders enabled their followers to fulfill their most important values, and provided them with important personal and social rewards. Foremost is the sense of accomplishing some worthwhile purpose, coupled with the belief that following the leader will make the venture succeed. Above all, the leader should enfuse his followers with a sense of hope.

Effective leaders operate through agreement power and persuasive power, *not* structure power. T. E. Lawrence, a young officer in the British army, led an Arab uprising against the Turks during World War I, a most remarkable feat. Lawrence was a Westerner and an infidel, two big strikes against him. He had no legitimate structure power among the Arabs whatsoever—quite the contrary. Nevertheless, he galvanized an agglomeration of feuding Arabian desert tribesmen into a fighting force instrumental in the British defeat of the Turks, who were allies of the Germans. How he did it contains lessons for any would-be leader.

- By persuading Sheik Feisal of their common interests, he secured the Sheik's blessing and support. Feisal, a highly respected member of the ruling family, was diligently working to politically unify all of Arabia. Both he and the British wanted the Turks out of there.
- Lawrence spoke the Arabian language fluently. He respected, and in many ways admired, the Arab culture and the desert way of life. He adapted completely to it, at all times wearing Arabian garb (to the occasional bewilderment of his British colleagues).
- Throughout the campaign he rode, lived, ate and fought side-by-side with his followers, never asking for, and rarely accepting, special privileges. This fit well with the high value the Arabs

placed on equality, as well as demonstrating that Lawrence was one of them.

■ His structure power as a British army officer gave him access to the resources (money, supplies and weapons) the Arabs needed to do their job.

■ The Arabs were anxious to rid their country of the Turks, having been under their thumb for five hundred years. Lawrence realized he could unite the Arabs around this idea. In fact, he declined followers on any other basis. The tribes were "tangibly compensated" with British gold for their assistance, but Lawrence refused to use the promise of gold to bribe wavering potential followers. As far as he was concerned, the gold was a confirmation of the agreement, not the main inducement.

■ Lawrence shaped his "army's" tactics around its own natural capabilities. Warfare according to European conventions at the time would have been suicidal and fruitless. But his forces excelled at hit-and-run tactics, having over countless generations honed their fighting skills by raiding one another's flocks and camel herds. Rather than trying to turn them into imitation British cavalry, he developed a style of guerrilla warfare that capitalized on their existing talents.

■ Just as important, he capitalized on the Arabs' fierce independence and individuality. He felt that British army discipline strove to make obedience an instinct, to submerge every individual down to the lowest common denominator. This approach would have been a disaster among the Arabs; but by arousing their love for the cause of freedom from the Turks, Lawrence realized their full support and loyalty, and their maximum enthusiasm on the battlefield. Letting them share in the spoils of their raids helped too, of course.

The elements of effective leadership are all there: uniting followers around an Idea (which is to say, some supremely important value); organizing the effort; furnishing the necessary resources; and inspiring their hopes of success. Neither Lawrence, nor even Sheik Feisal, ever *ordered* either tribes or individuals to do anything. Rather,

■

they worked by persuasion to arouse and extend loyalties to the greater goal of freedom from Turkish rule. While Feisal's support was essential, Lawrence had to establish his own credibility as leader through fairness, justice, example and performance. He was right there with them, blowing up Turkish railroads and leading assaults.

The modern "professional management" mentality tends to place its faith in the organization chart. Corporations are rationally structured. Jobs are tightly defined. Industrial engineers time-and-motion study the assembly line. Computers organize the delivery routes. Workers are closely tracked, their output counted, their comings and goings scrutinized and their mistakes carefully toted up. This style of management strives to turn every job, as much as possible, into a restrictive cage of no-choice decisions.

This helps guarantee *predictable* performance throughout the organization, but by itself rarely leads to *maximum* performance. Organization members react both to the box *and* to the person occupying it. Loyalty to the box ensures minimum acceptable performance, but it takes leadership to get much more than that. In recent decades the United States Army has been putting an increasing emphasis on management by its officers; but as skeptics continue to point out, "You can lead men to their deaths, but you can't *manage* men to their deaths."

Actually, it is possible to manage men to their deaths, but the men don't like it very much. Many an officer who tried it has been shot by his own troops. (Witness the fraggings during the Vietnam War.) Arbitrary, dictatorial treatment is a sure pathway to grief, not only in military organizations but elsewhere. In the heyday of the labor movement, organizers had a saying that "one bad foreman is enough to unionize a whole plant."

In large corporations and bureaucracies most work is so routinized that few genuine leaders are really needed. Companies must have leadership at the top, but true leaders in the middle ranks can pose a threat to others around them. Also, it takes a Power Person to be a leader, and most people are not up to it. While a little leadership helps just about everyone to do a better job, the typical large organization is content to slog along with the minimum amount necessary.

Power in the Middle

Let's not be too tough on Hardy Charger. He's not a bad guy. The fact is, he'd like to work more closely with his people, but he doesn't know how to go about it. Also, he's not sure it's the proper thing to do. None of the other managers he knows at HugeCo work closely with their people, leaving him uncertain how it would go over if he tried it. With no organizational models for even a modicum of leadership, he's vaguely fearful that trying it might result in his losing control. Give the people under you a little slack, and who knows *what* they might do? So Hardy's management style is more an outcome of the situation than of his own character.

In any case, bigger problems are preying on Hardy's mind right now. He's under the gun to come up with some market-busting ideas. His boss, Mr. Deal, has made that the cornerstone of his Five-Year Marketing Strategic Plan. Hardy Charger is running on adrenaline these days.

But no complaints. Unlike Rosemary he has no conflicts about working after quitting time. Or on weekends. Or any time at all. Just last Thursday his home phone rang at 10:27 P.M., and the next morning he was on the daybreak plane to Toledo. Does he do it for the money? Of course, but that's far from the whole story. He doesn't take home much more than the guys in the factory do. But his attitude about working at HugeCo is quite different from theirs.

You see, Hardy brings to his job an entirely different array of rewards, penalties and values. Foremost in his mind is the reward of *advancement*. His big payoff is further up the pyramid, where power, status, success and big bucks await those who prevail in the upward scramble. That's why he doesn't mind working so many hours that his true pay rate isn't much higher than Rosemary's. If he doesn't do it, the guy in the next office will.

His *values* too are different. Win, don't lose. Work hard. Look good. Be wealthy. Be important. Be influential. Compete. At every step he weighs important penalties. Just one big mistake may bring him embarrassment, humiliation, loss of power, stunted career or even loss of position. That last could be real trouble for Hardy. The world is full of would-be top managers, and his experience here with HugeCo might be too specialized to travel very well.

Hardy Charger must make decisions—not whether or not to work after hours ("No problem, Mr. Deal. Shall I make arrangements to spend the night in town?")—but *managerial decisions*. Do we do this, or do we do that? Each time he makes one of these decisions, he faces some troublesome constraints:

- He has more to lose (his career) if they turn out badly, than he has to gain if they come out well.
- He has more responsibility than he has authority. That is, he can be blamed for things over which he has no real control. In fact, his corporate rivals may do all they can to make sure he is blamed for failures that were in no way his fault—it's a jungle out there.
- It isn't easy to tell how a decision is going to come out. Uncertainty prevails. If he decides to do *this* rather than that, it *might* come out the way he intended . . . but who knows for sure?

Figure 4, using what game theorists call a "payoff matrix," illustrates the spot Hardy Charger is in when he makes a typical middle management decision. If he makes a good one he picks up a few brownie points. If things go sour, he gets a big load of egg on his face. If he can legitimately *not* make a decision, nothing happens either way. This may not seem fair, but that's how it works at HugeCo.

For one thing, good performance is *expected*. Nobody pins a rose on Hardy for just doing his job. For another, it isn't that easy to rack up stunning successes in middle management positions. Being largely routine, most of the work requires no big, high-potential, risky decisions. When those infrequent successes do occur, everybody who was involved (especially those above him on the ladder) are quick to claim a share of the credit (funny how they're all out of their offices when the disasters descend).

Finally, HugeCo tends to *not* promote people with black marks on their records, rather than *to* promote people with good records. Too many are trying to clamber up the ladder, just about all of them well qualified for the next rung. So the smart money shrinks from risky decisions. "Keep your head above water," say the old corporate veterans, "and eventually you'll float to the top."

The Hardy Chargers of the world survive according to how well they can *avoid making decisions*. They can't just tell their bosses, "Thanks, but if it's all the same to you, I'd like to sit this one out." Instead, they rely on such time-tested tactics as these:

■ *Get someone else to make the decision.*
  Write a memo. Call attention to the fact that if things go terribly wrong, it will be somebody else's responsibility. Finance decided to shortchange your budget. Purchasing decided to go with an unreliable supplier. Research decided to put other people's market studies ahead of yours in the schedule. This may help them to see things your way. Otherwise it may be *their* ass in the sling, not yours.
■ *Put in extra effort.*
  If you have the responsibility but not the control, things can turn out poorly through no fault of your own; and you may not be in a position to pin it on someone else. A "decision-maker" may

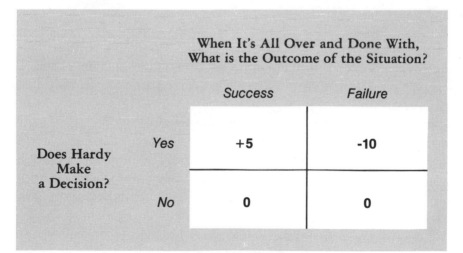

		When It's All Over and Done With, What is the Outcome of the Situation?	
		Success	Failure
Does Hardy Make a Decision?	Yes	+5	-10
	No	0	0

Figure 4
A PAYOFF MATRIX
for Hardy Charger's Managerial Decisions

try to step in and try to *do* something, but if things are out of control, this risks making things even worse, while at the same time calling attention to it. Better just to "give it your all." Spend mucho hours in the office, evenings and weekends. Have your people working overtime. Overspend your budget (but just a little). That way it will be on the record that you did everything you possibly could.

■ *Be a "minimaxer."*

Another game theory term, this one has to do with payoff matrices. "Minimax" means going with the decision that guarantees the player the smallest possible maximum loss. In figure 4, Hardy's "minimax" solution is to make no decision at all. He won't gain anything, that's true. The main thing is that he is guaranteed not to lose.

■ *Go by the book.*

When in doubt, follow a safe precedent. Do what the policy manual says. Do what your predecessor (if he or she was a success) used to do. Do what "everybody around here always does." If things then inadvertently go down the tubes, anyone who criticizes what you did is really criticizing standard operating procedure.

■ *Go for the "Safe Buy."*

Do whatever is the easiest to justify in the event of disaster. "How could I have known? I gave the contract to the biggest and most reliable company in the business." As contemporary corporate wisdom puts it: Nobody ever got fired for recommending that the company buy from IBM.

■ *Put off the consequences for as long as possible.*

Pick the alternative that will require the longest amount of time to pass before anyone can tell whether it was a hit or a miss. With any luck at all, by the time things go sour you'll have been promoted or will be working for some other company, safely out of harm's way.

■ *Share the responsibility with everybody.*

If you and a lot of other people are in a "no way to win" situation, often you will find that everybody coalesces around the same survival strategy. For example, one large engineering firm tries to get each manager periodically to forecast whether or not he will make the budget for his part of the project. That way, thinks top management, we'll have some advance warning and some time to figure out how to cope with potential budget overruns. But, thinks each manager, if *I* do that, all I'll reap is trouble and grief. Therefore all the managers put off mentioning their overruns until the last minute, at which time myriad overruns sprout like wildflowers in the Spring. No individual manager gets singled out, top management being so distracted by trying to cope with all the overruns that they don't have time to come down on *anybody*.

So, what about that market-busting new product idea? Hardy does in fact have a good one cooking, but he must get it okayed by the Review Committee. The Committee, comprised of middle managers from other departments, is in a no-win situation similar to Hardy's. If they pass a new product that turns out to be a big success, they get no credit. But if they endorse an idea that turns out to be the worst invention since Frankenstein's monster. . . . That is why they've been blasting down Hardy's proposals like space invaders in a video arcade. Any idea they approve represents a potential problem at some point in the future.

But Hardy wasn't born yesterday. In addition to his one good product idea, he plans to propose three total turkeys. He has already mentioned to Mr. Deal his problems with getting things through the Review Committee; and Mr. Deal has made it clear that those new, innovative products had better start rolling out, or he'll find out why not. They have to endorse *something* this time around, and Hardy has made sure that they have only one choice—his choice.

There you have the quintessential organizational power-play. Not, as some might suspect, holding a gun to somebody's head (that might work once or twice, but it's no way to build a career), but something far gentler. Set up the situation so that somebody has to make the decision that you want. If it turns out well, *you* get the credit ("That was my idea," says Hardy triumphantly). If it turns out badly, *they* get the blame. ("I sent them a bunch of ideas," says Hardy innocently. "That's the one they picked.")

Don't feel too sorry for the Committee, though. It has six members, none of whom asked for the job. Nobody keeps records on who votes for what, and by the time anyone knows whether The Product was successful or not, different people may be on it. This system makes it hard to pin the blame for failure on any individual. What did you think committees are for? They are the quintessential "cover-your-ass" maneuver. Nobody wants to be "it" in someone else's power-play, and decision-making by committee is an ideal way to avoid that.

Organizational Climate

Sounds like a lot of aggravation and wasted effort, doesn't it? It goes right back to the organizational situation: who is responsible for what, who reports to whom, and what is rewarded and what is punished. Mr. Deal is wondering what it would take to light a fire under Hardy Charger. Actually, Hardy already has more motivation than is good for either his heart or his marriage. But executives at HugeCo generally lean toward variations of "Use a bigger whip," or some other Control approach. You've heard of Theory X, Theory Y and Theory Z? HugeCo operates according to Theory KGB: Any slip-up will be punished swiftly and severely. This guarantees power-plays and cover-your-ass maneuvers. The managers, their careers perpetually on the line, put their best efforts into playing control games with their people and with one another, so as to avoid getting zapped.

A Power Person would have a different question: "How can we get our people to come up with more, and better, new product ideas?" This focuses on achieving the main objective, not on controlling what everybody does. Innovative companies such as Texas Instruments and 3M go about it quite differently from HugeCo. They encourage their people to take risks. They reward the successful innovators. They allow for the fact that most new ideas are not going to be stunning successes. They don't come down hard on people for the occasional, inevitable duds.

The character of the organization to a great extent determines what its people will do. The nature of the business is an important part of its character: A coal mine, a computer software development company and a corporate law firm are going to be quite different types of organizations, by necessity.

Beyond that, "organizational climate" takes over, and that is the responsibility of top management. They set up the formal organization—the organization chart, and the policy and procedures manual. Just as important, by example and leadership (or lack of it) they set the tone of the organization by *showing* the people below them the approaches and the kinds of behavior that win in that particular game. Just *telling* them isn't enough. If the example is at odds with the official word, which do you follow? A few years ago a candidate was elected governor of Ohio largely on the strength of a "Buy Ohio" campaign slogan. In office, he soon announced that he was considering some non-Ohioans for important cabinet posts. Later he announced a much ballyhooed plan to promote tourism within the state, then promptly climbed on a plane for an out-of-state vacation. Or consider the large management consulting firm that launched a major internal push for "excellence." Up until that time the firm had been a big money machine—very lucrative for the partners. During a high-level discussion on how to pursue the goal of "excellence," a partner remarked to the chairman: "Your mouth says 'excellence' but your eyes still say 'profits.' "

Contrast those examples of neg-leadership with this vignette about Russian General Georgi Zukhov, the commander who won the battles of Stalingrad and Moscow, and took Berlin, in World War II. Encountering a group of several wounded soldiers along a road trying to get a ride, he stopped his staff car to inquire. He found them quite discouraged. Officers were the only ones who had cars, and the officers just drove right by them. He told them to stay there and keep trying. Then he had his driver take him down the road out of sight and stop. He proceeded to pull over every officers' car that came along, until he saw the wounded soldiers ride by, finally picked up. He summarily demoted all fifty-odd officers he had pulled over and sent them straight to the front. News of this "policy suggestion" reached every soldier in the Red Army by word-of-mouth within a matter of days.

Power at the Top

Speaking of top management, let's ride the elevator up to the tenth floor and look in on B. F. Deal, vice-president of marketing.

Mr. Deal moves through a world less structured and more political than Hardy Charger's. There aren't as many day-to-day "have-to's." In fact, much of Mr. Deal's job consists of making up the "have-to's" for the people below him—the policies and procedures they are to follow. At Mr. Deal's level, structure power doesn't count so much (except, of course, in the downward direction), and agreement power, performance power and persuasive power count more. He doesn't concentrate so much on pleasing his boss (as a middle manager would), as on building strong friendships and alliances. He tries to reward his friends and neutralize his enemies. He strives to maintain an image as a "guy who delivers." In his job as V.P. of marketing, that means coming up with new product lines, new markets and new strategies. Depending on the company, the type of business and their positions, other top managers would have to deliver access to sources of finance; favorable labor or political relations; new sources of business or revenues; or new and better ways to manufacture The Product. And bringing in big profits never hurt either, of course. At the top just about anything will be forgiven someone who is perceived as effectuating vast improvements in the bottom line.

It is the same in other organizations besides business, the only difference being in the ultimate bottom line. In government agencies the executives most valued are those who persuade legislators to vote them broader responsibilities and ever-expanding budgets. In the armed forces top management (i.e., the generals and admirals) must deliver military victories. In political parties, those who run the campaigns had better bring in both big contributions and winning numbers of votes.

At the top, big decisions can't be so easily evaded. Executives are much more visible than middle managers, and they are individually under close scrutiny by many parties both inside the company and out. But the decisions still carry risks, and bad ones can be career-disenhancing. At this level another set of tactics—"situation management"—comes into play. Those wise in the ways of large organizations realize that a *real* decision is not simply a matter of choosing the best from among options X, Y and Z. For top managers, a major decision is a process extending from the initial recognition of a need for action, to the final evaluation of results. This may involve many people and extend over a period of years. This offers Mr. Deal and his peers a lot of situation to manage, and plenty of tools to use. For example:

At the beginning of the decision process—

- *Set your goals so as to give yourself a break.*
  Usually a savvy decision-maker has some idea of what the most likely outcomes of a decision are. By initially framing the objectives so that they are pretty close to what the most likely outcome will be, one's chances of perceived effectiveness can be markedly improved. "He delivered, just like he promised."
- *Have consultants and experts support the decision you want to make.*
  A good consultant understands that the consultant's function is to help the person who hired him get the job done. New ideas, great discoveries, or the pure and unvarnished truth, are not necessarily the point. Rather, the consultant is hired to bring in the proper facts, arranged to support the correct goals. Thus you will notice that in big disputes between business and the government, each side has its all-star lineup of experts. The trick is not to bribe people to tell lies on your behalf, but to hire experts who happen to subscribe to the same version of the truth that you do.
- *Incorporate "the best thinking of all your people" into the planning stages.*
  Being the decision-maker, you can easily enough hang onto the credit for a successful decision, but having others involved helps diffuse the blame and avoid pinpointing anyone as the cause of failure. We've already seen how handy committees can be.
- *Position yourself as the "architect" of the venture.*
  The "architect" is the one with vision who understands the need and formulates the Grand Design. "Engineers" and "bricklayers" are then given the job of bringing it off. If the result is a success, the architect gets the credit. If it isn't so successful, well, maybe

the engineers and the bricklayers just didn't have what it takes to bring a Grand Design to fruition. If you aren't convinced that this tactic works, try to come up with the names of some of the engineers who worked for Frank Lloyd Wright, Philip Johnson or I. M. Pei.

During the process of implementing the decision—

- *Be ready to move on to "other opportunities."*
  At all times closely monitor how implementation of the decision is progressing. At the first unmistakable signs of impending disaster, declare the venture to be a "two-phased" program. Take credit for the "concept and design" phase, and pass the "implementation" phase over to someone else. Yes, it's time to start working on your *next* big decision.
- *Manage the perceptions that others have of your progress.*
  Any sign of difficulties will have the same effect on your corporate rivals that blood in the water has on sharks. An aura of competence, progress and success is essential. Hopefully this is no more than an accurate reflection of the reality of the situation. If in fact things really are crashing and burning all around you, you of course will be working like the devil behind the scenes to ensure that everything will come out all right by the project deadline.

At the end of the process, when the success of the decision is evaluated—

Hopefully Mr. Deal's decision-making is right on target, and his Five-Year Marketing Strategic Plan will be a stunning financial triumph. That will impress the Board of Directors, who will soon make him president and CEO of HugeCo. He will then appoint Hardy Charger as his vice-president of marketing, and Rosemary will be elevated to the position of executive secretary. But if the outcome of a big decision falls short of what everybody had been led to expect, there are still a few tricks in the nimble executive's bag that may help salvage the situation. For instance:

- *Rearrange the original goals.*

  Try to recast the objectives stated at the outset so that they conform to the actual, final outcome. After all, over time the situation may have changed, new needs may have arisen, and new facts may have come to light. "Knowing what we know now, it is clear that we did much better than anyone could reasonably have expected." Wait until you see where the arrow hits, then draw your bullseye around it. This is easier to do if the initial goals were framed a bit vaguely at the time the process was set in motion.

- *Bury your mistakes.*

  What do you think "government security" is for? Information isn't always classified to keep the enemy from finding out. Sometimes items are declared Top Secret to preserve the reputations of the decision-makers. The old saying is that the graveyards are where doctors bury their mistakes. Organizations have their own "graveyards" where, short of being subpoenaed, mistakes disappear never to be seen again. For records that need not be kept, shredders work just fine.

HugeCo's immediate concern is how to improve the profit picture in the face of withering competition. At the beginning of this chapter it looked as though B. F. Deal was in deep, deep trouble: But here's a little secret. B.F. himself had a hand in fostering that impression. He saw an excellent opportunity for advancing the fortunes of the marketing division (not to mention the fortunes of its vice-president). By shaping the Board's perceptions into viewing the situation as a marketing problem, he had them all primed for his solution—the Five-Year Marketing Strategic Plan. He has laid it out for the Board, and he can tell they are going to go for it. They are impressed by its boldness, and the minority of members (financial and accounting types, as usual) who are counselling caution will certainly be overridden.

Are old B.F. and his marketing division going out on a limb, high-rolling some big risks as they aim to shoot the moon? It may look that way to the Board, but in truth B.F. has the outcome in his back pocket. He has left the objectives "flexibile" in case they need to be re-evaluated as events unfold. He has the report from The

Consulting Firm that analyzes the situation and recommends HugeCo base their near-term marketing efforts on new product introductions. He has carefully set the stage for the "implementation" phase of the effort. Marketing will design the products and develop prototypes. When they are ready for the rollout, marketing will be responsible for advertising, sales and distribution. In between, it will be manufacturing's responsibility to produce the goods "at cost levels, and meeting quality standards, commensurate with profit targets and the competitive picture." Well, what could the vice-president of manufacturing say, that they couldn't do it?

This way marketing has two ways to win—if the venture turns out profitably; or if they come up with the new products but "manufacturing drops the ball." The only way marketing (and B.F.) can wind up looking bad is if they don't produce any new product ideas at all. That's unlikely, even in the current organizational climate. In any case, B.F. isn't going to let that happen. His scheming may sound a bit cynical, but he genuinely believes HugeCo needs his Strategic Plan to emerge from its slump. He has listened to Hardy Charger's problems with the Review Committee, and he is determined to get rid of that bottleneck, as well as others. He wants those innovative ideas to flow. Come Monday he will announce the appointment of a task force to revamp the entire product development process. He will demonstrate his serious intent by sitting in on the meetings himself.

The Curse of the Control People

Rosemary, Hardy Charger and B. F. Deal give us a basis for understanding how reasonable people behave in organizations:

- Analyze the situation the person is in.
- Understand how he views his rewards, penalties and values.
- Follow his decisions through the Action Decision Sequence, paying special attention to the no-choice decisions imposed by the organizational structure, the constraints of the job, and the organizational culture.

Since reasonable people tend to have similar arrays of work-related rewards, penalties and values, you'll find that, provided they are competent to do the job in the first place, any two people will perform a given job in about the same way. They'll each have their own style, but the job is designed so that their content won't differ substantially.

But not all people are reasonable. Some are obvious misfits or bad apples. These are troublesome but can be dealt with, provided that they aren't the owner's son, civil service or shielded by some other invulnerable job protection. Once identified, they can be replaced with someone else who is willing and able to do the job.

The real problem in organizations comes when Control People get into positions of power, people who are more concerned with being in control than with furthering the aims of the organization.

I'm thinking now of Gretta, supervisor of the Research Laboratory at the Medical School. The head of The Lab, Dr. Zorders, is world-renowned as a medical researcher, but a manager, no way. Plus his marriage has become boring, and Gretta is, ah, inclined to be affectionate. He happily leaves Gretta to run The Lab while he writes research reports, journal articles and grant proposals, and travels around the world presenting papers to his research colleagues.

Dr. Zorders has established a good reputation for The Lab, and the people working there are well-trained, well-educated and hardworking. Were Gretta a Power Person, this would be a fine opportunity. She could coordinate the work, schedule the equipment, keep the stockroom supplied and handle all the routine paperwork. The Lab would run efficiently, and everyone could produce a lot of research results.

Sad to say, Gretta is a Control Person. She doesn't have the kind of education, training or experience that would truly qualify her for this job. Therefore she resents that everyone under her is smarter and more competent than she is. Also, many of them are attractive young women, and Dr. Zorders seems to like them (actually, he is just a naturally friendly person). This makes her jealous of them, and she may even be a bit jealous of The Lab itself: Sometimes Dr. Zorders seems to think it is more important than *she* is. In any case, she doesn't care about The Lab so much as she cares about bossing it. She may not be equipped to be powerful in this job, but control she can certainly handle.

Gretta makes it clear that Lab personnel are not to communicate with Dr. Zorders directly, but only through her. ("He's got so many important things on his mind—we mustn't distract him with every petty problem that comes along.") If any of them do talk to him or go into his office, she rants about their "going over her head." Thus she controls the flow of information between him and them. He tells her what he wants The Lab to do. However, Gretta doesn't always relay it to the staff. This results in screwups and missed deadlines, giving Gretta the opportunity to get people in trouble and providing her with crises to handle.

"Honestly, I don't know what is wrong with those people!" she tells him. As far as *he* can tell, Gretta is the only thing holding the operation together. She also comes in early and will take things off people's desks and sabotage their experiments. She collects gossip, including what she picks up by eavesdropping on telephone conversations. Anything that will discredit someone, she passes along to Dr. Zorders, so as to set him against them. He feels fortunate to have her in charge: Who else could handle that zoo? Certainly not him. And she does have such a pleasant way of, ah, expressing her loyalty.

Every organizational position has certain powers—tasks to perform, resources with which to perform them, and relationships with other positions. Problems come when people get into positions for which they really aren't suited. Dr. Zorders has no taste for directing the behavior of other people. He'd rather write research articles and give talks at conferences. Being director of The Lab, he should be running it, delegating enough authority to Gretta to ensure that his orders are carried out. Instead, by his lack of interest he has created a "power vacuum."

Gretta is running The Lab herself, using what little authority her job carries, plus Dr. Zorders' agreement that she should be in charge, plus her dishonest use of rewards, penalties, values and information. She has worked a neat reversal of "authority" here. The person with authority has responsibility for the situation, as well as control over it. Gretta has seized control of the situation but has no responsibility for it, leaving Dr. Zorders with responsibility but no control (though

.

of course she lets him *think* he has control). That is what we commonly call "manipulation."

This can happen in any organization, from one as small as a family, to one as large as a government or a multinational corporation, whenever someone is placed in a position whose power and authority they aren't equipped to handle. Thus we find many American households run by their children, offices run by their secretaries and even mental institutions and prisons run by their inmates. Allow a power vacuum to develop, and all too often a Gretta is there to ooze in and take over, partly out of self-advantage, but also just to have control for its own sake. One of history's famous examples of this happened in pre-revolutionary Russia. The czar, Nicholas II, was a weak and ineffectual man with a religious-fanatic wife. He fell under the control of Rasputin, the "mad monk," through the influence Rasputin had over the czarina. Rasputin shaped the czar's policies to suit his own interests and contributed significantly to the failures of the Imperial government that led to the Bolshevik Revolution.

Control People in organizations use various tactics. They may play on fears and ignorance and lack of information. If they tell you something the boss told them, for example, how can you verify that the boss *really* told them that? Straight out ask the boss? That's courting trouble.

They can get holds on people through compromising information, or through control over rewards or penalties. If it looks as though someone can make you rich, or get you promoted, or put an end to your career, you'll certainly be responsive to his or her wishes. Often they don't really have that much power over you; but as long as they can control the information flow, how are *you* to know that?

They can hire employees who are "tainted" in one way or another, for example people with criminal records. That might sound risky, but if carefully selected, often such people cannot only be easy to control but can even come in handy. They may be more willing to do dirty work than other employees, and if a fall guy is needed they are easy to set up or frame. The executives of one pet supply firm escaped prosecution for providing prostitutes to their buyers by having men with conviction records handle the arrangements. In the early stages of subsequent legal proceedings these men perjured themselves

.

to protect the company. They were convicted, but by the time the executives went on trial the testimony of these men, who were the chief witnesses against them, was too tainted to stand up in court.

Organizations that fall into the hands of a Gretta or a Rasputin generally are doomed, unless legitimate authority steps in and straightens things out. At the very least they lose their effectiveness as morale, cooperation and productivity grind to a halt. What about the Control People themselves? It is not a recommended approach for anyone seeking a long-term, prosperous and successful career. If the organization fails, they fail with it. Even if it doesn't, eventually it will probably decline to the point where others will be motivated to root them out, a messy but necessary task that may be distressingly similar to an exorcism (which, in a sense, it is).

Unfortunately, many people loyal and valuable to the organization may be hurt in the meantime. Rasputin's influence contributed to Russia's defeat in World War I and the Imperial government's collapse. Rasputin was assassinated by others around the czar who may have wanted to control the czar themselves. Gretta drove a number of people to quit The Research Laboratory before she was finally fired (and, because of the status of her work visa, deported). By that time the productivity of The Lab had gone South, and Dr. Zorders lost the federal grant that had been supporting his research. Oh, and his wife filed for divorce too. But don't waste your sympathy on him. He isn't a Victim, just an amateur Control Person who got in over his head by tangling with a professional. He learned a few lessons from this little escapade, but Gretta never will learn anything. To this day she can't understand why everybody got so upset. After all, it was their own damned fault. If they didn't want a strict and efficient supervisor, then why did they hire her in the first place?

Control People try to run things by being tough, tricky, devious and ruthless. Sooner or later most of them come up against somebody who is tougher, trickier, more devious and more ruthless, and down they go. Mao and Stalin both died of old age in office, after many years of running governments based primarily on iron-fisted control of vast nations with huge populations. That tells you something about how truly tough, tricky, devious and ruthless those two fellows were.

Power Organizations and Control Organizations

As with people, most organizations are blends of power and control, with very few pure examples of either extreme. Championship amateur athletic teams come close to pure power. Within the constraints of the particular sport, every team member puts out maximum effort in concert with the others, and as an organization they achieve their objective, which is to do better than the competing teams. This may be why we find college sports and the Olympic Games so captivating, and why we are so concerned about keeping them "pure." They are one of the few ways in which the average person can experience, appreciate and identify with nearly pure power.

At the other extreme, maximum security prisons and certain mental institutions for the criminally insane operate by nearly pure control. While lip service may be paid to rehabilitation, in practice the primary objective of such organizations is to keep a very tight lid on a large number of dangerous social misfits.

A "Power Organization" is one in which every member, to the maximum extent possible, is able to contribute to achieving the organization's objectives, and at the same time achieve his own. Everyone concurs on the organization's goals, and the group's energy all goes in the same direction. Cooperation increases the group's overall effectiveness, moving everyone ahead together.

Small, entrepreneurial businesses and crack military units tend to be Power Organizations. Many of the "high technology" success stories of the late 1970s and early 1980s celebrate Power Organizations. United around a New Idea, a bunch of hotshot young engineers and programmers work in a basement every night until 4:30 A.M. for eight straight months and produce a revolutionary computer. It's heady stuff. People in Power Organizations find great joy in what they are doing. Many would do it for nothing: Being part of that kind of group is a priceless reward in and of itself.

Why then can't we all work in a place like that?

The problem is that they require special circumstances: (1) a common, important, attainable objective; (2) high commitment from every member; (3) a leader who can organize their efforts in the right direction; (4) members capable of doing the required tasks and who individually have the potential for being Power People themselves; and (5) just one hell of a lot of luck. These all come together but rarely. When they do, it's a once-in-a-lifetime experience for most of the people involved. Few entrepreneurs follow up their first stunning success with another, though many try. Lawrence's Arab army took Damascus before his thirtieth birthday, and from that point his life was all downhill.

Most organizations start off on a power premise but as they achieve success begin to shift more toward control. This seems almost inevitable, because as organizations achieve success, they also become larger. It becomes more difficult to maintain the high degree of cohesion and commitment among the larger, more heterogeneous workforce. The original leaders can no longer stay in close touch with the large number of employees, and must delegate more and more authority to intermediate managers. Tasks become more specialized, which means that less and less is demanded of each individual's total range of capabilities. Formal reporting channels are set up, choking off the opportunities for cooperation and synergy that characterized the company in its formative stage.

Finally the organization reaches HugeCo's stage of development. People are hired to do one specific job which, being mostly routine, they aren't especially committed to. The organization's goals—keeping the dividend and the stock price high—are so remote from what most employees do that they focus more on their own survival and prosperity than that of the company. Faced with a decision hinging on whether to help the company or help themselves, they are inclined to decide in their own favor. Hence the territoriality, the internal rivalries, the risk avoidance and the self-serving behavior.

As growth levels off or even declines, control takes precedence. Effort and attention focus on self-preservation, not the group's collective welfare. People fight to protect what they have, not to move the organization ahead. Distracted from positive objectives, people put more time, effort and energy into controlling one another. People don't like to be controlled, so resistance builds; as times goes on more and more effort is required to keep things under control. As a result of internal strife and misplaced energies, the organization stagnates and eventually is eclipsed by an upcoming Power Organization that has some technological, conceptual or ideological advantage going for it.

The theories on which modern corporate and bureaucratic structures are based are sound enough. Adam Smith over two hundred years ago illustrated the superiority of division of labor with his example of the pin factory. Frederick W. Taylor at the turn of the century showed the effectiveness of scientific management, the practice of figuring out the best way to do a thing and then making everybody do it that way. Modern technology and management structures make it possible to centrally control a huge, geographically wide-ranging organization, thereby focusing every employee's energies on accomplishing a specific range of tasks programmed to be as routine as possible. (It has been said of the United States Navy, for example, that it is a system "designed by geniuses to be run by idiots." That is more or less what designers of large organizations hope will be the final outcome of their efforts.)

The problem is that this sort of structuring focuses each member on accomplishing the *organization's* objectives, in a specific environment. Should the environment change, the structure will lose its effectiveness, to some degree. If the organization's objectives are very far removed from the individual *members'* objectives, belonging to the organization becomes dysfunctional for them.

This has happened time and time again over the centuries, among businesses, among governments, among nations, and even among the tiniest of organizations—clubs, families and friendships. The environment changes, or the objectives of the organization and its members drift apart. Some organizations last longer than others, religions seeming particularly long lived: Judaism has been extant for more than three thousand years, Christianity for nearly two thousand and Islam for more than thirteen hundred. (Needless to say, organizations that have lasted this long are quite different now from how they were when they began—but the ideas on which they were founded have stayed constant.) The Roman Empire lasted for almost one thousand years, and the Academy established by Plato in ancient Athens for several hundred (as have Harvard and several other universities here in the United States). In general the principle applied by Lawrence seems to hold true: Organizations founded around an idea are more stable than those founded on personal advantage or interest.

But modern technologies have quickened the pace of growth, and the life cycle has been shortened. Some of the industrial giants founded before the turn of the twentieth century, for example Standard Oil (now Exxon), Procter and Gamble, and Eastman Kodak are still going strong, but others such as Pullman Corp., Swift & Co. and numerous railroads no longer count for much. World maps constantly change as governments rise and fall.

The organizational life cycle of Power—Stagnation—Control—Disintegration historically has been practically inescapable in the long run. In the short run, organizations may be able to keep their power premises alive by understanding, and acting upon, the difference between power and control. Some control is necessary in every organization. The trick is to use it in the service of, and not as an obstacle to, power. Such tools as time-and-motion studies, management information systems and "Management By Objectives" can, if used thoughtfully, help employees (and therefore the organization itself) to be powerful. Too often these are used instead to keep them under control, with the result that the organization itself becomes less, rather than more, effective.

At least, this life cycle has been held true in societies that have placed a high value on the individual. One exception to it has emerged in the twentieth century—the totalitarian government. Based on a completeness of control made possible by modern technologies—specifically mass communication, rapid transportation and the machine gun—communist governments *start out* as Control Organizations. Since 1917, none has yet progressed beyond that stage.

The problem is that the control of a totalitarian organization's structure is virtually inescapable. All-pervasive no-choice and routine activities, stringently enforced, control every member's behavior to the extent that free action is smothered. If one wants to exist there is no other path than to do his job. Those who administer tyrannical governments typically are not motivated by hatred for their charges. Even in such an extreme case as the Nazi death camps, the horrible truth is that the majority of people involved in operating them were *just doing their jobs*. How many can honestly say that, in the same circumstances, they are sure they would behave any differently? (In a series of experiments in the 1950s psychologist Stanley Milgram discovered the majority of his subjects—average American citizens—would willingly electrocute a stranger if directed to do so by an authority figure in a "job" situation. Many were not comfortable about it, but they did it in spite of their discomfort, apparently accepting it as a no-choice action.)

The humane imperative is to keep those kinds of circumstances from developing, wherever we can prevent it. However, as history has proved time and again, tearing down existing authority structures is not the answer.

Worker Power

With all the different kinds of organizations, and all the different kinds of jobs and positions in each one, it would be impossible to lay out a list of specific guidelines to help you, or anyone else, improve your job, your performance or your career. But there are some general principles for dealing more effectively with power in the workplace.

Principle Number 1: *Understand where the* real *power lies.*
The real power over any organization lies in the hands of its market. If a business doesn't please its customers, good-bye, business. The market of a bureaucracy usually is those who control its budget, typically elected officials who must please *their* market, the voters and the special interests who contribute campaign funds. The power over any sub-unit of a larger organization—a department, or a division, or a subsidiary—generally belongs to the person to whom that unit reports to.

Often this comes down to the power of the purse strings—"He Who Has the Gold Makes the Rules." But not always. Voluntary organizations such as clubs, churches or professional associations, are not obliged to please anyone outside the organization—the power resides in the members themselves.

Whatever organization you are in, always keep in mind the ul-

.

timate market the organization must please, because that determines the group's overriding values, the ones it must fulfill when the chips are down. Realistically, the situation may not be that simple. Big corporations now have to please not only their customers but also the government, consumer activists, the financial community, the news media, and other constituencies, each of which has its own criteria. That can spawn a lot of uncertainty and complexity. We know what *those* do to effective decision-making.

One type of organization—the American family—currently is in the peculiar situation of having no "market." Families traditionally have "reported" to God, if the household was religious, and also to the cultural group, the immediate community, and/or to the spouses' families. Thus decisions in the family unit could be banged off some external reference points. But with the trend in modern America to maximize each individual's freedom of choice, the institution of marriage has been chopped loose from its moorings and is now culturally adrift. Many families, of course, still maintain stability by taking guidance from religious principles. Those that don't may find themselves with an identity crisis: How is this supposed to work, and what is the point of it anyway?

Some such households manage to work out a satisfactory "government by mutual agreement," but in many the two principals never reach accord as to who is going to be the final authority on what. The result too often is a snakepit of manipulation and control games, with the real Victims being the children who, as children always have, learn how to deal with the world from their parents' example. The rampant American divorce rate is a poignant indicator of the power problems that arise when traditional authority structures are corroded and none emerge to replace them.

Principle Number 2: *Understand how the organization works.*

Know the job descriptions (who is supposed to do what) and the lines of reporting (who tells whom what to do). Don't stop there. Learn how the organization *really* works. The ways that things *do* get done are never the same as the ways they are *supposed* to get done. The "have to's" are a starting point, not the whole story. Find out who influences whom; what informal maneuvers are necessary to get around bottlenecks and roadblocks in the "official" procedures; things like that. Don't take the formal policies and procedures too literally. There are few organizations whose operations wouldn't come to an immediate halt if the members seriously tried to follow them all to the letter. Find out what the definite "have to's" are, and which ones must be set aside in the interests of getting the job done.

Principle Number 3: *Don't fight the system.*

Knowing how the organization works, go with it, not against it. "Grass roots" agitation may succeed in democratic organizations such as volunteer groups or political movements, but change in authoritarian, hierarchial organizations nearly always comes from the top down, and rarely from the bottom up. Coming from the top, everybody down below "has to" do it (at least in theory). They can get in trouble if they don't. Anyone down below who tries to make changes in this type of organization has to fight a structure of no-choice and habitual decisions, manned by people who have a lot at stake (their livelihoods) if they screw up. Lots of luck.

Principle Number 4: *Be clear about what organization you are in.*

People usually are members of several organizations at the same time. For example, you work for a company. You have a family. You are a law-abiding citizen of some nation, and you try to be a normal member of some cultural group. You may belong to a union or a professional society.

Hopefully you have your life neatly arranged, all consistent and free of cross pressures. Otherwise you may have to face some hard decisions. Am I a union man, or a company man? What comes first here, my job or my family? Do I do what is best for my department, or what is best for the firm? As a law-abiding citizen do I blow the whistle, or as a loyal employee do I help with the cover-up? Office romances often end up in this kind of conflict, which companies used to resolve by requiring the lower-placed one to leave. Having your own priorities straight helps to avoid these gut-wrenchers in the first place, or to sort them out when you have to.

.

207

Having made up your mind, support the organization. Live up to its values, in fact but also symbolically. Wear the uniform, speak the language and eat the food (it's not for nothing that politicians hoping to get votes from the Italian district make sure to be seen eating some spaghetti). The leaders of any organization are expected to "live it." If you want to be among them, start early.

Above all, steer well clear of corrupted situations. They can put you in conflict with every other organization that touches your life. Worse than that, they can entangle you in a network of "devil's bargains," in which everyone is bound together through their fear of detection and their mutual need to cover up the corruption. Needless to say, this is neither a healthy working situation or a promising career path.

Principle Number 5: *Perform.*

To the best of your abilities, do the job they are paying you for. If you want to progress, develop the skills for the job you *want* to do. Don't try to do *every*body's job, just make certain to do your own. Carry out your duties and responsibilities faithfully, never miss a chance to improve your skills, and put out at least 110 percent of what is expected of you.

■ ■ ■

Fortunate indeed is the one who works with love. Psychologists tell us that meaningful work is essential for human happiness. We need to use our abilities, and we need to accomplish something in our lives. Just about everyone would like to make a solid contribution to the world, if given the chance.

The problem for many is that their jobs deny them that chance. More often than not the fault lies in those jobs. Too many at the lower levels are constrained into robot-like routines of no-choice decisions, offering no possibility of fulfillment or any sense of real accomplishment. Too many jobs at the middle level are shaped by their power situations into political struggles for survival. The best advice is to figure out what you really want to do and then steadfastly work toward it, making the most of whatever you do along the way. There's nothing new about that advice, you say? True enough. There's nothing new about organizations either.

If any organizational situation becomes unbearable, you can always decide to leave. That decision, like any other, hinges on your perceptions of your rewards, penalties and values relevant to the alternatives: Am I better off sticking it out, or should I leave and cut my losses?

These can be among the hardest decisions a person ever has to make; but sometimes there's simply no doubt about the right course of action. Take inspiration from the story of Marilyn S., freshly graduated with a liberal arts degree from Ivy League University. Searching for her first job, she answered an ad for a "personal aide" and was invited for an interview. A celebrated actress/Hollywood personality, now a few years past her prime (well, more than just a few), had come to her city to star at a local dinner theater. She needed a woman to handle correspondence and appointments, run errands and take care of odds and ends. Marilyn was offered the job. She accepted and was told she could start immediately. As if on cue, the aging beauty's white toy poodle pranced in from the next room, frisked a couple of circles around Marilyn's feet by way of welcome, then went to the exact center of the oriental carpet and laid a row of little doggy diamonds. "Take care of that, dahhhling," purred her new employer.

"I'm sorry, Miss _____," said Marilyn as she gathered up her coat and purse, "but I don't do dogshit."

8

DO YOU SINCERELY WANT TO BE POWERFUL?

What Having Power Means

I hope this book has amused as well as informed you. But do not be fooled by the tone of *The Power of Persuasion*. Power is a deadly serious matter. Repeat: DEADLY. It is right up there with degenerative, parasitic and infectious diseases, as one of the world's leading causes of death.

Wars are waged because of power. Violent crimes such as assaults, homicides, and rapes result from power. Many instances of suicides, accidents and stress-related maladies, as well as self-destructive behaviors such as alcoholism, drug addiction, sexual deviance and gambling are rooted in power problems. Historians have estimated that during this century alone as many as one hundred million souls—including not only armed warriors but also hordes of non-combatant Africans, Armenians, Cambodians, Chinese, Jews, Latin Americans and Russians—have perished, either by violence or by intentional neglect, because of power. The two "superpower" nations, the United States and the Soviet Union, are so-called because between them they have in their hands the capability of exinguishing all life from the face of the earth. Perhaps the government would have been wise to require a warning label:

POWER MAY BE HAZARDOUS TO YOUR HEALTH
READ THIS BOOK AT YOUR OWN RISK

Strictly speaking, as you know by now, *control* is the real problem, not power. But as long as we understand the difference, there's no point in quibbling over words. Whatever we call it, the urge of some people to push other people around has always bedeviled humanity. All that makes today different from times past is technology. We have managed, with modern weapons, communication and transportation, to do it much more effectively and on a much vaster scale than was ever possible before.

Even in the more commonplace contexts of our lives, power and control remain *extremely* touchy topics. You now appreciate their pervasiveness and subtlety—truly, they touch each of us many times every day. Viewed from a safe distance, power and control may be fascinating, perhaps entertaining; but even in their most petty and mundane forms, the people involved can take them very, very seriously. In the early 1980s a novel by a renowned British comic novelist, Kingsley Amis, was virtually boycotted for a time by the American publishing industry.* The reason? Mr. Amis committed the heinous crime of basing his satirical book *Stanley and the Women* on the premise that educated, successful women are capable of being Control People who inflict living hell on the hapless men in their lives. Worse than that, he had the temerity to make the women doing it appear ridiculous (their male victims didn't come off much better). I mention it only as one of many examples of the gravity of power and control even in commonplace, non-lethal contexts (and I'll leave it as an exercise for you to puzzle out why this happened and who was behind it).

For all that we have covered, we barely scratched the surface. We established a framework for understanding power and control, then hung a few bits and tatters of substance upon it. Every sentence in

---

* Reported by Hilton Kramer in a review of the book, *Wall Street Journal*, September 23, 1985.

the book could be easily elaborated to paragraph length. Every paragraph could be expanded to a section, each section to a chapter, and each chapter to an entire book. And think of the chapters, only hinted at here, that remain to be written: Power Between the Sexes; Power in the Family; Political Power; Power in Sports and Games; Power and Religion; Money Power; Power and the Legal Process; Power Out on the Street; Power and Mental Health . . . the possibilities are as unlimited as the Human Condition. For power and control *are* the Human Condition—"still the same old story, the fight for love and glory, on that you can rely," as Dooley Wilson played it for Ingrid Bergman and Humphrey Bogart in *Casablanca*.

Thus there can never be a cookbook *The Joy of Power and Control*. A few recipes, useful in special, limited situations, can be found in the better how-to books, for example, Dale Carnegie's *How to Win Friends and Influence People*, and *Getting to Yes* by Fisher and Ury. Attempts to condense power and control in all their aspects into any list of simple, easy to follow steps will always be defeated by the sheer immensity of the topic. In the end, everyone must make his or her own way through the Power Jungle. A guide can aim us down the right path, but we have to hack away the vines and underbrush with our own machetes, and face down the lurking dangers with our own boldness.

I don't pretend to offer anybody a cookbook. However, I may be able to help out as a guide.

The Two Sides of Being Powerful

Start by recognizing that there are two sides to being powerful:

1. Being able to act effectively.
2. Staying out of other people's control.

A Power Person must do both. Either by itself will take you nowhere. You may know someone who has perfected staying out of other people's control. At any rate, you will recognize the type. They are suspicious of everything and everybody. They read the fine print. They know their rights inside and out, and they never miss a chance to stand up for them. Nobody is going to put one over on *them*. Nobody is going to beat them out of *anything*.

The problem is, they never get around to accomplishing anything. All their energy goes into self-defense. They can't seem to get anywhere. Life for them is a joyless struggle with no decisive victories. Perpetually preoccupied with staving off defeat, they make no forward progress. The price of freedom may be eternal vigilance, but that alone will never lead to a happy life.

Just as futile are the lives of those who have an ability to act effectively, but are defenseless against Control. Many entertainers, athletes and inventors fall into this category. Joe Louis, undeniably one of the greatest boxers who ever lived, made a lot of money. Tragically, he died poorer than he should have, picked clean by the vultures who surrounded him in his heyday. Marilyn Monroe had magical powers over a whole nation of men, which still left her less than a match for the sharks that infest the entertainment world. The people who invented magnetic recording, television and the ballpoint pen were not the ones who reaped the riches. William Kennedy's Pulitzer Prize–winning novel *Ironweed* illustrates the tragedy of this kind of single-faceted life approach. The central character, Francis Phelan, a man with a genuine potential for power, is perpetually thwarted by his helplessness before the control forces that pervade his life. Able to cope only by dropping out of society and living as an alcoholic bum, he is finally redeemed by love (unlike most people forced into that path in real life, who live and die miserably and anonymously).

Being powerful thus is a twofold challenge; and if a cookbook isn't possible, a guidebook can still be an invaluable aid. Follow the Eleven Paths to Power. They will lead you toward being able to act more effectively. Avoid the Levers of Control. Those are what the Control People will use to try to manipulate your actions.

Follow the Eleven Paths to Power

Powerpath 1: *Know yourself intimately.*
One of the two inscriptions on the temple of the oracle at ancient Delphi was "Know thyself." This is absolutely Rule Number One for

being powerful. Know every aspect of yourself thoroughly, from your halo all the way down to your hemorrhoids. Don't flinch, don't hold back, and don't deceive yourself. Know what is best about yourself, and what is the worst. Know your strengths and also your weaknesses. Know what you can do, and what you can't. Adam Smith two hundred years ago noted that people tend to overestimate their chances of success and underestimate their chances of failure (hence the timeless lure of lotteries). Equally as big a hinderance is the tendency many have to underestimate their abilities and let themselves be hobbled by mis-perceived shortcomings.

Never stop working at trying to get closer and closer to the truth about yourself. Especially, come to understand what you really, *really* want to accomplish, what you want out of your life. Know what you *believe in*. After all, how can you be powerful if you don't know what you want in the first place?

Powerpath 2: *Be an information filter and a knowledge sponge.*

"Knowledge is power," Francis Bacon wrote in 1597, about two thousand years after the Hebrews said much the same in Proverbs (24:5). They in turn likely lifted it from the men who composed the Kabbalah a thousand or so years before *they* came on the scene.

This is an old and proven precept, but times are a little different now. The Hebrews have always put a high value on learning, but in most Western cultures, until moveable-type printing was invented knowledge was at a premium—carefully guarded, and accessible only to those literate in Latin or Greek. Now, with mass communication, we are smothered by information, most of it useless at best, and confusing and misleading at worst. But knowledge—*information that you can use*—is as precious and as elusive as ever.

If you want to be powerful, learn to winnow the knowledge out of the information. Filter out all the trivia, the hype and the drivel that comprises the bulk of what you see, hear and read. Instead, go for the truth—important facts, accurate theories and well-informed opinion. Start with a sound education and good books. Steer clear of the commercial news media as sources of knowledge until you un-derstand how they work. With very few exceptions, their primary mission is not to transmit knowledge, but to sell products, images and ideas to the audience (and true knowledge often tends to get in the way of that). Talk to people. Expose yourself to new ideas and new experiences. Always be alert to what is going on around you. Pay attention. If in doubt, check it out.

How can knowledge help you to be powerful? Four ways:

- Knowledge of a wider range of possibilities in life can give you better goals and objectives to aim for.
- Knowledge of human nature can give you a better understanding of how other people see the world, how they think, what they do and why they do it.
- Knowing how things work and why things happen can give you a basis for estimating what is likely to result from different kinds of actions, in different situations.
- Greater knowledge of yourself and the world can give you a wider range of possible actions from which to choose.

Take advantage of every opportunity to learn, and keep learning all your life. Don't worry if you can't answer all the questions in "Trivial Pursuit," or you aren't up on the latest sports stars or celebrities: that's only information. It won't help you, but knowledge will. Your life is not a trivial pursuit, and you cannot be powerful if you are ignorant. Learn what is important for your own life, and leave the junk-info to others.

Powerpath 3: *Get it together.*

Sir Galahad had the strength of ten because his heart was pure. What is a pure heart but one free of contradictions and wrong motives? According to Plato a person can be effective only when he has the separate parts of himself properly linked together in well-tempered harmony—one man instead of many. Russian mystic G. I. Gurdjieff likened the typical person to a house with many masters. From moment to moment different masters are in control, directing the person in ways inconsistent with the others.

Power People have focus in their lives. They concentrate on what they want to accomplish. They aren't being pulled in a dozen different directions at once, and they aren't entangled in contradictory motives and values. Work on achieving consistency among your goals and objectives, your capabilities, your values, your actions, the organizations to which you belong and your relationships with other people. Most people live in a constant turmoil of contradictions, and most people aren't very powerful. There is a connection.

Powerpath 4: *Live an upright life.*

The beginning of wisdom is fear of the Lord, the Scriptures tell us. That may be translated to: "Tell the truth and follow the rules." This is ethically correct, and our system of ethics evolved over the eons because it works. In addition to being right, this Powerpath also is just plain smart.

Stick to the truth and you don't have to remember so much. Follow the rules, and decent people will side with you rather than against you. Stay free of transgressions and infractions, and other people will have a harder time controlling you—you give them less leverage.

Dishonesty creates bad feelings and opposition in others, and guilt and contradictions in the perpetrator. In the real world little white lies are sometimes necessary in the service of some greater good, but overall honesty is the best policy. As best you can, follow both the written and unwritten rules you are supposed to live by. Always keep in mind that if you flout a rule you are setting yourself up for trouble in the future, no matter what anyone tells you at the time. One young woman transgressed the rule about keeping her clothes on and struck some erotic nude poses with another woman in front of a camera. This little indiscretion came to a light a few years later, resulting in a bundle of money and publicity for *Penthouse* magazine, and forfeiture of the Miss America title the young woman had won just a few months before.

Powerpath 5: *Take a shot.*

There once was an old man who had lived a good and pious life but in his waning years felt he had nothing to show for it. Finally he fell to his knees and prayed, crying out: "God, hear me. I've been a good man. I've never asked anything of you before, and I'm grateful for all you have given me. So please grant me just one request—let me win the lottery." Weeks passed and nothing happened, so he prayed again to win the lottery. Still nothing. After months of fruitless praying he cried out to the heavens: "God, will you give me a break? All I'm asking is, let me win the lottery!" A voice thundered down out of the sky: "Will you give *me* a break? At least buy a ticket!"

The point is that if you don't play, you won't win. As Ben Gold, my college buddy from Brooklyn, used to say. "You'll always be a boogeyman if you don't take a shot." If you want to attain some goal or reach some objective, you have to go after it. And . . .

Powerpath 6: *Hang in there.*

"If I had to write a handbook for the American entrepreneur and put everything in one sentence I'd say, 'Persevere, no matter the pain, persevere.' " Those are the words of H. Ross Perot, a selfmade billionaire who, among other things, once organized his own commando raid to free two of his employees being held prisoner in Iran.

Nobody can *make* things happen, except God. The best we mortals can do is put ourselves into positions where good things can happen to us, with better or worse odds. When you go after something give it the best shot you can, and if it doesn't happen on the first try, figure out why not, make the necessary adjustments and try again. Keep going after it until you get it. Persistence pays off.

Powerpath 7: *Pick do-able objectives.*

Your chances for success are much better if in the first place you pick objectives which you have a reasonable chance of achieving. Powerpaths 1 and 2 can help you here. You don't want to waste your time and energy trying to batter your way through a stone wall, but neither should you pass up worthwhile goals that you could in fact attain. If you dream of accomplishing something on a grand scale, don't be daunted by the apparent scope of the task. See if you can sort it out into a chain of do-able objectives that lead you to final success.

Powerpath 8: *Don't make a big deal about being the boss.*

Bossing other people is not the same thing as achieving your objectives, unless control is your only objective. Other people's efforts may be necessary for obtaining your goals, but use their help wisely and well. If in a position of power or authority, perform your job carefully and correctly, and don't abuse your position. When in command, command—but above all else, *be fair*. Especially . . .

Powerpath 9: *Don't motivate other people to oppose you.*

Lord knows accomplishing something with everything going in your favor is hard enough. Causing people to seek revenge, and giving others reason to rejoice in your failures and downfall, will only make it more difficult, if not impossible, to reach your objectives. Don't challenge people. Don't threaten them. Don't give others reason to want to get even or to put you in your place. Make friends, not enemies. Being a bad guy can have this kind of impact, as we all know. Bear in mind that shoving your success in other people's faces can do it as well. The ancient Greeks, very equality-minded people, practiced ostracism—banishing undesirable citizens for long periods of time. Generally, they did this not to criminals, but to men whose success provoked envy and jealousy. Enjoy your good fortune and achievements for what they are. Don't use them, as a Control Person would, as a means of putting other people down.

Powerpath 10: *Put your adversities to good use.*

Some people never had a chance to begin with. One man grew up so poor that as a small boy he had to help out the family by selling his mother's homemade silver polish door-to-door, and he was permitted no other activity on Sunday except Bible reading. Another fellow, well, you have to give him credit for a good try. A black man, he survived as a youth by doing stoop labor in farmers' fields. He scraped through college and law school on menial night work—short order cook, night watchman, anything he could get. Once out of law school, none of the city's big law firms would hire him, and he wound up in the ghetto defending pimps, prostitutes and drug dealers. Not exactly a stairway to the stars. But talking about trouble—how about the man who in his early forties was diagnosed as having a heart disease? What could be more hopeless than that?

Actually, the young Bible-reading door-to-door salesman went on to become the most famous, wealthiest advertising copywriter of his time. Claude C. Hopkins learned, from his early selling forays, the psychology of the housewife. His total immersion in the Scriptures taught him a simple, forceful style of writing, and solid, work-oriented values. We met him in Chapter 6 as the author of the Pepsodent campaign.

Our young black lawyer didn't do so badly either. Willie Brown has found in the San Francisco ghetto an impregnable power base. The voters in his district return him, one of their own, time and again to the California State Legislature, where, as Speaker, he is one of the most powerful political figures in the entire nation.

No doubt Nathan Pritikin was discouraged to learn of his heart disease, but it led him to developing a diet and exercise program that kept him going for nearly thirty more years. The Longevity Centers he instituted have similarly benefited thousands of others.

Many of history's greatest books and ideas were born in adversity. Dante wrote *The Divine Comedy* while he was in exile. Would Alexander Solzhenitsyn have won the Nobel Prize for literature in 1970 had he not spent all those miserable years in Stalin's Gulags? Defeats often are only temporary, and they can be more valuable than triumphs. For one thing, they can be very motivating. Also, mistakes and setbacks can give priceless feedback. They can tell you what you are doing wrong; what others do who succeed; and whether you are going after the right thing in the first place. Try to avoid making mistakes, but of course you will make a bunch anyhow. When they happen, use them wisely.

As a personal note, I was delighted to discover that when I became interested in persuasion, power and control, every time somebody gave me grief I could turn it into a field trip. If this book has excited your interest, you can do the same.

And finally . . .

Powerpath 11: *Calm down.*

The *other* inscription on the temple at Delphi was: "Nothing in excess." Centuries of wisdom and the thinking of the great philosophers all point to one conclusion: Be content with what you have. That doesn't mean that you have to give up on trying to improve your life, but think of this. No matter how far you go, there is always something that looks just a little better, just a few steps further ahead. That being the case, slow down and enjoy where you are right now. It looked pretty good just a few steps back, didn't it? Open-ended desires lead to nothing. Plato put it well—"No man is rich whose needs can never be satisfied." Translated to the terms used in this book, keep a lid on the importances you attach to your desires. Don't let them enslave you. The less important they are, the less they hinder you from being truly powerful. If they are too obsessive, they can cause you considerable trouble indeed—look at all the distress precipitated by Captain Ahab's fixation on getting even with Moby Dick.

Don't feel frustrated if you haven't gone as far, or as fast, as you wanted to. What is the ultimate goal of human endeavor, anyway? Hey, don't ask *me*. Smarter people than I have been trying to figure that one out for thousands of years. They're still working on it. Until they come up with The Answer, why not take things just a little easy? Why not join them in their quest?

Subvert the Levers of Control

One side of being powerful is to follow the Eleven Paths to Power. They may seem a bit "square" to someone looking for a quick fix, but, as centuries of experience have demonstrated, in the long run they are infallible. If that isn't obvious, then I have failed in my attempt to explain power to you.

The other side of being powerful is to keep free of other people's control. By that I mean, don't let them manipulate you into doing what is beneficial for them, if it isn't also beneficial for you. People with "street smarts" know something about that already. But decent people often tend to be simple-minded about such matters, particularly when they are young, because they lack the Control Person's instinct for evil (Plato said *that*, too). To make life a little easier for the decent people, here is a quick rundown on how the Control People go about it.

Control Lever 1: *Get into positions or agreements that give you control.*

Set the situation up so that others have to do what you say. As Mel Brooks remarked in his movie *History of the World*—"It's good to be the king!" It's also good to be the owner, the president, the boss or even the boss's wife. There are a multitude of jobs, offices or roles that will let you lord it over somebody. Even just having a flunky assistant is enough for many Control People to vent their tyrannical urges. If you are going to enter an agreement with someone, exploit every weakness and vulnerability, and drive him to the wall with hard bargaining. Be the one to make and/or enforce the rules. Seize every advantage. Always have *your* lawyer draw up the contract. Be sure to be married in *your* church. Conduct the negotiations in *your* office. Anything to ensure that you get the benefit of every doubt.

Control Lever 2: *Surround yourself with weak people.*

Power People are hard to control. You'll have much better luck if you try to control people who are confused, ignorant and disorganized, who are without resources or who are driven by the wrong motives. If you really want to swing with this lever, find people who are obsessed with gambling, addictive drugs and/or illegal sexual practices. Get people like *that* into the right position and they will do anything (I said *any*thing) you tell them. Be careful though, as such as those are unreliable and even dangerous to be around. You'll generally be better off sticking with everyday weaknesses—people saddled with fears and insecurities about jobs, health, loneliness, love or personal worth. You may recall an incident in 1978—the Reverend Jim Jones induced over nine hundred followers in his settlement in Guyana to kill themselves in a massive death orgy. Jones by all accounts was an archetypal Control Person; but his grand finale could never have happened had he not made sure, even before he left the United States, that the people who accompanied him to Guyana were a collection of archetypal Victims.

Control Lever 3: *Eliminate all opposition.*

Cement overshoes? Death squads? *I* never said that. We are talking about the everyday lives of ordinary people. Lethal force will get you in more trouble than it is worth. Try gentler approaches. Send rivals out on errands at opportune times. Talk them into taking jobs at other firms. Get them transferred to positions in faraway locations. Help them decide to go away to college or to try their luck in another town. Don't tell them about the upcoming policy meeting. Get their names removed from the routing list. Discredit their authority or expertise (wit or ridicule may help here). Fix them up with somebody else so as to get their mind off the one you are after. Have them committed or declared incompetent. Bribe them to butt out. If there are more than one, get them to fight among themselves. Isolate your victims from people who might be able to interfere on their behalf. Eliminate them *psychologically* by undermining their self-confidence with doubts and confusion; *legally* by rigging the rules to prevent them from meddling with your plans; *financially* by cutting off their funds; or *politically* by co-opting or corrupting their support. Remember, elimination needn't be permanent, just long enough to get the job done.

Control Lever 4: *Rid yourself of troublesome values.*

Controlling other people will be much easier if you cast off certain values. You do not want your ability to take decisive action hindered by such considerations as kindness, honesty, fairness, compassion, integrity and the like.

Control Lever 5: *Get some kind of hold over people you have to deal with.*

Sometimes you can control people through rewards such as their livelihoods, sexual favors or flattering their vanity. Or you can control them through penalties, based on their fear of being destitute, or being humiliated, or being made to look ridiculous, or being unloved. With a bit of probing and jockeying around, you can often put yourself in control at minimum cost to yourself. Maybe you can get them to compromise themselves by breaking a law, cutting some important corner or doing something disgraceful (Handy hint: Show them only the *prints*. Keep negatives locked up in a safe deposit box.) Sometimes gifts help. For example, get an official to take a bribe (preferably not directly from you). If you can prove he took it, you've got someone there you can count on.

In families, double-binds work wonders. Tie the other members up in value conflicts (for example, "Be manly" . . . but . . . "Don't assert yourself"/"Succeed at your career" . . . but . . ."Don't neglect me and the children"). No matter what they do, you can prove that they were wrong. Then pile on the guilt! A corporate equivalent is "management by multiple criteria." Give your people enough different kinds of objectives to meet, and you can be sure that nobody will measure up on *all* of them. If you then want to get rid of someone, point to the ones he "failed" on as cause for dismissal.

Control Lever 6: *Stay out of sight.*

It's easier to control people if they don't know what you are up to. And if things go sour, you surely don't want the inconvenience of having the police show up at *your* address. So keep a low profile. Use assumed names, and be hard to find. Have others front for you. Work at night, or behind closed doors, or far from the action. Disguise yourself in dress, manner and appearance. Stay behind the scenes. Remember, you're not after glory—you want control.

Control Lever 7: *Show strength, not weakness.*

Don't give anyone any openings. Don't reveal your vulnerabilities. Keep up appearances at all costs. Always be in the right, and put others in the wrong. Make sure that you always come out on top, no matter what you have to do to win. Take the offensive, keep them off balance. Keep the ball in their court, let *them* do the reacting. When you intimidate, retaliate or punish, be swift and merciless. Don't let anybody get away with anything. Don't get mad, get even.

Control Lever 8: *Never . . .*

. . . but that's enough. You get the idea. From a distance Control may to some people seem glamorous or exciting, but from up close it is nothing but shabby. Once the concept of Control is pointed out, most people can recognize it when they encounter it. Control is a constant impediment to Power, and dealing with it is not always easy. If possible stay out of Control situations—circumstances that bring out the Control Person in yourself or that are dominated by someone else in a Control frame of mind. Work on subduing your own Control impulses, and identify the kinds of events and stimuli that trigger them. Your internal Control Person only creates trouble for yourself. Deny it the opportunity.

If the Control problem seems to be at someone else's initiative, try to determine whether you are up against a jerk, a bully or just some ordinary, decent person like yourself who for some reason or other is having a bad day (yes, it happens to everybody, not just you). This is important, because while a jerk may taint your day, a mishandled bully can ruin your life.

Start by trying to get the situation off the Control premise. "A soft answer turneth away wrath," the Scriptures tell us. If you can defuse the impulse (either the other person's, or your own) to make the adversary lose, that may resolve the conflict. Remove the threat or the challenge. Most Control situations can be converted to "I win— you win" propositions if the people involved are of good will. Both parties have legitimate objectives, and things can be worked out so both can achieve them. This approach usually works with the decent people, who are as relieved as you are to be out of a Control situation. Fortunately, most of these encounters do involve decent people, because they so greatly outnumber the others.

A *jerk* has learned through experience that ignoring other people's rights works. They are the ones who leave their cars parked by the gas pumps while they and their families go to the restroom, *after* they have filled their tanks. They are the ones who, no matter how close you stand to the paintings in the museum, crowd in front of you. They aren't against you. They simply don't care about you. Usually, calling their attention to what they are doing is sufficient. They'll give you a blank stare, and they won't apologize. But they'll quit doing it.

Bullies are rare, but resolute. They come in many forms—physical bullies, social bullies, moral bullies, intellectual bullies—but all of them have one common characteristic: They get a thrill out of jerking other people around. That is their main payoff. The final outcome of the situation may not be as important to them as the fact that *they made you lose*. The best tactic with bullies is to avoid having to deal with them in the first place; and over time that is the story of their lives. They become progressively more alienated from humanity, as people learn to steer clear of them. But then, bullies are psychologically alienated right from the start—that's what makes them bullies.

Even if you can avoid them, standing up to them may be the socially responsible course, because as long as they are allowed to get away with it, everybody loses. Bullies pick on Victims, people they know cannot offer effective resistance. For your part, there's no future in being a Victim. But not everyone is up to that kind of confrontation, and there is a chance that it might touch off a never-ending enmity. Some bullies force the issue all the way, ultimately "winning" by making the other person do something despicable in self-defense. You may recall the 1981 incident in Skidmore, Missouri, when parties unknown shot the town bully, Kenrex McElroy. He had left them no choice. It was an embarrassment to law enforcement, but the legal system had proved unable to protect the townspeople from him. In 1985 a Philadelphia radical group, MOVE, bullied their neighbors and the city government so relentlessly that the world finally was treated to the television spectacle of seeing 61 homes burned to the ground, the result of the city's ill-conceived attempt to deal with them. Eleven MOVE members died in the fire, but from their own point of view perhaps they came out on top even at that. Their beliefs and behavior were based on rejecting all established authority as "evil," and their supporters and apologists now point to the debacle as evidence of the "evils of the system."

If you are a mischievious sort, try ordering a Control Person to do something that he or she wants to do anyway. "Go ahead, buy the dress." "I think you *ought* to go out with the guys." This puts *them* in a "no-win" bind. If they don't do it, they deprive themselves; but if they do it, they'll be plagued by the posssibility that you bossed them around. In either case, you spoil the fun of getting away with it.

In one-shot, one-on-one encounters, kindness may be the best weapon of all against bullies. Graciously let them have their way. That also denies them their Big Payoff of getting away with something.

And it ensures that you won't be unjustly unpleasant to someone whose motives you mistook. It also is the most difficult weapon to use, for it requires extinguishing entirely the Control Person streak that we all harbor. Would that we all were capable of such genuinely saintly behavior.

More Power to You!

Control People present one set of potential frustrations to people trying to be powerful, and Control Organizations present another. Organizations are not evil in themselves: only individual people can have motives. Organizational control nevertheless can be an obstacle to those who aspire to be Power People.

"The System" has *always* constrained people's actions, whether it was the church, the king, the government, tradition or some other structure of "have-tos." At the present time, business corporations exert more influence on American behavior than any other type of organization. Most citizens depend upon them for their livelihoods, and they spend the bulk of their daylight hours doing what their employers tell them to. Business also exerts considerable influence on our economic decisions, shaping our desires, fashions, tastes, and leisure activities toward what it can sell us in the marketplace. And since the mass media exist primarily to give advertisers a means by which they can deliver their sales pitches to us, business interests largely shape the picture of the world communicated by our most prevalent information sources. Of course the legal system, the government, the educational system and our culture in general also place structural restrictions on our decisions to do, and not to do, things.

Throughout history, people have always chaffed at the tangle of "have-tos" their respective social organizations have imposed on them. Expression of resentments against "The System" has taken many forms, recently including punk fashions, drug use, graffiti, shoplifting, rude public manners (boom boxes, littering and jabbering in movie theaters, for instance), and protest movements. Certain such movements, for example civil rights in the 1960s and unions in the early part of the century, were in response to genuine social injustice—some classes of

.

226

society were getting badly mauled by it, and structural changes had to be made. More recently, Ralph Nader's consumer movement and the environmentalists have tapped public resentments against control by Big Business, and the women's movement has given expression to frustrations some women feel with what they perceive to be traditional authority relationships between the sexes. In a sense, jazz and rock-and-roll music can be seen as American protests against control—we'll enjoy *our* music, and we'll play it *our* way, not how somebody else has written down that we *should* play it. It is no accident that these originated with blacks and initially appealed primarily to young people and others outside the establishment. Nor should it surprise us that various governments have tried to ban them or at least keep them tightly restricted.

Sadly, many Americans confuse thwarting "The System" with being free or being powerful. It is easy enough to resist social control in America. Many people make a good living doing that. But resisting control takes us only half way toward power. One also must be moving forward toward his or her own important objectives. And here is an astonishing fact—individuals can do that in just about any social system, democratic or dictatorial, free or slave. Freedom and power are states of minds, and "fighting the system" sometimes is not a powerful response at all, but merely the only thing a Control Person or a Victim can think to do. Human beings have never existed for long without some kind of system, for life is next to impossible without social organization. The idea is to master the system and use it to attain your own objectives—it can be a great help, if you know how to tap it.

If it hasn't come through clearly by now, let me say it one last time. Power is a positive thing. Control is for losers. Plato in his *Republic* explored the way to the Just Life, and ever the lover of mathematics, he calculated that the "kingly life" (the Power approach) is 729 times more pleasant than the life of a despot (the Control approach). Christianity is an empowering belief system, as are other religions. Speaking to the everyday life of the common man, the Gospel of Mark (4:20) tells us that "Those who take the Word to heart yield at thirty- and sixty- and a hundredfold."

That is my advice to you. Screw Control. Go for Power. We began the book with some apparently skeptical remarks about love. Let's bow to symmetry and close on the same subject. Did you understand what I've been saying? Then this will make sense: Love means helping the other person to be powerful. It's not poetic. It's not romantic. It's not sentimental. But it's entirely functional. Think about it. And . . . more power to you!

APPENDIX

The Choice Evaluation Array:
The criteria by which choices are weighed at each step
in the Action Decision Sequence

$$\text{Relative Appeal (RA)} = f(M) - f(D)$$

WHERE

M = Motivators (potential rewards and prescriptive values)
D = Demotivators (potential penalties and proscriptive values)

More specifically, at any instant, t,

$$RA = f\left(\sum_{i=1}^{m} I_{Ri} * P_{Ri} + \sum_{i=1}^{n} I_{VPi} * S_{VPi}\right) - f\left(\sum_{i=1}^{j} I_{Pi} * P_{Pi} + \sum_{i=1}^{k} I_{VNi} * S_{VNi}\right)$$

m = number of potential rewards perceived by Actor

I_{Ri} = importance of reward Ri to Actor

P_{Ri} = Actor's estimate of the probability that reward Ri will result from making that choice

n = number of prescriptive (positive) values perceived by Actor

I_{VPi} = importance of positive value VPi to Actor

S_{VPi} = perceived salience of prescriptive value VPi to the decision being considered

j = number of potential penalties perceived by Actor

I_{Pi} = importance of penalty Pi to Actor

P_{Pi} = Actor's estimate that penalty Pi will result from making that choice

k = number of proscriptive (negative) values perceived by Actor

I_{VNi} = importance of negative value VNi to Actor

S_{VNi} = perceived salience of negative value VNi to the choice being considered

BIBLIOGRAPHY

Aaker, David A., and J. G. Myers (1975), *Advertising Management*. Englewood Cliffs, N.J.: Prentice-Hall.

Abernathy, William J., and James M. Utterbeck (1978), "Patterns of Industrial Innovation," *Technology Review*, 80 (June/July) 141–47.

Ahtola, Olli T. (1975), "The Vector Model of Preferences: An Alternative to the Fishbein Model," *Journal of Marketing Research*, 12 (February): 52–59.

Alderson, Wroe (1957), *Marketing Behavior and Executive Action*. Homewood, Ill.: Richard D. Irwin.

Allport, Gordon W. (1967), "Attitudes" in M. Fishbein (ed.), *Readings in Attitude Theory and Measurement*. New York: John Wiley.

Ansoff, H. Igor, and John M. Stewart (1967), "Strategies for a Technology-based Business," *Harvard Business Review* (November–December): 71–83.

Aronson, Elliot (1968), "Dissonance, Expectation and the Self," in R. Abelson, *et al.*, (eds.), *Theories of Cognitive Consistency: A Sourcebook*. Chicago: Rand McNally.

———— (1969), "The Theory of Cognitive Dissonance: A Current Perspective," in L. Berkowitz (ed.), *Advances in Experimental Psychology*, Vol. 4. New York: Academic Press.

Atkinson, J. W. (1964), *An Introduction to Motivation*. Princeton: D. Van Nostrand Co.

Axelrod, Robert (1984), *The Evolution of Cooperation*. New York: Basic Books.

Bach, George R., and P. Wyden (1968), *The Intimate Enemy*. New York: William Morrow.

Bagozzi, Richard P. (1981), "Attitudes, Intentions and Behavior: A Test of Some Key Hypotheses," *Journal of Personality and Social Psychology*, 41, 4: 607–27.

———— (1982), "A Field Investigation of Causal Relations Among Cognitions, Affect, Intentions and Behavior, *Journal of Marketing Research*, 19 (November): 562–83.

———— and F. M. Nicosia, (1980), "On the Distinction Between Cognition and Motivation in Consumer Research," Alfred P. Sloan School of Management, Massachusetts Institute of Technology, Cambridge, Mass.

Barker, Roger C. (1968), *Ecological Psychology*. Stanford: Stanford University Press.

Barnard, Chester I. (1968), *The Functions of the Executive*. Cambridge, Mass.: Harvard University Press.

Bauer, Raymond A. (1964), "The Obstinate Audience," *American Psychologist*, 19 (May): 319–38.

Baum, L. Frank (1900), *The Wizard of Oz*. New York: Grosset & Dunlap.

Bearden, William O. and A. G. Woodside (1976), "Interaction of Consumption

Situations and Brand Attitudes," *Journal of Applied Psychology*, 61 (December): 764–69.

Becker, Ernest (1974), *The Denial of Death*. New York: The Free Press.

——— (1975), *Escape From Evil*. New York: The Free Press.

Belk, Russell W. (1974), "An Exploratory Assessment of Situational Effects in Buyer Behavior," *Journal of Marketing Research*, 11 (May): 156–63.

——— (1975), "Situational Variables and Consumer Behavior," *Journal of Consumer Research*, 2 (December): 257–64.

Bell, Gerald D. (1967), "Self-confidence and Persuasion in Car Buying," *Journal of Marketing Research*, 4 (February): 46–53.

Benson, John M. (1981), "The Polls: A Rebirth of Religion?" *Public Opinion Quarterly*, 45 (Winter): 576–85.

Benson, Purnell H. (1960), *Religion in Contemporary Culture*. New York: Harper and Brothers.

Bernardo, John J. and J. M. Blin (1977), "A Programming Model of Consumer Choice among Multi-Attributed Brands," *Journal of Consumer Research*, 4 (September): 111–19.

Berne, Eric (1964), *The Games People Play*. New York: Grove Press.

Berryman, Jack W. (1975), "From the Cradle to the Playing Field: America's Emphasis on Highly Organized Competitive Sports for Pre-adolescent Boys," *Journal of Sport History*, 2 (Fall): 112–44.

Bettman, James R. (1970), "Information Processing Models of Consumer Behavior," *Journal of Marketing Research*, 7 (August): 370–76.

———, N. Capon and R. J. Lutz (1975), "Cognitive Algebra in Multi-Attribute Attitude Models," *Journal of Marketing Research*, 12 (May): 151–64.

Bither, Stewart and P. Wright (1977), "Preference Between Product Consultants: Choice vs. Preference Functions," *Journal of Consumer Reserach*, 4 (June): 39–47.

Bittman, Ladislav (1985), *The KGB and Secret Disinformation: An Insider's View*. New York: Pergamon-Brassey's.

Blake, Robert R., and J. S. Mouton (1964), *The Managerial Grid*. Houston: Gulf Publishing Co.

Blumstein, Philip, and P. Schwartz (1983), *American Couples*. New York: William Morrow.

Bogart, Leo, S. B. Tolley and F. Orenstein (1970), "What One Little Ad Can Do," *Journal of Advertising Research*, 10 (August): 3–14.

Boorstin, Daniel J. (1961), *The Image*. New York: Harper Colophon Books.

——— (1965), *The Americans: The National Experience*. New York: The Vintage Press.

——— (1973), *The Americans: The Democratic Experience*. New York: Random House.

Boy Scout Fieldbook (1978). New York: Workman Publishing.

Boyd, Harper W. Jr., M. L. Ray and E. C. Strong (1972), "An Attitudinal Framework for Advertising Strategy," *Journal of Marketing*, 36 (April): 27–33.

Burnett, John J. and R. E. Wilkes (1980), "Fear Appeals to Segments Only," *Journal of Advertising Research*, 20 (October): 21–24.

Burns, Edward McNall, R. E. Lerner and S. Meacham (1980), *Western Civilizations* (9th ed.). New York: W. W. Norton.

Burton, Richard F. (1932), *The Arabian Nights*. New York: Blue Ribbon Books.

Busch, Paul and D. T. Wilson (1976), "An Experimental Analysis of a Salesman's Expert and Referent Bases of Social Power in the Buyer-Seller Dyad," *Journal of Marketing Research*, 13 (February): 3–11.

Campbell, Donald T. (1975), "On the Conflicts Between Biological and Social Evolution and Between Psychology and Moral Tradition," *American Psychologist*, 30 (December): 1103–26.

Carnegie, Dale (1936), *How to Win Friends and Influence People*. New York: Simon & Schuster.

Caro, Robert A. (1982), *The Years of Lyndon Johnson: The Path to Power*. New York: Alfred A. Knopf.

Carroll, Lewis (n.d.), *Alice's Adventures in Wonderland and Through the Looking Glass*. New York: Illustrated Editions Company.

Cartwright, Dorwin (1959), *Studies in Social Power*. Ann Arbor, Mich.: Institute for Social Research.

Castenada, Carlos (1972), *Journey to Ixtlan*. New York: Simon & Schuster.

Caudill, Harry M. (1983), *Theirs Be The Power: The Moguls of Eastern Kentucky*, Urbana, Ill.: University of Illinois Press.

Chandler, Alfred D. Jr. (1962), *Strategy and Structure*. Cambridge, Mass: M.I.T. Press.

——— (1977), *The Visible Hand*. Cambridge, Mass.: The Belknap Press.

Chaucer, Geoffrey (1952), *The Canterbury Tales*. Translated by N. Coghill. Baltimore: Penguin Books.

Clawson, C. Joseph and D. E. Vinson (1978), "Human Values: A Historical and Interdisciplinary Analysis," in H. K. Hunt (ed.), *Advances in Consumer Research*, 5: 392–402.

Clemmens, Samuel (1928), "The Man That Corrupted Hadleyburg," "My First Lie and How I Got Out of It," and "The Mysterious Stranger," in *The Complete Works of Mark Twain*, New York: Harper and Brothers.

Cochran, Thomas C. (1972), *Social Change in Industrial Society: Twentieth Century America*. London: G. Allen & Unwin.

Colley, Russell H. (1961), *Defining Advertising Goals for Measured Advertising Results*. New York: Association for National Advertisers.

Cox, Donald F. and R. A. Bauer (1964), "Self-confidence and Persuasibility in Women," *Public Opinion Quarterly*, 28 (Fall): 453–66.

———, and S. Rich (1964), "Perceived Risk and Consumer Decision Making," *Journal of Marketing Research*, 1 (November): 32–39.

Crespi, Irving (1971) "What Kinds of Attitude Measures Are Predictive of Behavior?" *Public Opinion Quarterly*, 35 (Fall): 327–334.

Cummings, William H. and M. Vankatesan (1976), "Cognitive Dissonance and Consumer Behavior: A Review of the Evidence," *Journal of Marketing Research*, 13 (August): 303–8.

Cunningham, Francis L. B. (1959), *The Christian Life*. Dubuque, Iowa: The Priory Press.

Cyert, Richard M., and J. G. March (1963), *A Behavioral Theory of the Firm*. Englewood Cliffs, N.J.: Prentice-Hall.

Davis, Harry L. (1976), "Decision Making Within the Household," *Journal of Consumer Research*, 2 (March): 241–60.

Day, George S. (1972), "Evaluating Models of Attitude Structure," *Journal of Marketing Research*, 9 (August): 279–86.

Doob, Leonard W. (1949), "The Strategies of Psychological Warfare," *Public Opinion Quarterly*, 13 (Winter): 635–44.

——— (1950), "Goebbel's Principles of Propaganda," *Public Opinion Quarterly*, (Fall): 419–42.

Dostoyevski, Fyodor. *The Brothers Karamazov*. Translated by Constance Garnett. New York: Signet, 1957.

Drucker, Peter F. (1973), *Management*. New York: Harper & Row.

Dunstan, J. Leslie (1962), *Protestantism*. New York: George Braziller.

Edwards, A. L. (1953), "The Relationship Between the Judged Desirability of A Trait and the Probability that the Trait will be Endorsed," *Journal of Applied Psychology*, 37: 90–93.

Emerson, Richard M. (1962), "Power-Dependence Relations," *American Sociological Review*, 27: 31–41.

Engel, James F., and R. D. Blackwell (1982), *Consumer Behavior* (4th ed.). Hinsdale, Ill.: The Dryden Press.

Epstein, Edward Jay (1982), "Have You Ever Tried to Sell a Diamond?" *Atlantic Monthly* (February): 23ff.

Ettema, James S., and D. C. Whitney (eds.) (1982), *Individuals in Mass Media Organizations*, Beverly Hills: Sage Publications.

Etter, William L. (1975), "Attitude Theory and Decision Theory: Where is the Common Ground?" *Journal of Marketing Research*, 12 (November): 481–83.

Evans, Franklyn B. (1963), "Selling as a Dyadic Relationship," *American Behavioral Scientist*, 6 (May): 76–79.

Fabun, Don (1967), *The Dynamics of Change*. Englewood Cliffs, N.J.: Prentice-Hall.

Farris, George F. (1981), "Groups and Informal Organization," in R. Payne and C. Cooper (eds.), *Groups at Work*. New York: John Wiley.

Festinger, Leon (1957), *A Theory of Cognitive Dissonance*. Stanford: Stanford University Press.

——— and J. M. Carlsmith (1959), "Cognitive Consequences of Forced Compliance," *Journal of Abnormal and Social Psychology*, 58: 359–66.

——— and N. Maccoby (1964), "On Resistance to Persuasive Communications," *Journal of Abnormal and Social Psychology*, 68: 359–66.

Fishbein, Martin (1967), "A Consideration of Beliefs and their Role in Attitude Measurement," in M. Fishbein (ed.), *Readings in Attitude Theory and Measurement*. New York: John Wiley.

———— (1967), "A Behavior Theory Approach to the Relations Between Beliefs and an Object and Attitudes Toward the Object" in M. Fishbein (ed.), *Readings in Attitude Theory and Measurement*. New York: John Wiley.

———— (1967), "Attitude and Prediction of Behavior," in M. Fishbein (ed.), *Readings in Attitude Theory and Measurement*. New York: John Wiley.

———— (1973), "The Search for Attitudinal-Behavioral Consistency," in H. II. Kassarjian and T. S. Robertson (eds.), *Perspectives in Consumer Behavior*. Glenview, Ill.: Scott, Foresman and Co.

———— and I. Ajzen (1975). *Belief, Attitude, Intention and Behavior: An Introduction to Theory and Research*. Reading, Mass.: Addison-Wesley.

Fisher, Roger, and William Ury (1981), *Getting to Yes*. Boston: Houghton Mifflin.

Frank, Adolphe (1967), *The Kabbalah*. New Hyde Park, N.Y.: University Books.

Frame, Donald M. (1948), *The Complete Works of Montaigne*. Stanford, Calif.: Stanford University Press.

French, John R. P., and B. Raven (1959), "The Basis of Social Power," in D. Cartwright (ed.), *Studies in Social Power*. Ann Arbor, Mich.: Institute for Social Research.

Friedman, Milton, and R. Friedman (1984), *Tyranny of the Status Quo*. New York: Harcourt, Brace, Jovanovich.

Fromm, Eric (1941), *Escape from Freedom*. New York: Farrar & Rinehart.

———— (1947), *Man For Himself*. New York: Rinehart.

———— (1955), *The Sane Society*. New York: Rinehart.

———— (1956), *The Art of Loving*. New York: Harper and Brothers.

Funkhouser, G. Ray (1973), "The Issues of the '60s: An Exploratory Study in the Dynamics of Public Opinion," *Public Opinion Quarterly*, 37 (Spring): 62–75.

———— (1973), "Trends in Media Coverage of the Issues of the '60s," *Journalism Quarterly*, 50 (Autumn): 220–26.

———— (1979), "How Cost Accounting Systems Can Affect Organizational Behavior," *Management Review* (October): 71–73.

———— (1980), "Attitudes and Morale Assessment," in K. A. Albert (ed.), *Handbook of Business Problem Solving*. New York: McGraw-Hill, 5:13–5:32.

———— (1980), "A Model of Persuasion as a Pure Power Game" (Roundtable discussion), Annual Conference of the American Association for Public Opinion Research, Kings Island, Ohio, May 31.

———— (1984), "A New Approach to Understanding the Persuasion Process," Annual Conference of the American Association for Public Opinion Research, Delavan, Wisconsin, May 18.

———— (1984), "A Practical Theory of Persuasion Based on Behavioral Science Approaches," *Journal of Personal Selling of Sales Management*, 4 (November): 17–25.

―――― (1984), "Using Qualitative Historical Observations in Predicting the Future," *Futures* (April): 173–82.

―――― (forthcoming), "The Engineering of Decisions: An Action-Based Theory of Persuasion," in R. P. Bagozzi (ed.), *Advances in Communication and Marketing Research*. Greenwich, Conn.: JAI Press.

―――― and David Popoff (1969), "Your Thoughts on Crime and Punishment," *Psychology Today* (November): 53–58.

―――― and R. R. Rothberg (1985), "The Dogma of Growth: A Reexamination," *Business Horizons*, 28 (March/April): 9–16.

―――― with R. Richard Ritti (1977), *The Ropes to Skip and the Ropes to Know: Studies in Organizational Behavior*. Columbus, Ohio: Grid Publishing Inc.

Galbraith, John K. (1975), *Money*. Boston: Houghton Mifflin.

―――― (1983), *The Anatomy of Power*. Boston: Houghton Mifflin.

Gay, Peter (1967), *The Enlightenment: An Interpretation*. New York: Alfred A. Knopf.

Gemperlein, Joyce (1985), "The Power of Politeness," (Philadelphia) *Inquirer* (January 6): 22 ff.

Gibran, Kahlil (1923), *The Prophet*. New York: Alfred A. Knopf.

Goffman, Erving (1952), "On Cooling the Mark Out: Some Aspects of Adaptation to Failure," *Psychiatry*, 15.

―――― (1959), *The Presentation of Self in Everyday Life*. New York: Doubleday.

Goldman, Eric S. (1981), in *Reflections on America*. Washington, D.C.: U.S. Bureau of the Census.

Green, Paul E., and Y. Wind (1973), *Multiattribute Decisions in Marketing*. Hinsdale, Ill.: The Dryden Press.

Greenberg, Marshall G., and P. E. Green (1974), "Multidimensional Scaling," in R. Ferber (ed.), *Handbook of Marketing Research*. New York: McGraw-Hill.

Greenstein, Fred I. (1983), *The Hidden Hand Presidency: Eisenhower as Leader*. New York: Basic Books.

Griffin, Donald R. (1984), *Animal Thinking*. Cambridge, Mass.: Harvard University Press.

Haley, Russell I. (1968), "Benefit Segmentation: A Decision-Oriented Research Tool," *Journal of Marketing*, 32 (July): 30–35.

Hansen, Flemming (1969), "Consumer Choice Behavior: An Experimental Approach," *Journal of Marketing Research*, 3 (December): 132–37.

―――― (1976), "Psychological Theories of Consumer Choice," *Journal of Consumer Research*, 3 (December): 132–37.

Harris, Thomas (1969), *I'm OK, You're OK*. New York: Harper & Row.

Harsanyi, John C. (1977), *Rational Behavior and Bargaining Equilibrium in Games and Social Situations*. Cambridge: Cambridge University Press.

Hayakawa, S. I. (1968), "Mass Media and Family Communications," 76th Annual Convention of the American Psychological Association, San Francisco, September 2.

Hartley, Robert F. (1981), *Marketing Mistakes*. Columbus, Ohio: Grid Publishing Inc.

Heider, Fritz (1958), *The Psychology of Interpersonal Relations*. New York: John Wiley.

Heilbroner, Robert L. (1976), *Business Civilization in Decline*. New York: W. W. Norton.

Heller, Joseph (1974), *Something Happened*. New York: Alfred A. Knopf.

Hendrick, Clyde, J. Mills and C. A. Kiesler (1968), "Decision Time as a Function of the Number and Complexity of Equally Attractive Alternatives," *Journal of Personality and Social Psychology*, 8 (June): 313–18.

Henry, Walter A. (1976), "Cultural Values do Correlate with Consumer Behavior," *Journal of Marketing Research*, 13 (May): 121–27.

Herzberg, Frederick (1966), *Work and the Nature of Man*. New York: World Publishing Company.

Hilgard, Ernest and R. Atkinson (1967), *Introduction to Psychology*. New York: Harcourt, Brace and World.

Hirschman, Elizabeth C. (1981), "American Jewish Ethnicity: Its Relationship to Some Selected Aspects of Consumer Behavior," *Journal of Marketing*, 45 (Summer): 102–10.

Hoffer, Eric (1951), *The True Believer*. New York: Harper & Row.

———— (1964), *The Ordeal of Change*. New York: Harper Colophon Books.

Hofstadter, Richard (1955), *The Age of Reform*. New York: Alfred A. Knopf.

Holden, Constance (1978), "The Criminal Mind: A New Look at an Ancient Puzzle," *Science*, 199 (3 February): 511–14.

Hopkins, Claude C. (1936), *My Life in Advertising*. New York: Harper and Brothers.

Homans, George C. (1983), "Steps to a Theory of Social Behavior," *Theory and Society*, 12 (January): 1–46.

Homer (1950), *The Iliad*. Translated by A. Lang, W. Leaf and E. Myers. New York: Modern American Library.

———— (1950), *The Odyssey*. Translated by S. H. Butcher and A. Lang. New York: Modern American Library.

Hooper, Michael (1983), "The Motivational Bases of Political Behavior: A New Concept and Measurement Procedure," *Public Opinion Quareterly*, 47 (Winter): 497–515.

Hovland, Carl I., A. A. Lumsdaine and F. D. Sheffield (1949), *Experiments on Mass Communication*. Princeton: Princeton University Press.

————, I. L. Janis and H. H. Kelley (1953), *Communication and Persuasion*. New Haven, Conn.: Yale University Press.

Howard, John A. (1977), *Consumer Behavior: Application of Theory*. New York; McGraw-Hill.

————, and J. Sheth (1969), *The Theory of Buyer Behavior*. New York: John Wiley.

Hoyer, Wayne D. (1984), "An Examination of Consumer Decision Making for a Common Repeat Purchase Product," *Journal of Consumer Research*, 11 (December): 822–29.

Huber, Joel (1975), "Predicting Preferences on Experimental Bundles of Attributes: A Comparison of Models," *Journal of Marketing Research*, 12 (August), 290–97.

Hughes, G. David and J. L. Guerrero (1971), "Testing Cognitive Models Through Computer-Controlled Experiments," *Journal of Marketing Research*, 8 (August): 291–97.

Hull, Clark L. (1943), *Principles of Behavior*. New York: Appleton-Century.

Hyman, Herbert H. and P. B. Sheatsley (1974), "Some Reasons Why Information Campaigns Fail," *Public Opinion Quarterly*, 11: 413–23.

Jacoby, Jacob, D. Speller and C. Kohn (1974), "Brand Choice Behavior as a Function of Information Load," *Journal of Marketing Research*, 11 (February): 63–69.

Janis, Irving L. (1963), "Personality as a Factor in Susceptibility to Persuasion," in W. Schramm (ed.), *The Science of Human Communication*. New York: Basic Books.

———, and L. Mann (1977), *Decision Making*. New York: The Free Press.

Johnson, Paul (1983), *Modern Times*. New York: Harper & Row.

Johnson, Richard M. (1974), "Trade-off Analysis of Consumer Values," *Journal of Marketing Research*, 11 (May): 121–27.

Kahneman, Daniel and A. Tversky (1979), "Prospect Theory: An Analysis of Decision Under Risk," *Econometrika*, 47 (March): 263–91.

Kassarjian, Harold H. (1973), "Consumer Behavior: A Field Theoretical Approach," in H. H. Kassarjian and T. S. Robertson (eds.), *Perspectives in Consumer Behavior*. Glenview, Ill.: Scott-Foresman.

——— (1978), "Presidential Address, 1977: Anthropomorphism and Parsimony," in H. Keith Hunt (ed.), *Advances in Consumer Research*, Vol. 5, Ann Arbor, Mich.: Association for Consumer Research.

Katona, George (1953), "Rational Behavior and Economic Behavior," *Psychological Review*, 60 (May): 307–10.

Katz, Daniel, and R. L. Kahn (1966), *The Social Psychology of Organizations*. New York: John Wiley.

Kazantzakis, Nikos (1959), *Zorba the Greek*. New York: Simon & Schuster.

Keidan, Bruce (1977), "How Lou Brock Has Come to Steal Immortality," *Philadelphia Inquirer*, (28 August): 1–E.

Kelman, Herbert C. (1961), "Processes of Opinion Change," *Public Opinion Quarterly*, 25 (Spring): 57–78.

Kennedy, William (1984), *Ironweed*. New York: Penguin Books.

Kiley, Dan (1983), *The Peter Pan Syndrome*. New York: Avon Books.

Korda, Michael (1976), *Power!* New York: Ballantine Books.

Korzybski, Alfred (1948), *Science and Sanity*. Lakeview, Conn.: Institute of General Semantics.

Kotler, Philip (1980), *Marketing Management* (4th ed.). Englewood Cliffs, N.J.: Prentice-Hall.

Krech, David, R. S. Crutchfield and E. L. Ballachey (1962), *Individual in Society*. New York: McGraw-Hill.

Krugman, Herbert E. (1965), "The Measurement of Advertising Involvement," *Public Opinion Quarterly*, 29 (Fall): 349–56.

——— (1972), "Why Three Exposures May Be Enough," *Journal of Advertising Research*, 12 (December): 11–14.

LaPierre, Richard T. (1934), "Attitudes vs. Actions," *Social Forces*, 13: 230–37.

Laqueur, Walter (1980), *The Terrible Secret*. New York: Little, Brown.

Larson, Erik (1980), "Mafia's Frank Sindone Gladly Provided Loans—at Interest of 180%," *Wall Street Journal* (22 December): 1.

Lasch, Christopher (1984), *The Minimal Self*. New York: W. W. Norton.

Lasswell, Harold D. (1967), *Power and Personality*. New York: The Viking Press.

Lawrence, T. E. (1926), *Seven Pillars of Wisdom*. New York: Doubleday.

LeCarre, John (1963), *The Spy Who Came in from the Cold*. New York: Coward-McCann.

Lee, Gary R., and R. W. Clyde (1974), "Religion, Socioeconomic Stature and Anomie," *Journal for the Scientific Study of Religion*, 13 (March): 35–47.

Levitt, Theodore (1967), "Communications and Industrial Selling," *Journal of Marketing*, 31 (April): 15–21.

Levy, Alan (1983), *Ezra Pound: The Voice of Silence*. Sag Harbor, N.Y.: The Permanent Press.

Levy, Sidney J. (1981), "Interpreting Consumer Mythology: A Structural Approach to Consumer Behavior," *Journal of Marketing*, 45 (Summer): 49–61.

Lewin, Kurt (1935), *A Dynamic Theory of Personality*. New York: McGraw-Hill.

——— (1951), *Field Theory in Social Science*. New York: Harper and Brothers.

Linton, Harriet and E. Graham (1959), "Personality Correlates of Persuasibility," in C. I. Hovland and I. L. Janis (eds.), *Personality and Persuasibility*. New Haven: Yale University Press.

Lipman, Joanne (1984), "Owners Who Stay Put Play a Part in Shaping the American Skyline," *Wall Street Journal* (22 May): 1.

Lipset, Seymour M. and W. Schneider (1983), *The Confidence Gap*. New York: The Free Press.

Lomax, Alan (1960), *The Folk Songs of North America*. New York: Doubleday.

Lutz, Richard L. (1975), "Changing Brand Attitudes through Modification of Cognitive Structure," *Journal of Consumer Research*, 1 (March): 49–59.

Maccoby, Nathan (1963), "The New Scientific Rhetoric," in W. Schramm (ed.), *The Science of Human Communication*. New York: Basic Books.

Machiavelli, Niccolo (1961), *The Prince*. Baltimore: Penguin Books.

Mackay, Charles (1932), *Extraordinary Popular Delusions and the Madness of Crowds*. New York: Farrar, Straus and Giroux.

Malinowski, Bronislaw (1948), *Magic, Science and Religion and Other Essays*. New York: The Free Press.

Manchester, William R. (1978), *American Caesar, Douglas MacArthur 1880–1964*. Boston: Little Brown.

Mao Tse-tung. *Quotations from Chairman Mao Tse-tung.* Peking: Foreign Languages Press, 1967.

March, James G. and H. A. Simon (1958), *Organizations.* New York: John Wiley.

Maslow, Abraham H. (1970), *Motivation and Personality.* New York: Harper & Row.

Mayer, David and H. M. Greenberg (1964), "What Makes a Good Salesman?" *Harvard Business Review* (July–August): 119–25.

Mazzei, George (1983), *The New Office Etiquette.* New York: Poseidon Press.

McClelland, David C. (1961), *The Achieving Society.* Princeton: D. Van Nostrand Co.

——— (1970), "The Two Faces of Power," *Journal of International Affairs,* 24 (January): 29–47.

McCombs, Maxwell E., and Donald L. Shaw (1972), "The Agenda-Setting Function of the Mass Media," *Public Opinion Quarterly,* 36 (Summer): 176–87.

McGregor, Douglas (1960), *The Human Side of Enterprise.* New York: McGraw-Hill.

McGuire, William J. (1969), "The Nature of Attitudes and Attitude Change," in G. Lindzey and E. Aronson (eds.), *The Handbook of Social Psychology* (2nd ed.). Reading, Mass.: Addison-Wesley.

——— (1969), "An Information-Processing Model of Advertising Effectiveness," paper presented at the Behavioral and Management Science in Marketing Symposium, University of Chicago, June 29–July 1.

——— (1973), "Source Variables in Persuasion," in Ithiel de Sola Pool, et al. (eds.), *Handbook of Communication.* Chicago: Rand McNally.

McLuhan, Marshall (1964), *Understanding Media.* New York: Signet Books.

McMurry, Robert N. (1961), "The Mystique of Supersalesmanship," *Harvard Business Review,* 39 (March–April): 113–22.

Michaud, Stephen G., and H. Aynesworth (1983), *The Only Living Witness.* New York: The Linden Press.

Michener, James A. (1976), *Sports in America.* New York: Random House.

Milgram, Stanley S. (1965), "Some Conditions of Obedience and Disobedience to Authority," *Human Relations,* 18: 57–76.

Miller, George A. (1956), "The Magical Number Seven, Plus or Minus Two: Some Limits on Our Capacity for Processing Information," *Psychological Review,* 63 (March): 81–97.

Miller, Neil E. and J. Dollard (1941), *Social Learning and Imitation.* New Haven: Yale University Press.

Mills, Judson (1965), "Effects of Certainty About a Decision upon Post Decision Exposure to Consonant and Dissonant Information," *Journal of Personality and Social Psychology,* 2: 749–52.

Milton, John (1963), "Paradise Lost," in John T. Shawcross (ed.) *The Complete English Poetry of John Milton.* Garden City, New York: Anchor Books.

Mindell, Mark G., and W. I. Gordon (1981), *Employee Values in a Changing Society,* New York: American Management Association.

Miniard Paul W., and Joel B. Cohen (1983), "Modeling Personal and Normative Influences," *Journal of Consumer Research,* 10 (September): 159–80.

Mishima, Yukio (1965), *The Sailor Who Fell from Grace with the Sea.* New York: Alfred A. Knopf.

Mitchell, Arnold (1983), *The Nine American Lifestyles.* New York: Macmillan.

Molloy, John T. (1975), *Dress for Success.* New York: Warner Books.

Monroe, Kent B. (1973), "Buyers' Subjective Perceptions of Price," *Journal of Marketing Research,* 10 (February): 70–80.

Murray, Henry A., et al. (1938), *Explorations in Personality.* New York: Oxford University Press.

Musashi, Miyamoto (1982), *The Book of Five Rings.* New York: Bantam Books.

The New American Bible (1970). Encino, California: Benziger, a division of Glencoe Publishing Company.

Newcomb, Theodore M. (1958), "Attitude Development as a Function of Reference Groups: The Bennington Study," in E. E. Maccoby, T. M. Newcomb and E. L. Hartley (eds.), *Readings in Social Psychology.* New York: Holt, Rinehart and Winston.

Newell, Alan and H. A. Simon (1972), *Human Problem Solving.* Englewood Cliffs, N.J.: Prentice-Hall.

Newman, Joseph W. (1977), "Consumer External Search: Amount and Determinants," in A. G. Woodside, et al., (eds.) *Consumer and Industrial Buying Behavior.* New York: North-Holland Publishing Co.

Nicosia, Francesco M. (1966), *Consumer Decision Processes.* Englewood Cliffs, N.J.: Prentice-Hall.

——— (1978), "Brand Choice: Toward Behavioral-Behavioristic Models," In H. L. Davis and A. J. Silk (eds.), *Behavioral and Management Science in Marketing.* New York: Ronald Press.

Noelle-Neumann, Elisabeth (1974), "The Spiral of Silence: A Theory of Public Opinion," *Journal of Communication,* 24 (Spring): 43–51.

——— (1985), "Identifying Opinion Leaders," 38th ESOMAR Congress, Wiesbaden (September 1–5).

Norris, Vincent P. (1980), "Advertising History—According to the Textbooks," *Journal of Advertising,* 9 (March): 3–11.

North, Douglas C., (1981), *Structure and Change in Economic History.* New York: W. W. Norton.

Ogilvy, David (1963), *Confessions of an Advertising Man.* New York: Dell.

Olshavsky, Richard W. and D. H. Granbois (1979), "Consumer Decision Making—Fact or Fiction," *Journal of Consumer Research,* 6 (September): 93–100.

Ordiorne, George S. (1965), *Management by Objectives.* Belmont, Calif.: Pitman Publishing.

Ortega y Gasset, Jose. *Man and Crisis.* New York: W. W. Norton, 1958.

Ortiz, Darwin (1984), *Gambling Scams.* New York: Dodd, Mead & Co.

Orwell, George (1956), *The Orwell Reader.* New York: Harcourt, Brace.

•

———— (1979), *1984*. New York: Harcourt, Brace, Jovanovich.

———— (1985), *Orwell: The Last Writings*. New York: Arbor House.

Orwell, Sonia, and I. Angus (eds.) (1968), *The Collected Essays, Journalism and Letters of George Orwell, Vol. 2: My Country Right or Left, 1940–1943*. New York: Harcourt, Brace & World.

Osgood, Charles E., and P. H. Tannenbaum (1955), "The Principle of Congruity in the Prediction of Attitude Change," *Psychological Review*, 62: 42–55.

Ouspensky, P. D. (1949), *In Search of the Miraculous*. New York: Harcourt, Brace.

Packard, Vance (1958), *The Hidden Persuaders*. New York: Pocket Books.

Park, C. Whan (1978), "A Conflict Resolution Choice Model," *Journal of Consumer Research*, 5 (September): 124–27.

Parsons, Talcott (1963), "On the Concept of Influence," *Public Opinion Quarterly*, 27 (Spring): 37–62.

Parsons, Talcott and E. A. Shils (eds.) (1951), *Toward a General Theory of Action*. Cambridge, Mass: Harvard University Press.

Pasternak, Boris (1958), *Doctor Zhivago*. Translated by Max Hayward and Manya Harari. New York: Pantheon.

Payne, John W. (1976), "Task Complexity and Contingent Processing in Decision-Making: An Information Search and Protocol Analysis," *Organizational Behavior and Human Performance*, 16: 366–87.

Peck, M. Scott (1983), *People of the Lie: The Hope for Healing Human Evil*. New York: Simon & Schuster.

Perrett, Geoffrey (1982), *America in the Twenties*. New York: Simon & Schuster.

Peters, Thomas J., and R. H. Waterman, Jr. (1982), *In Search of Excellence*. New York: Harper & Row.

Pfeffer, Jeffrey (1981), *Power in Organizations*. Marshfield, Mass.: Pittman Publishing.

Pickthall, Mohammed Marmaduke (1953), *The Meaning of the Glorious Koran*. New York: Mentor Books.

Pitts, Robert E., and A. G. Woodside (1983), "Personal Value Influences on Consumer Product Class and Brand Preference," *Journal of Social Psychology*, 119: 37–53.

Plato (1980), *The Republic of Plato*. Translated by F. M. Cornford. Oxford: Oxford University Press.

Plutarch (1910), *Plutarch's Lives*, London: J. M. Dent & Sons, Ltd.

Pollard, William E. and T. Mitchell (1972), "Decision Theory Analysis of Social Power," *Psychological Bulletin*, 78 (November): 433–46.

Popielarz, Donald T. (1967), "An Exploration of Perceived Risk and Willingness to Try New Products," *Journal of Marketing Research*, 4 (November): 368–72.

Potter, David M. (1954), *People of Plenty*. Chicago: University of Chicago Press.

Potter, Stephen (1948), *Theory and Practice of Gamesmanship*. New York: Henry Holt & Co.

Pruden, Henry O., and D. S. Longman (1972), "Race, Alienation and Consumerism," *Journal of Marketing*, 36 (July): 58–63.

Puzo, Mario (1969), *The Godfather*. New York: G. P. Putnam and Sons.

Rabelais, Francois (1955), *The Histories of Gargantua and Pantagruel*. Baltimore: Penguin Books.

Raiffa, Howard (1982), *The Art and Science of Negotiation*. Cambridge, Mass.: The Belknap Press.

Rand, Ayn (1957), *Atlas Shrugged*. New York: Random House.

Rapoport, Anatol (1953), *Operational Philosophy*. New York: Harper and Brothers.

Raven, Bertram H. (1965), "Social Influence and Power," in I. D. Steiner and M. Fishbein (eds.), *Current Studies in Social Psychology*. New York: Holt, Rinehart and Winston.

Ray, Michael L. and W. L. Wilkie (1970), "Fear: The Potential of an Appeal Neglected by Marketing," *Journal of Marketing*, 34 (January): 54–62.

Rieser, Carl (1977), "The Salesman Isn't Dead—He's Different," in H. A. Thompson (ed.), *The Great Writings in Marketing*. Tulsa, Okla.: Petroleum Publishing Co.

Riesman, David (1950), *The Lonely Crowd*. New Haven: Yale University Press.

Ringer, Robert L. (1974), *Winning Through Intimidation*. Greenwich, Conn.: Fawcett Publications.

Ritti, R. Richard, and G. R. Funkhouser (1977), *The Ropes to Skip and The Ropes to Know: Studies in Organizational Behavior*. Columbus, Ohio: Grid Publishing, Inc.

Roberts, Donald, and N. Maccoby (1973), "Information Processing and Persuasion: Counterarguing Behavior," in P. Clarke (ed.), *New Models of Communication Research*. Beverly Hills: Sage Publications.

Rokeach, Milton (1968–69), "The Role of Values in Public Opinion Research," *Public Opinion Quarterly*, 32 (Winter): 547–59.

——— (1973), *The Nature of Human Values*. New York: The Free Press.

——— (1974), "Change and Stability in American Value Systems, 1968–1971," *Public Opinion Quarterly*, 38 (Summer): 222–38.

Roloff, Michael E. and G. R. Miller, (1980), *Persuasion: New Directions in Theory and Research*. Beverly Hills: Sage Publications.

Rosenberg, Milton J. (1956), "Cognitive Structure and Attitudinal Affect," *Journal of Abnormal and Social Psychology*, 53 (November): 367–72.

Rosenhan, D. L. (1973), "On Being Sane in Insane Places," *Science*, 179 (January): 249–58.

Rosnow, Ralph L. and E. J. Robinson (eds.) (1967), *Experiments in Persuasion*. New York: Academic Press.

Rowsome, Frank Jr., (1959), *They Laughed When I Sat Down*. New York: Bonanza Books.

Rubenstein, Richard L. (1974), *Power Struggle*. New York: Charles Scribner's Sons.

——— (1983), *The Age of Triage*. Boston: Beacon Press.

Rubin, Jeffrey Z. (1981), "Psychological Traps," *Psychology Today* (March): 52–63.

Ryan, Michael J. and E. H. Bonfield (1975), "The Fishbein Extended Model and Consumer Behavior," *Journal of Consumer Research*, 2 (September): 118–36.

Sabatini, Arthur J., (1981), "Memoirs of a Well-Spent Youth," *TODAY/The Philadelphia Inquirer* (30 August): 22 ff.

Schmedel, Scott (1980), "Taking On an Industry Giant: An Interview with Gene M. Amdahl," *Harvard Business Review* (March–April).

Schramm, Wilbur, (1961), "How Communication Works," in W. Schramm (ed.), *The Process and Effects of Mass Communication*. Urbana, Ill.: University of Illinois Press.

Schumacher, Ernest F. (1973), *Small is Beautiful*. New York: Harper & Row.

Shakespeare, William (1984), *Complete Works*. London: Henry Pordes.

Sherif, Muzafer and C. W. Sherif (1967), "The Own Categories Procedure in Attitude Research," in M. Fishbein (ed.), *Readings in Attitude Theory and Measurement*. New York: John Wiley.

Sheth, Jagdish and W. Talaryzk (1972), "Perceived Instrumentality and Value Importance as Determinants of Attitudes, *Journal of Marketing Research*, 9 (February): 6–9.

Shook, Robert L. (1978), *Ten Greatest Salespersons: What They Say About Selling*. New York: Harper & Row.

Shugun, Steven M. (1980), "The Cost of Thinking," *Journal of Consumer Research*, 7 (September): 99–111.

Simison, Robert L. (1979), "Auto Salesmen Polish Old Moves, Add a Few to Peddle Costly '79's," *Wall Street Journal* (11 January): 1.

Skinner, B. F. (1983), *A Matter of Consequences*. New York: Alfred A. Knopf.

Smith, Adam (1937), *An Inquiry into the Nature and Causes of the Wealth of Nations*. New York: Modern Library.

Smith, B. L., H. D. Lasswell and R. D. Casey (1946), *Propaganda, Communication, and Public Opinion*. Princeton: Princeton University Press.

Smith, Gail (1967), "How GM Measures Ad Effectiveness," in K. K. Cox (ed.), *Readings in Market Research*. New York: Appleton-Century-Crofts.

Solzhenitsyn, Alexander (1963), *One Day in the Life of Ivan Denisovich*. New York: Bantam Books.

Sorokin, P. A. (1954), *The Ways and Power of Love*. Boston: The Beacon Press.

Spanier, David (1977), *Total Poker*. New York: Simon & Schuster.

Steinbeck, John (1965), *The Pearl*. New York: Viking Press.

Steiner, Claude (1974), *The Scripts People Live*. New York: Bantam Books.

Sterling, Claire (1981), *The Terror Network: The Secret War of International Terrorism*. New York: Holt, Rinehart and Winston.

Strong, E. K. (1925), *The Psychology of Selling*. New York: McGraw-Hill.

Suchman, Abe and M. Perry (1969), "Self-confidence and Persuasibility in Marketing: A Reappraisal," *Journal of Marketing*, 6 (May): 146–54.

Swanberg, W. A. (1961), *Citizen Hearst*. New York: Charles Scribner's Sons.

Sykes, Gresham M., and David Matza (1957), "Techniques of Neutralization: A Theory of Delinquency," *American Sociological Review*, 22 (December): 664–70.

Terkel, Studs (1972), *Working*. New York: Random House.

Thibaut, John W. and H. H. Kelley (1959), *The Social Psychology of Groups*. New York: John Wiley.

Tocqueville, Alexis de (1947), *Democracy in America*. New York: Oxford University Press.

Toffler, Alvin (1980), *The Third Wave*. New York: William Morrow.

Tolman, E. C. (1932), *Purposive Behavior in Animals and Men*. New York: Appleton-Century-Crofts.

Tolstoy, Leo (n.d.), *War and Peace*. Translated by C. Garnett. New York: Carlton House.

Toynbee, Arnold J. (1956), *An Historian's Approach to Religion*. Oxford University Press.

Train, John (1983), "The Lonely Voice of Alexander Solzhenitsyn," *Wall Street Journal* (23 June).

Trillin, Calvin (1984), *Killings*. New York: Ticknor & Fields.

Trow, George W. S., Jr. (1980), "Reflections: Within the Context of No-Context," *New Yorker* (17 November): 63 ff.

Tversky, Amos (1972), "Elimination by Aspects: A Theory of Choice," *Psychological Review*, 79 (July): 201–99.

———— and D. Kahneman (1974), "Judgments under Uncertainty: Heuristics and Biases," *Science*, 185 (27 September): 1124–31.

————, and ———— (1981), "The Framing of Decisions and the Psychology of Choice," *Science*, 211 (30 January): 453–58.

————, and ———— (1983), "Extensional Versus Intuitive Reasoning: The Conjunction Fallacy in Probability Judgment," *Psychological Review*, 90 (October): 293–315.

Tuhy, Carrie (1983), "What Price Children?" *Money*, 12 (March): 77–84.

Ursic, Michael (1980), " 'Consumer Decision Making—Fact or Fiction?' Comment," *Journal of Consumer Research*, 7 (December): 331–33.

Von Neumann, John, and O. Morgenstern (1947). *Theory of Games and Economic Behavior*. Princeton: Princeton University Press.

Wagner, Richard (1983), "Der Ring des Nibelungen," Bayreuth, West Germany.

Watkins, Julian L. (1959), *The 100 Greatest Advertisements*. New York: Dover.

Weber, Max (1930), *The Protestant Ethnic and Spirit of Capitalism*. Translated by T. Parsons. London: G. Allen & Unwin.

Weinstein, Fred, and Gerald M. Platt (1969), *The Wish to be Free: Society, Psyche and Value Change*. Berkeley: The University of California Press.

Wellman, Francis (1962), *The Art of Cross Examination*. New York: Collier Books.

West, Nathanael (1933), *Miss Lonelyhearts*. New York: New Directions.

White, Morton (1955), *The Age of Analysis*. New York: Mentor Books.

White, Theodore H. (1973), *The Making of the President 1972*. New York: Atheneum.

——— (1982), *America in Search of Itself*. New York: Harper & Row.

Whorf, Benjamin L. (1956), "Science and Linguistics," in J. B. Carroll (ed.), *Language, Thought and Reality*. Cambridge, Mass.: M.I.T. Press.

Wilkie, William L., and E. A. Pessemier (1973), "Issues in Marketing's Use of Multi-Attribute Models," *Journal of Marketing Research*, 10 (November): 428–41.

Williams, Robin M., Jr. (1962), "Individual and Group Values," *Annals of the American Academy*, 371 (May): 20–37.

Wilson, Edward O. (1975), *Sociobiology: The New Synthesis*. Cambridge, Mass.: The Belknap Press.

Wilson, James Q. (1975), *Thinking About Crime*. New York: Basic Books.

——— (1983), "Crime and American Culture," *The Public Interest* (Winter): 22–48.

Yao, Margaret (1980), "Agents Try Some Tricky Tactics to Survive Slump in Home Sales," *Wall Street Journal* (3 December): 31.

Zimbardo, Philip (1983), "To Control a Mind," *The Stanford Magazine* (Winter): 59–64.

——— and E. B. Ebbeson (1969), *Influencing Attitudes and Changing Behavior*. Reading, Mass.: Addison-Wesley.

Zipf, George K. (1949), *Human Behavior and the Principle of Least Effort*. Cambridge, Mass.: Addison-Wesley.

INDEX